MW01032449

"In a few short years, Ortl
ing Christian scholars. Thi
scholarly and inspiring. W
eminent plausibility of the
tion of Jesus. Ultimately, wh.. ...s ..is oook apart is that Ortlund
never overpromises and always engages the best counterarguments
with scrupulous fairness, demonstrating in the process an amazing
mastery of the Christian tradition and philosophical and scientific
literature. A book to savor, and to pass on to friends and family."

—**Matthew Levering**, Mundelein Seminary

"In this engaging book, Ortlund stirs our deepest hopes and longings for infinite beauty and perfect goodness, longings we often
ignore or repress. He goes on to argue that there are good reasons
to sustain these hopes and that truth, goodness, and beauty are
ultimately aligned. This is the ideal book to give thoughtful unbelievers, and one that believers will find most useful as a model
for intelligent evangelism in the twenty-first century."

—**Jerry L. Walls**, Houston Baptist University

"In this remarkably lucid and engaging book, Ortlund asks us to
reflect on the 'affective' dimensions of a belief in God as the supreme
source of truth, beauty, and goodness. When listening to music, or
reflecting on the laws of mathematics, or expressing profound moral
convictions, we sometimes experience longings for a transcendent
'beyond' that cannot be contained within the realm of 'the natural.'
The Christian story, Ortlund argues, offers us a profound story in
which these deepest yearnings of the human spirit are satisfied.
Ortlund's compelling case is made with philosophical clarity, can-
dor, and an impressive use of a wide variety of illustrations from
fiction, poetry, and film."

—**Richard J. Mouw**, Paul B. Henry Institute for the Study
of Christianity and Politics, Calvin University

"Ortlund has written a marvelous, engaging book that defends the
coherence, beauty, and power of the Christian story—the one story
to rule them all. He effectively shows how the naturalistic story in
particular fails to furnish an explanatory account of the nature of
the universe, of human experience, and of the deepest longings of
the human heart. Rather, all of these things hold together in Jesus

Christ, whose resurrection grounds the hope that everything sad will become untrue."

"Ortlund's considerable talents applied to the ultimate question have yielded an impressive and eminently readable treatise that is both academically rigorous and deeply personal. Impressively researched and beautifully crafted, this book makes contagious the author's obvious delight at exploring life's mysteries, and it casts an animating vision of gripping beauty and enchanting transcendence. Without triumphalism it features epistemically modest yet hearty reasoning that invites readers into a conversation and into close consideration of existentially central threads of evidence—from math to morals—that end up weaving a lovely tapestry and providing a needed corrective to the postmodern fragmentation of truth, goodness, and beauty."

"If you've long thought that Christianity is unsophisticated and by the looks of things a boring way to live, and yet every now and again you find yourself wondering, But just what if there is something to it? then *Why God Makes Sense in a World That Doesn't* is a book you should read. Gavin Ortlund avoids the overreach of attempting to 'prove' God. Instead, he argues that belief in God and the Christian story is more rational and desirable than believing in atheism and the story that naturalism tells about the world. Ortlund serves as a careful guide through the arguments, engages the other side fairly, and admits he knows what it feels like to doubt. At the core of Christianity are the claims that there is a God and that Jesus rose from the dead. If true, they change everything. If false, they are some of the biggest errors of all time. Either way, these claims are worth your attention. This book will help you consider how wagering on God and Jesus might surprisingly make sense to you after all."

WHY **GOD**
MAKES SENSE
IN A WORLD THAT
DOESN'T

WHY **GOD** MAKES SENSE
IN A WORLD THAT **DOESN'T**

The Beauty of Christian Theism

GAVIN ORTLUND

Baker Academic
a division of Baker Publishing Group
Grand Rapids, Michigan

© 2021 by Gavin Ortlund

Published by Baker Academic
a division of Baker Publishing Group
PO Box 6287, Grand Rapids, MI 49516-6287
www.bakeracademic.com

Printed in the United States of America

Library of Congress Cataloging-in-Publication Data
Names: Ortlund, Gavin, 1983– author.
Title: Why God makes sense in a world that doesn't : the beauty of Christian theism / Gavin Ortlund.
Description: Grand Rapids, Michigan : Baker Academic, a division of Baker Publishing Group, 2021. | Includes index.
Identifiers: LCCN 2021006694 | ISBN 9781540964090 (paperback) | ISBN 9781540964571 (casebound) | ISBN 9781493432455 (ebook)
Subjects: LCSH: God (Christianity) | Apologetics.
Classification: LCC BT103 .O78 2021 | DDC 231—dc23
LC record available at https://lccn.loc.gov/2021006694

The author is represented by the literary agency of Wolgemuth & Associates.

Baker Publishing Group publications use paper produced from sustainable forestry practices and post-consumer waste whenever possible.

22   23   24   25   26   27   7   6   5   4   3   2

For Isaiah, Naomi, Elijah, and Miriam,
whom I often feel I love more than my own life:
I wish peace, goodness, strength,
and joy upon each of you, forever.

The first thing that must strike a non-Christian about the Christian's faith is that it obviously presumes far too much. It is too good to be true.

—Hans Urs von Balthasar

Contents

Preface

This book comes from my heart, more than anything else I have ever written.

Don't get me wrong: It's an academic book. It seeks to be rigorous in argumentation and deep in the relevant secondary literature. Some passages get technical. At the same time, as it has overflowed from personal excitement, this book has also taken on a tone and quality that I hope will have a broader and more personal reach. I have labored to make it an accessible and enjoyable read, for any thoughtful and sincere reader, as much as possible. Down with boring books! Down with obligatory reading! The subject matter at hand is too enthralling. If we are not captivated and delighted along the way, something is amiss.

I tell you that I've given you my best effort as a writer so that I may invite you to give the book your best effort as a reader. We live in an age of distraction and sound bites. The careful reading of books is not our defining strength. But if you will give me your attention from cover to cover, I will do everything I can to make it worth your effort.

My passion for this book derives from my own experience. Over the last several years I have become utterly absorbed in philosophical literature pertaining to the question of God. I remember the day in December 2018, browsing around at Barth's Books (a famous bookstore where I live in Ojai, California), when I first self-consciously resolved to give myself to this task as my next great intellectual effort. I'd been a bit depressed, having just completed several other book projects in historical theology (my area of formal training) and wondering where to turn my energies next. Philosophy had been my first intellectual love—it was in college, reading Kierkegaard and Wittgenstein and Camus, that I first understood how fun it could be to *think*. And for several years my interest in apologetics had been steadily brewing, though fueled more by YouTube debates than academic reading.

That day I came across several of the so-called new atheist books: Richard Dawkins's *The God Delusion*, Christopher Hitchens's *God Is Not Great*, and Sam Harris's *The End of Faith*. I vividly remember the longing that came over me as I leafed through them. It felt like my feet finding the path again. I knew what my next adventure would be. I bought all three books and headed to the park.

Since that day, philosophical questions of a religious nature have become a central absorbing passion in my life, occupying my mind on bike rides, during swims and hikes, while playing soccer with kids in the backyard, and at various sleepless hours of the night. More than once since then I have prayed, *Lord, if you give me anything else to accomplish in my life, please let me write this book!*

In the process, I have come to feel that the needs of the times call for a slightly different approach to apologetics, which I explain in the introduction.

A couple of brief explanatory matters are in order, in the hope of avoiding misplaced expectations for your sake and one-star Amazon reviews for mine. First, as I explain in the introduction, this book is not a comprehensive treatment of all worldviews, but especially focuses on two options: Christianity and naturalism. My reason for restricting my focus to Christianity and naturalism is twofold: (1) those are the options most people I know are considering; and (2) those are the options I am best equipped to write about. So if you're trying to decide between, say, theism and pantheism, this book will not likely help you much. Furthermore, I don't address *every* difference between naturalism and Christianity (there are other books that give more of a survey approach to "top objections" or "top issues"). Rather, I'm trying to get at the big picture of how each worldview functions. I'm interested in the questions, What kind of story does each tell about our world? and, Which story is more satisfying to both mind and heart?

By "naturalism" I mean the philosophy that only physical laws and forces exist, such that there is nothing beyond the realm of nature. As I note in the introduction, some of my arguments are merely against naturalism; others are for theism generally; and others are for Christian theism specifically, which is what the arguments cumulatively entail. Thus, the word "supernaturalism" comes up now and again, for convenience. By it I simply mean any worldview that posits some entity, whether personal or impersonal, beyond the natural order. For my purposes here, I classify the multiverse hypothesis as within the bounds of naturalism *if* all the other universes in the multiverse are understood to be reductively physicalist and bound by the same natural laws as our observable universe.

I wish to give sincere thanks to Andrew Wolgemuth, my literary agent, for his wonderful encouragement, friendship, and hard work; to all of the team at Baker Academic, who were a delight to work with and contributed to this project in numerous ways (especially Dave Nelson for overseeing the project and James Korsmo for his careful editorial work); to Tim Keller, whose approach to the topics addressed in this book I relate to so sincerely and intuitively, and whose various sermons and books I have absorbed so appreciatively, that I almost regard him as an old friend even though we have actually met on only one occasion and I have no reason to expect him to reciprocate such interest; to those who read portions of the manuscript and gave feedback, especially Jeff Zweerink, Joel Chopp, and Eric Ortlund; to my wife, Esther, for her tireless support, love, and encouragement, in my writing and everything else; and to my children, Isaiah, Naomi, Elijah, and Miriam, who fill my daily life with laughter and delight, and to whom I dedicate this book.

Introduction

Beauty, Story, and Probability in the Question of God

Suppose Hamlet is searching for Shakespeare. He cannot find him in the way he might find other characters in the play, like Ophelia or Claudius. So where should he look? Hamlet's knowledge of Shakespeare will be different than anything else in his life. On the one hand, finding Shakespeare will be very difficult. Shakespeare is very far removed; Hamlet has never encountered him. On the other hand, the knowledge of Shakespeare might also prove unavoidable. For in a deeper sense, Shakespeare is very close; Hamlet has never done anything *but* encounter him. As Hamlet's creator, Shakespeare is at once beyond his every device and inside his every thought.

This book is about the knowledge of God, who, if he exists, is to us something like what Shakespeare is to Hamlet. For instance, if God is real, he will be both infinitely close and infinitely far. He is infinitely close because reality itself abides within him; each breath we breathe is a gift from him. As Augustine put it, God is closer to us than we are to ourselves.[1] He is infinitely far because

---

1. Augustine, *Confessions* 3.6, 2nd ed., ed. Michael P. Foley, trans. F. J. Sheed (Indianapolis: Hackett, 2006), 44: "You were more inward than the most inward place of my heart."

he is qualitatively different than anything we have ever known; he surpasses us constantly at every level; for all eternity we could search him out and still always have infinitely more to discover. As Job observed, "How faint the whisper we hear of him!" (Job 26:14 NIV).

The question of God is thus unparalleled in all of life, in several ways. It is, first, the most important and thrilling adventure of our lives. Nothing could be more urgent than whether he exists—and if so, what to do about it. For God is held to be the Supreme Good, who alone can fulfill the longings of the human soul. Therefore the stakes of finding him are literally infinite. Sex, achievement, food and drink, relationship—these are mere trifles to the human heart in comparison with God, the source of all things, the goal of all things, the ever-flowing fountain of all beauty and glory.

The question of God is, secondly, the most fascinating puzzle you will ever think about. Whether or not he is real, certainly a more interesting *idea* has never been conceived. The concept *God*—the infinite Person, the ground of being, the precondition of reality—is the most staggering, enthralling idea ever to confront the human mind. The mere idea of God outweighs the physical universe in grandeur and importance.

Finally, the question of God is the most difficult and humbling question we will face. Take the feeling of smallness you have when standing before the Grand Canyon, or approaching a king—then multiply that feeling many times over and you get the idea. That is what we are up against. It will take all our courage, all our hope, all our yearning.

This book is a journey into the question of God. It explores four classic arguments for the existence of God. We will approach these arguments, however, in three distinctive ways, and I want to explain these distinctives in advance.[2]

2. In each of the following three distinctives, but especially the first two, my book is situated within a larger movement of new approaches to apologetics, perhaps best represented and influenced by Tim Keller's *Making Sense of God: An Invitation to*

Appealing to Beauty

In his famous *Pensées*, Blaise Pascal proposed a threefold strategy for commending God, particularly the Christian God, to those who don't believe: "Men despise religion. They hate it and are afraid it might be true. The cure for this is first [1] to show that religion is not contrary to reason, but worthy of reverence and respect. Next [2] make it attractive, make good men wish it were true, and then [3] how that it is."[3] This is an intriguing strategy. To summarize, Pascal proposes a threefold order of apologetics:

1. Show religion to be *respectable*.
2. Show religion to be *desirable*.
3. Show religion to be *true*.

Many efforts at Christian apologetics start with Pascal's third step, as though having powerful arguments were the main task at hand. Pascal's approach reflects a kind of practical wisdom in starting further back, at the psychological level. After all, few decisions are the result of strictly rational factors. We are not robots. This is especially the case with the question of God, the most inward and poignant question of all. For this reason, Pascal also taught that the truth of God is such that it will never be recognized apart from love, inwardness, and longing.[4]

My approach in this book is especially alert to the second stage of Pascal's apologetic strategy. I'm interested in the affective dimension of these classical arguments, in their appeal to the whole

the Skeptical (New York: Viking, 2016). For an overview of this turn in apologetics, see Sarah Eekhoff Zylstra, "Ask and You Shall Evangelize," *The Gospel Coalition*, November 14, 2018, https://www.thegospelcoalition.org/article/ask-shall-evangelize/.

3. Peter Kreeft, *Christianity for Modern Pagans: Pascal's* Pensées *Edited, Outlined, and Explained* (San Francisco: Ignatius, 1993), 28. In context here, by "religion" Pascal has in mind Christianity.

4. E.g., Pascal says, "Truth is so obscured nowadays and lies [are] so well established that unless we love the truth we shall never recognize it." Kreeft, *Christianity for Modern Pagans*, 216.

person, and in what they reveal about the beauty of Christianity. Whatever else you conclude about the Christian story, my goal is that you will at least feel something of its wonder and enchantment. Even where you may remain unpersuaded, I hope you might, in some way or another, *wish* it were true.[5]

My own experience is that when the gospel is truly understood and embraced, particularly in contrast to naturalistic worldviews, it feels like stepping through the wardrobe into Narnia. The empty tomb means supreme happiness, like the feeling of waking up as a little child on Christmas morning, or of learning that your true love actually loves you back. You know you have gotten a whiff of it when this thought arrives: *Can it really be that good?* This book tries to help us *feel* that—as well as, in the other direction, feel something of the confinement and barrenness of naturalism.[6]

Of course, beauty *in itself* is not a sufficient criterion for adjudicating truth. The fact that we desire something to be true does not make it true. At the same time, desire is not irrelevant to truth, either. Desire is itself a piece of data that must be taken into account and interpreted alongside other data. For example, hunger might not prove you have food, but it might suggest to you that there is such a thing as food out there, somewhere. Similarly, if we notice within our hearts deep-seated longings for things

5. I'm also less focused on Pascal's first step. Skeptics who don't find Christianity even worth the time to investigate (as well as Christians who have no curiosity or angst about their faith) may want to start with a different book. The two I'd recommend are Tim Keller's *Making Sense of God* and Rebecca McLaughlin's *Confronting Christianity: 12 Hard Questions for the World's Largest Religion* (Wheaton: Crossway, 2019). These books start further back, explaining why the investigation is worth it in the first place. This book will have more traction for those who are already at least somewhat open to the possibility of faith, as well as for those who are somewhat sensitive to its difficulty.

6. As discussed in the preface, this book does not have a comprehensive scope: I am primarily interested in comparing two alternatives, Christianity and naturalism. Some of the arguments in this book go to support "supernaturalism" in general—i.e., the belief that there is something beyond nature (whether Plato's forms, God, gods, etc.). Other arguments are specifically aimed at theism, and others (esp. in chap. 4) specifically at *Christian* theism. The cumulative effort of them all is, of course, toward Christian theism.

like meaning, love, and lasting hope—longings so powerful that life seems unendurable without them—this very fact may prove relevant, alongside other considerations, to our overall assessment of the world that produces creatures with such longings.[7]

This interest in the interplay between beauty and truth is an ancient instinct. The Greek philosophers spoke of the three transcendentals: the good, the true, and the beautiful. Christians have historically put a great deal of reflection into how the gospel relates to each one of these three and why it is important to commend the gospel not only as true but as good and as beautiful. Hans Urs von Balthasar, who has perhaps more than anyone else developed a theology of aesthetics, argued that in the modern world, truth without beauty is powerless and ineffectual: "In a world that no longer has enough confidence in itself to affirm the beautiful, the proofs of the truth have lost their cogency. In other words, syllogisms may still dutifully clatter away like rotary presses or computers which infallibly spew out an exact number of answers by the minute. But the logic of these answers is itself a mechanism which no longer captivates anyone."[8] Similarly, von Balthasar claimed that goodness apart from beauty becomes unstable and

7. C. S. Lewis famously argued along these lines (though we are not in a position to assess this argument just yet): "Creatures are not born with desires unless satisfaction for those desires exists. A baby feels hunger: well, there is such a thing as food. A duckling wants to swim: well, there is such a thing as water. Men feel sexual desire: well, there is such a thing as sex. If I find in myself a desire which no experience in this world can satisfy, the most probable explanation is that I was made for another world. If none of my earthly pleasures satisfy it, that does not prove that the universe is a fraud." C. S. Lewis, *Mere Christianity*, in *The Complete C. S. Lewis Signature Classics* (San Francisco: HarperSanFrancisco, 2002), 76. For a more recent and more academic defense that, under certain conditions, desires are a guide to possibility, see Todd Buras and Michael Cantrell, "C. S. Lewis's Argument from Nostalgia: A New Argument from Desire," in *Two Dozen (or So) Arguments for God: The Plantinga Project*, ed. Jerry L. Walls and Trent Dougherty (Oxford: Oxford University Press, 2018), 356–71.

8. Hans Urs von Balthasar, *The Glory of the Lord: A Theological Aesthetics*, vol. 1, *Seeing the Form*, trans. Erasmo Leiva-Merikakis, ed. Joseph Fessio, SJ, and John Riches (San Francisco: Ignatius, 1982), 19. Readers who wish to pursue a robustly theological vision for beauty should give more attention to von Balthasar. A careful reading of von Balthasar's *The Glory of the Lord* would encourage another of the

arbitrary.[9] David Bentley Hart has likewise urged that the Christian gospel addresses the world not primarily as a series of arguments but as a story involving a unique interrelation of truth and beauty: "Making its appeal first to the eye and heart, as the only way it may 'command' assent, the church cannot separate truth from rhetoric, or from beauty."[10]

This vision of the unity of the transcendentals is an ancient one, but it has fresh relevance in our current cultural moment, for at least three reasons. First, we live in a time of disillusionment and disenchantment (and, stemming from this, a time of apathy about truth). Accordingly, the greatest impediment to the hearing of the gospel is usually not opposition but indifference. Søren Kierkegaard famously used aesthetic writing to engage those not already interested in religious questions.[11] When people are under the illusion that they have no dire spiritual need, Kierkegaard considered it necessary to communicate indirectly, "because direct communication presupposes that the receiver's ability to receive is undisturbed."[12] Though Kierkegaard's context ("Christendom") differs from our own, the genius of his general strategy of communication is ever relevant.[13]

---

convictions undergirding this book: that apologetics is the task of theology (as has been the case throughout church history), not merely philosophy.

9. Von Balthasar, *The Glory of the Lord*, 1:19: "In a world without beauty . . . the good loses its attractiveness, the self-evidence of why it must be carried out. Man stands before the good and asks himself why *it* must be done and not rather its alternative, evil. For this, too, is a possibility, and even the more exciting one: Why not investigate Satan's depths?"

10. David Bentley Hart, *The Beauty of the Infinite: The Aesthetics of Christian Truth* (Grand Rapids: Eerdmans, 2003), 4.

11. Søren Kierkegaard, *The Point of View for My Work as an Author: A Direct Communication, Report to History*, in *The Kierkegaard Reader*, ed. Jane Chamberlain and Jonathan Rée (Oxford: Blackwell, 2001), 306–7. He spoke of this as a "deception into the truth," by which he meant a dialectical strategy of indirect communication. The word "aesthetic" should be understood here in the context of Kierkegaard's famous three categories: the aesthetic, the ethical, and the religious.

12. Kierkegaard, *The Point of View for My Work as an Author*, 307.

13. Kierkegaard, *The Point of View for My Work as an Author*, 307: "There is an immense difference, a dialectical difference, between these two cases: the case of a man who is ignorant and is to have a piece of knowledge imparted to him, so that

Beauty is a powerful tool for cutting through disenchantment and apathy because it has a kind of persuasive power that reaches down to the heart. As Sarah Zylstra put it, "Even as our neighbors lose belief in the truth of the gospel, they're still, on a gut level, looking for its goodness and beauty."[14] Beauty speaks at this "gut level." It travels at a wavelength that even the disenchanted can hear.[15] I have known many people, for example, who have come to Christ through reading *The Lord of the Rings* or C. S. Lewis's fiction. I suspect that part of the reason is that there is a *beauty* in these stories that simply cannot be accounted for within the limits of a nihilistic worldview.

Second, we live in an age of distraction and diversion.[16] Pascal famously wrote, "The sole cause of man's unhappiness is that he does not know how to stay quietly in his room."[17] I used to think this was an interesting sentiment but something of an overstatement for effect. It was only recently, when I gave the *Pensées* a

---

he is like an empty vessel which is to be filled or a blank sheet of paper upon which something is to be written; and the case of a man who is under the illusion and must first be delivered from that. Likewise there is a difference between writing on a blank sheet of paper and bringing to light, by the application of a caustic fluid, a text which is hidden under another text."

14. Zylstra, "Ask and You Shall Evangelize."

15. I have often heard apologists speak about how the appeal to the heart, rather than a strictly logical case, can reduce defensiveness and gain a hearing. E.g., the apologist William Lane Craig shares this story: "I remember once, when I was delivering a series of talks at the University of Birmingham in England, that the audience the first night was very hostile and aggressive. The second night I spoke on the absurdity of life without God. This time the largely same audience was utterly subdued: the lions had turned to lambs, and now their questions were no longer attacking but sincere and searching. The remarkable transformation was due to the fact that the message had penetrated their intellectual façade and struck at the core of their existence." *Reasonable Faith: Christian Truth and Apologetics*, 3rd ed. (Wheaton: Crossway, 2008), 88.

16. Alan Noble, *Disruptive Witness: Speaking Truth in a Distracted Age* (Downers Grove, IL: InterVarsity, 2018), 24, notes that our distracted culture is not well equipped to wrestle with deep ideas, and therefore it is harder to leverage truth to call for a response. In fact, sometimes it is even difficult to get people to comprehend when you are making a truth claim, because the gospel can easily be co-opted by the surrounding cultural narratives to become simply one more option among others, as a matter of preference or image (see Noble, *Disruptive Witness*, 4, 25, 38, 59).

17. *Pensées* 136, in Kreeft, *Christianity for Modern Pagans*, 173.

thorough read in preparation for this book, that the genius and relevance of Pascal's comment fully dawned on me. In context, he is arguing that our inability to consider the one central, certain fact of life (death, and what lies beyond it) represents a kind of supernatural spell or torpor: "All I know is that I must soon die, but what I know least about is this very death which I cannot evade."[18] The way we avoid facing the ultimate questions (meaning and death) is by filling our lives with distractions: "However sad a man may be, if you can persuade him to take up some diversion he will be happy while it lasts."[19] This is Pascal's point: if we could stay quietly in our room, we'd be forced to slow down enough to attend to our true condition.

Beauty can help the distracted just as it can help the disenchanted. Beauty conveys a sense that there is something richer beneath the surface of our hurried lives and that it is worth slowing down to consider it. Peter Kreeft calls beauty "goodness's prophet."[20] Beauty has its own kind of testimonial power, helping us *feel the stakes* of religious questions, compelling us to stop and listen.

Third, we live in a time of outrage and polarization. Intriguingly, as our culture has grown more morally pluralistic, it has also grown more morally incensed. There is also a great deal of pessimism about the future and a deep longing for transcendent experience. Beauty is one way to engage people more effectively, because it enables us to appeal more comprehensively to the various questions and anxieties that people have. It might allow us to strike a more winsome, invitational tone than is usually present amid the entrenchment and rancor that often characterize public dialogue.

An appeal to beauty can better speak to the moral concerns of our polarized culture as well. A Christian apologist once remarked to me that on university campuses thirty years ago he was asked

18. *Pensées* 427, in Kreeft, *Christianity for Modern Pagans*, 192.
19. *Pensées* 136, in Kreeft, *Christianity for Modern Pagans*, 175–76.
20. Peter J. Kreeft, *The Philosophy of Tolkien: The Worldview behind "The Lord of the Rings"* (San Francisco: Ignatius, 2005), 152.

more questions about Christianity's truth (Does God exist? Did
Jesus rise from the dead? etc.); today he is asked more questions
about Christianity's goodness (Is the church intolerant? Are Christians homophobic? etc.). I think this is broadly representative of our
whole culture. Thus, if we commend only the truth of Christianity
and neglect the appeal to beauty and goodness, we are actually not
hitting the central, animating concerns of our culture. That is why, in
the chapters that follow, we explore not only the strength of the arguments in view but also their beauty and relevance to human desire.

Seeking a Better Story

A second characteristic of this book is that I approach arguments in
a narrative frame. That is, I treat them not as stand-alone proofs but
rather as entry points into a larger, more cohesive question: What
is the overall shape of reality? What kind of *story* best explains our
world? This simultaneously entails more of a cumulative approach.

Alister McGrath defines "narrative apologetics" as "an approach to affirming, defending, and explaining the Christian faith
by telling stories."[21] This is part of what I'm pursuing here, but
I'm also after something more—I'm interested not only in how
stories show truth but also in how truth presents itself to us as,
ultimately, a story. (Hence the Shakespeare/Hamlet metaphor at
the start of this book, to which we will return.)[22]

I believe narrative has a unique power to convince in our current
context, for a variety of reasons: (1) it appeals more naturally to the
heart, will, and imagination; (2) it can be less confrontational and
more inviting; (3) it is better able to furnish meaning and convey
beauty; (4) it conveys truth more concretely; (5) it has greater ability

21. Alister E. McGrath, *Narrative Apologetics: Sharing the Relevance, Joy, and
Wonder of the Christian Faith* (Grand Rapids: Baker Books, 2019), 7.
22. For a helpful overview of the power of story in apologetics, see Josh Chatraw,
Telling a Better Story: How to Talk about God in a Skeptical Age (Grand Rapids:
Zondervan, 2020).

to break through cynicism and apathy; (6) it has greater explanatory reach; (7) it is better positioned to address the problem of evil.
Why are stories so powerful? Storytelling is one of the most
fundamental human activities. Stories are part of how all cultures,
ancient and modern, seek to make sense of the world (movies are
probably our culture's dominant method of storytelling).[23] As
Ursula Le Guin puts it, "There have been great societies that did
not use the wheel, but there have been no societies that did not
tell stories."[24] In other words, human beings have *always* made
sense of the world through stories. For good or ill, this is how we
tend to navigate ultimate questions.

Christians, in particular, have often interpreted our humanity in terms of our tendency to tell stories. Dorothy Sayers, for
example, argued that storytelling is at the heart of what it means
to be made in the image of God.[25] For J. R. R. Tolkien as well,
storytelling is a function of being created in God's image: "We
make in our measure and in our derivative mode, because we are
made: and not only made, but made in the image of a Maker."[26]
Tolkien developed the notion of "sub-creation" to describe this
reality, suggesting that the human tendency is to tell stories that
are unconsciously patterned after the great story, the true story,
the story of Christ. (This point was significant in the famous
conversation that he and Hugo Dyson had with C. S. Lewis in
September 1931 that was instrumental in Lewis's conversion.)[27]
We will return to Tolkien's idea of sub-creation later.

23. N. T. Wright, *The New Testament and the People of God*, Christian Origins
and the Question of God 1 (Minneapolis: Fortress, 1992), 123, discusses the power
of narrative for worldview formation, suggesting that narrative "is the most characteristic expression of worldview." We will discuss the cultural significance of movies
in chapter 3.
24. As quoted in Chatraw, *Telling a Better Story*, 34.
25. See Dorothy L. Sayers, *The Mind of the Maker* (San Francisco: Harper &
Row, 1941), 22.
26. J. R. R. Tolkien, "On Fairy-Stories," in *The Tolkien Reader* (New York: Bal-
lantine, 1966), 75.
27. See the discussion in McGrath, *Narrative Apologetics*, 31, 45–47.

In line with this interest in story, the four arguments of this book are situated in a narrative form, as four of the essential aspects of any good story:

- Chapter 1 explores the possibility that our world has a *beginning*.
- Chapter 2 explores the possibility that our world has a *meaning*.
- Chapter 3 explores the possibility that our world has a *conflict* or *drama*.
- Chapter 4 explores the possibility that our world has an ultimate *hope* or *denouement*.

Each chapter thus gets progressively more ambitious. Chapter 1 proposes supernaturalism of some kind, favoring theism or possibly deism. Chapter 2 furthers the appeal for supernaturalism, this time more concretely a *personal* supernatural reality (again with theism as the lead candidate). Chapter 3 argues more definitively for theism, emphasizing that supernatural reality appears not only to be a personal entity but also a righteous, moral one. Chapter 4 hones in on the Christian deity specifically.

Thus, this book considers Christianity versus naturalism in relation to the basic elements that all stories have: origins, meaning, conflict, and hope. The constant question will be: Which is telling us a better story—a story that better accounts for the strangeness, the incompleteness, the brokenness, and the beauty of our world?

Using Abductive Arguments

A final characteristic of my approach to apologetics in this book is that I tend to use abductive arguments more than deductive and inductive arguments. In formal logic, abduction is a distinct form of inference from deduction and induction. Deductive arguments start with premises and then reason toward a conclusion that is logically necessary. Inductive arguments work similarly, but yield only a probable conclusion.

Abductive reasoning, however, works *backward* from a present set of conditions to the most likely explanation. Sometimes it is called "inference to the best explanation." So, for example, suppose you have a roommate who loves eating Wendy's, and one morning you wake up and you see a half-eaten Baconator on the counter. No one else lives with you, and you are not aware of visitors. It is reasonable to abduce, *It's probably from my roommate.* But it's not logically guaranteed that that is the case. There could have been an unknown visitor, or even a burglar.

While abductive reasoning yields a less certain conclusion, it can still be persuasive, especially in the context of a cumulative case. Abduction should not be thought of as an untrustworthy method of inference—it plays a significant role in everyday life (for instance, trusting the speech of others), and it is regularly used by diagnosticians, juries, mechanics, detectives, and by those in many other professions. In some ways, abductive reasoning even has some advantages. For example, here it will help us not get bogged down chasing specialized knowledge that lies beyond the typical reader. So when I'm talking about the origins of the universe or the fine-tuning argument, an abductive approach allows us to ask: What is the *best* explanation? What is *most* likely? I think such arguments have plausibility value for most readers even if they fall short of pressing the issue as far as a more technical presentation could. In fact, I find that many people, especially younger people, find the modesty involved in abductive approaches actually *more* compelling.[28]

28. Keller, *Making Sense of God*, 215, suggests, "Neither religion nor secularity can be demonstrably proven—they are systems of thinking and believing that need to be compared and contrasted to one another in order to determine which makes the most sense. That is, which makes the most sense of our experience, of things we know and need to explain?" This is similar to the approach I adopt here. (Keller is particularly good at asking what make sense *culturally*, as well as logically and

Another benefit of abductive arguments is that they allow us to consider a greater variety of data, including data from the realm of human experience. It is possible to suggest God, not as the conclusion of a thread of reasoning, but as the *premise* of human experience. This approach says, in effect, "If God doesn't exist, so much of life—so much of what we *already assume* in the way we function—becomes more mysterious and inexplicable." This kind of appeal does not necessarily prove God, but it can draw attention to what a powerful explanatory framework belief in God provides for understanding things like love, meaning, beauty, and so forth.

So you might think of the four chapters of this book each as a sort of Pascalian wager. Pascal famously emphasized the unavoidability of the question of God. Short of intellectual certitude, we must still live on the basis of some kind of decision (even if that decision is simply to not think about the question). In this book we are pursuing this kind of realistic approach to the deepest question we all face: What is, all things considered, the *best* choice regarding the God question?

Help from Puddleglum

Let me conclude this introduction on a personal note. The kind of apologetics I am proposing here is not a theoretical exercise. It has been to me like a life raft in stormy seas. I am a Christian, and I have never rejected faith. But during certain seasons of my life, I have agonized my way through various doubts and intrusive thoughts. I've had a number of friends who have been through similar seasons of doubt and deconstruction. If you've been there, or are there, you know how confusing and painful that experience can be.

---

emotionally—in this book I'm more interested in what makes *emotional* and *intuitional* sense.)

I think we can expect that, in our cultural context, such experiences will not be going away any time soon. The modern West is marked by a deep sense of the loss of transcendence and certainty—a feeling of disenchantment, as though life has been drained of its former glory and meaning. The general drift is away from stability and toward despair. I worry that many within the church, especially in younger generations, are ill-equipped to navigate these times. Frankly, it seems to me that Christians often fail to take the challenges seriously enough.

Sometimes in dark moments I have been gripped by the dreadfulness of the naturalistic view that tugs at us from all around. In those moments, I have found enormous relief and comfort in the kind of beauty-oriented, narrative, abductive approach I'm taking here. As a summative expression of this approach, consider this passage from the character Puddleglum in C. S. Lewis's Narnia stories.

Puddleglum is a rather gloomy character based on Lewis's pessimistic gardener. In the book *The Silver Chair*, Puddleglum and his friends are held underground and tempted by an evil sorceress to doubt all that they believe is good about the world—the sun, the stars, and Aslan himself (the Christ figure). Puddleglum's reply sums up several of the intuitions involved in the approach in this book, especially my interest in the emotional factor of belief:

One word, Ma'am. . . . One word. All you've been saying is quite right, I shouldn't wonder. I'm a chap who always liked to know the worst and then put the best face I can on it. So I won't deny any of what you said. But there's one thing more to be said, even so. Suppose we *have* only dreamed, or made up, all those things—trees and grass and sun and moon and stars and Aslan himself. Suppose we have. Then all I can say is that, in that case, the made-up things seem a good deal more important than the real ones. Suppose this black pit of a kingdom of yours *is* the only world. Well, it strikes me as a pretty poor one. And that's a funny thing, when you come to think of it. We're just babies making up a game, if you're right. But four babies playing a game can make a play-world which licks your real world hollow. That's why I'm going to stand by the play-world. I'm on Aslan's side even if there isn't any Aslan to lead it. I'm going to live as like a Narnian as I can even if there isn't any Narnia. So, thanking you kindly for our supper, if these two gentlemen and the young lady are ready, we're leaving your court at once and setting out in the dark to spend our lives looking for Overland. Not that our lives will be very long, I should think; but that's small loss if the world's as dull a place as you say.[29]

I have always found this passage to be a forceful statement against nihilistic worldviews. Some will dismiss its relevance, of course, since it comes in a children's book. But Lewis was a master of stating profound ideas in simple, clear language. Here Lewis is utilizing a particularly powerful and profound idea (the ontological argument, my favorite idea of all time) and applying it to modern despair.[30]

Puddleglum is not advocating for a mere wishful thinking here; he is not saying, "It doesn't matter what is true; it only matters what is beautiful." Rather, Puddleglum is bringing considerations of beauty to bear *on* the question of truth. He is adopting the sorcerer's outlook as a hypothetical (note the repeated word "suppose") and noting its utter desolation even on its own terms. Taken in the best way, Puddleglum's appeal does not amount to "Your world is true, but I reject it anyway" but rather to "Supposing

29. C. S. Lewis, *The Silver Chair* (New York: Scholastic, 1953), 181–82 (italics original).

30. Some regard this passage as a sort of inversion of Plato's famous allegory of the cave, but Lewis himself correlated it with the ontological argument for God's existence. In a 1963 letter to Nancy Warner, responding to Warner's mentioning that her son noticed an "ontological argument" in *The Silver Chair*, Lewis wrote, "I suppose your philosopher son . . . means the chapter in which Puddleglum puts out the fire with his foot. He must thank Anselm and Descartes for it, not me. I have simply put the 'Ontological Proof' in a form suitable for children. And even that is not so remarkable a feat as you might think. You can get into children's heads a good deal which is quite beyond the Bishop of Woolwich." C. S. Lewis to Nancy Warner, October 26, 1963, in *The Collected Letters of C. S. Lewis*, ed. Walter Hooper (San Francisco: HarperCollins, 2007), 3:1472. Obviously Puddleglum's sentiments do not entail the ontological argument proper, in all its nuance. What is at play is the essential impulse of the argument—from the idea to the reality, on the principle of greatness.

your world were true, I would reject it anyway—and that may well suggest it might not be true."

Puddleglum's sentiments point to the sheer *oddity* of a nihilistic world. If all the really stable, happy doctrines of Christianity (say, God, or heaven, or the triumph of good over evil) are false, and in reality our lives are a meaningless blip in a vast and indifferent cosmos, then the ideas in our brain are in a very real sense more weighty than the reality that brought our brains into existence. That is not very easy to swallow, and it is even more difficult to live off of.

Puddleglum is also saying (and my eyes well up with tears as I write this): at the deepest existential level, a true faith perseveres in hope, even when it does so blindly and forlornly ("setting out in the dark," as Puddleglum puts it). The mere possibility of God drives it on, in the blackest moments. It fights with all the strength it can muster.

For all of us, the question of God is likely to take on this poignant feel at some time or another. Honest believers will likely have foreboding moments of disquiet (*What if it's all a sham?*); honest skeptics will likely have panicky moments of hesitation (*What if it's true after all?*). Whether we are in one of these camps or somewhere in the confusing middle, we must admit that we care deeply about the truth of the matter at hand. It's personal. There is no good in pretending that we are completely objective and rational about it. The thing to do is—with all the courage we can muster—acknowledge our biases, face our fears, and unendingly seek truth.

Whatever your personal angle of approach, my hope is that this book will help you feel, in perhaps some new way, the *beauty* of the gospel—that feeling of hope and goodness like when, at long last, the night is over and the sun starts to rise. This way, even if you are not yet convinced of its truth, you may at the very least be better positioned to feel the immensity of what is at stake in the question. For it is the question of all questions, the question that concerns the deepest places in our hearts, the question that will determine the fate of literally everything.

1

The Cause of the World

*Why Something Is More Plausible
(and Much More Interesting) Than Nothing*

The idea that things don't come into being without a reason
is pretty intuitive. That the entire *universe* didn't come into
existence without a reason—even more so. One might suppose that the rejection of such a possibility (a universe that began,
but lacks a cause for its beginning) is among those constraints
with which rational reflection generally begins. Arguments for
God as the first cause, or cosmological arguments, draw upon
this intuition that if the universe began, it must have had a cause.[1]
Such arguments can feel very powerful—often when I reconsider

1. One version of the argument can be formulated very simply: things that begin
to exist have a cause; the universe began to exist; therefore, the universe has a cause.
William Lane Craig has popularized this version of the argument, the kalam cosmological argument. See, e.g., William Lane Craig, *The Kalām Cosmological Argument*
(London: Macmillan, 1979). However, as we shall see, this is simply one version of
the argument; it has some strengths but also some drawbacks in relation to other
cosmological arguments.

them I feel their forcefulness all over again, as if it were hitting me for the first time.

But *did* the universe come into being from nothing? It turns out that this is no easy question. Today there is a complicated body of views on the origins of the universe, many of which affirm some kind of cyclical or self-caused start to the universe—and engaging this discussion pulls you into some pretty technical areas within cosmology (the branch of astronomy concerned with the origin and evolution of the universe). You start off wanting to say, innocently enough, that the universe didn't go "Poof!" from nothing, but to defend the point you find yourself talking about oscillating universes, quantum mechanics, eternal inflation theories, various definitions of the word "nothing," "no-boundary" conceptions of time, and so forth (more on all this later).

To complicate matters further, many forms of the cosmological argument don't involve the claim that the universe began to exist. In fact, putting all the focus on the universe's origins can actually obscure the deeper metaphysical point that has animated cosmological arguments throughout the classical theistic tradition— namely, how do we account for existence as such? Why is there anything at all? A beginningless universe doesn't actually take this question off the table.

So in this chapter we attempt an abductive approach that will allow us to traverse more lightly through the technical issues involved while also keeping an eye on the larger metaphysical and worldview implications throughout. We first consider what the *best* explanation for the origins of our universe is. Short of getting a PhD in theoretical physics, what is the most responsible and reasonable hypothesis with regard to whether the universe began? Following this, we turn to the larger philosophical question: Whether our universe (or the multiverse it inhabits) had a beginning or not, does it make more sense to understand it as deriving its being from something else or as a kind of self-existent "brute fact"?

In response, I suggest two modest conclusions: first, some kind of transcendent Cause to the universe/multiverse is more plausible than not; second, it is more interesting and evocative.

So think of this chapter as simply putting a foot in the door against naturalism. More work will need to be done; here at the outset we're simply trying to crack open the metaphysical possibilities and suggest some initial, provisional impressions.

What Made the Big Bang Go "Bang"?

The term "big bang" was first coined by the English astronomer Fred Hoyle during a radio address in March 1949. Hoyle was advocating for a steady-state model of the universe, in which new matter is continually created as galaxies move away from each other. He set this theory in contrast to the major rival theory at the time, which he described as the view that "all the matter in the universe was created in one *big bang* at a particular time in the remote past."[2] For Hoyle, the idea of a beginning to the universe was pseudoscientific and irrational, too closely resembling creationism.

Hoyle was trying to account for one of the great surprises of the twentieth century: the discovery that our universe is expanding. This had been recognized since the 1920s, in the wake of Einstein's general theory of relativity. In 1922, the Russian physicist Alexander Friedmann first theorized the expansion of the universe and offered a set of equations to describe it. In 1927, the Belgian Catholic priest and astronomer Georges Lemaître proposed a model for the expansion of the universe that was subsequently confirmed by a variety of observational science, such as Edwin Hubble's explanation of the "red shift" of galaxies in 1929, which established that they are moving away from the earth at velocities proportional to their distance.

2. As recounted in Simon Mitton, *Fred Hoyle: A Life in Science* (Cambridge: Cambridge University Press, 2011), 128 (italics original).

For several decades during the mid-twentieth century, the big bang theory and the steady-state theory competed as rival explanations for the expansion of our universe. But eventually, despite Hoyle's continued protests (even late into his life), the big bang model won out, supported by a wide variety of data. This led to theories about an initial singularity, which represents the boundary or edge of space-time itself. In 1970 Stephen Hawking and Roger Penrose proposed that, given the validity of general relativity and a few other conditions (such as that energy is always positive), going back in time leads to an initial state at which the density of time, space, matter, and energy is infinite and the laws of physics break down. This is the standard "hot" model of the big bang, based on the Hawking-Penrose singularity theorems and building on the earlier work of Friedmann and Lemaître.

There are all kinds of continuing disputes about how we should understand big bang cosmology, some of which we will engage in a moment. But the core claim that our universe traces back to an absolute beginning and is therefore finite in history has been the standard cosmological view since the 1960s.

It is hard to convey just how explosive (forgive the pun) this discovery has been in the history of science. Science is stereotypically seen as an objective and dispassionate pursuit of evidence—but the notion of an absolute beginning has created surprisingly emotional reactions. The distinguished physicist and astronomer Robert Jastrow observed that many scientists have found the idea downright *disturbing*.[3] Why is this? Jastrow suggests that it is because it violates scientists' faith in the sufficiency of natural causes.[4] Scientists seek to explain the world in terms of natural laws; but natural laws are formulated in relation to space and time and thus cannot apply to the singularity at which space and time break down. The big bang opens the door to the possibility of reality outside

3. Robert Jastrow, *God and the Astronomers* (New York: Norton, 1992).
4. E.g., Jastrow, *God and the Astronomers*, 123.

of the purview of what can be accounted for by science. It leads us to the very boundary of the physical and thus gestures toward the metaphysical.

Jastrow argues that if any scientist "really examined the implications, he would be traumatized."[5] Having opened his book stating he is an agnostic, he closes the book gesturing toward the theological implications: "For the scientist who has lived by his faith in the power of reason, the story ends like a bad dream. He has scaled the mountains of ignorance; he is about to conquer the highest peak; as he pulls himself over the final rock, he is greeted by a band of theologians who have been sitting there for centuries."[6] Why should the big bang have such theological connotations? In order to appreciate this point, we must understand that the big bang does not arise out of some prior physical reality, like a cosmic vacuum or a state of minimal energy. As Paul Davies notes, people often misconceive of the big bang as "the explosion of a concentrated lump of matter located at some particular place in a pre-existing void."[7] But the big bang was not the beginning of matter *within* space and time; rather, it was the beginning of space-time itself (recall that from Einstein we learned that space, matter, and time are interdependent). This means that, on the standard model, before the big bang there was *literally nothing*.

It is difficult to grasp this because we cannot possibly imagine *nothing*. When we try, we tend to envision *something* and then hollow it out in some way and give it the label "nothing." When I try to picture *nothing*, for example, I typically find myself thinking of blackness. But blackness, of course, is something—opposite of whiteness and light. Moreover, blackness requires space in which to exist. It cannot be nowhere. It also requires time in which to exist. It cannot exist never.

---

5. Jastrow, *God and the Astronomers*, 123.
6. Jastrow, *God and the Astronomers*, 107.
7. Paul Davies, *The Mind of God: The Scientific Basis for a Rational World* (New York: Simon & Schuster, 1992), 48.

The difficulty of conceptualizing *nothing* can help us appreciate how mysterious and provocative it is to consider the emergence of the universe from nothing. Davies reflects on the sheer wonder of it:

> The significance of this result cannot be overstated. People often ask: Where did the big bang occur? The bang did not occur at a point in space at all. Space itself came into existence with the big bang. There is similar difficulty over the question: What happened before the big bang? The answer is, there was no "before." Time itself began at the big bang. As we have seen, Saint Augustine long ago proclaimed that the world was made with time and not in time, and that is precisely the modern scientific position.[8]

It is interesting that Davies, who is an agnostic like Jastrow, correlates big bang cosmology with theology (as Jastrow also did). But it makes sense: the notion of space-time itself coming into being has a striking resonance with the classic Judeo-Christian doctrine of creation *ex nihilo* (from nothing). The seeming religious associations of twentieth-century cosmological progress have been frequently observed. In 1951, for example, Pope Pius XII hailed big bang cosmology as "bearing witness" to the original *Fiat lux*.[9] And apologists have regularly appealed to the triumph of the big bang over the steady-state model as a confirmation of arguments for God as the first cause of the universe. On atheism, in contrast, this historical development is rather disquieting. The philosopher Anthony Kenny sums up the challenge the big bang puts to the atheist: "According to the big bang theory, the whole matter of the universe began to exist at a particular time in the

8. Davies, *The Mind of God*, 50. Later Davies proposes that the universe can create itself (e.g., 73).

9. Pope Pius XII, "The Proofs for the Existence of God in the Light of Modern Natural Science," address to the Pontifical Academy of Sciences, November 22, 1951, https://www.ewtn.com/catholicism/library/proofs-for-the-existence-of-god-in-the-light-of-modern-natural-science-8950.

remote past. A proponent of such a theory, at least if he is an atheist, must believe that the matter of the universe came from no thing and by nothing."[10]

So far this historical sketch will seem rather triumphant for the theistic side. But this is simply because we've not gotten to the challenges yet. Christians sometimes leap too glibly from "the universe began" to "God is the first cause"—from the big bang to Genesis 1:1—as though it were immediately obvious that the two are equivalent. More caution is in order. For starters, there has been a steady barrage of challenges to the standard model of the big bang that must be considered. In addition, we must consider what kind of causation we are dealing with when it comes to the first moment (and here we must humble ourselves under the sheer abstruseness of the subject we are dealing with).

We will touch on various concerns like these in a moment. But there is a different kind of response that is so exceedingly common that we should get it out of the way first (perhaps it has already crossed your mind).

If Everything Needs a Cause, What Caused God?

Many years ago, Bertrand Russell summarized his reason for rejecting first cause arguments this way:

> For a long time I accepted the argument of the First Cause, until one day, at the age of eighteen, I read John Stuart Mill's *Autobiography*, and I there found this sentence: "My father taught me that the question, 'Who made me?' cannot be answered, since it immediately suggests the further question, 'Who made God?'" That very simple sentence showed me, as I still think, the fallacy in the argument of the First Cause. If everything must have a cause, then God must have a cause. If there can be anything without a

10. Anthony Kenny, *The Five Ways* (New York: Schocken Books, 1969), 66.

cause, it may just as well be the world as God, so that there cannot be any validity in that argument.[11]

Today, this "What caused God?" question seems to be the stock-in-trade response to cosmological arguments. Christopher Hitchens utilized it in his engagement with both cosmological and design arguments: "The postulate of a designer or creator only raises the unanswerable question of who designed the designer or created the creator."[12] In the opening pages of the preface of his *A Universe from Nothing*, Lawrence Krauss starts off the book by making the same point: "The declaration of a First Cause still leaves open the question, 'Who created the creator?' After all, what is the difference between arguing in favor of an eternally existing creator versus an eternally existing universe without one?"[13] This argument sets up the whole book and gives him a rationale at various points throughout the book to allow for a spontaneous coming-to-be of the universe (because, after all, on Krauss's view theism faces the same problem of an arbitrary starting point).

I will never forget encountering this same response while reading through Richard Dawkins's *The God Delusion*, where it also features prominently.[14] In chapter 3, Dawkins is addressing arguments for God's existence. He begins by considering the first three

11. Bertrand Russell, *Why I Am Not a Christian: And Other Essays on Religion and Related Subjects*, ed. Paul Edwards (New York: Simon & Schuster, 1957), 6.

12. Christopher Hitchens, *God Is Not Great: How Religion Poisons Everything* (New York: Twelve, 2007), 71.

13. Lawrence Krauss, *A Universe from Nothing: Why There Is Something Rather Than Nothing* (New York: Atria Books, 2012), xii.

14. I'd been familiar with Dawkins through watching various debates and interviews over the years, but had never given his works a thorough reading. So I was excited to give a careful read to *The God Delusion*—based on reviews I had seen, I did not have high expectations of its philosophical rigor, but I looked forward to whatever challenges it might contain. In the interests of not being too impolite, I shall articulate my disappointment by simply stating that there is one sentence of the book with which I wholeheartedly agree, and that is on p. 82 when Dawkins asserts, "I am a scientist rather than a philosopher." Richard Dawkins, *The God Delusion* (New York: Houghton Mifflin, 2006).

of Thomas Aquinas's five "ways," which are essentially arguments for God as the first cause or ground of the universe. Dawkins responds to all three arguments at once: "All three of these arguments rely upon the idea of a regress and invoke God to terminate it. They make an entirely unwarranted assumption that God himself is immune to the regress. . . . It is more parsimonious to conjure up, say, a 'big bang singularity,' or some other physical concept as yet unknown."[15]

There are several intriguing aspects to this passage. For one, it is perplexing to consider how a "physical concept" could be the first cause of physical reality. Similarly, Dawkins references a "big bang singularity" as a possible way to terminate the regress of causation—but this is the very thing for which we are seeking a cause. This seems like replying to the question "Who wrote this book?" by saying, "Perhaps it has a preface we don't know about."

But here let's focus on Dawkins's claim that God is not immune from a regress of causation. This sentiment comes from the same angle as the common question, "If everything needs a cause, what caused God?" It's worth engaging this point, because this is such a frequent claim, and Dawkins himself comes back to this point again and again throughout the book (one might interpret it as one of the primary themes of the book).[16]

The problem with this objection is that it misunderstands what is meant by the term "God." In the standard conception of theism in the Western, Abrahamic traditions, God is *by definition* the utterly unique, uncaused, necessary, self-existent Being. He is not simply one entity among others in the chain of causation, who is somehow given a special pass to not play by the rules. (Dawkins seems to be thinking of God like this; that is why he can say things like, "The existence of God is a scientific hypothesis like any other.")[17]

15. Dawkins, *The God Delusion*, 77–78.
16. E.g., see also Dawkins, *The God Delusion*, 125, 143, 155.
17. Dawkins, *The God Delusion*, 50.

One can deny that an uncaused being exists; but to ask what *caused* him only reveals that the subject in view has not yet been understood. It's like asking, "Who is the bachelor's wife?" or, "What is the number that is larger than infinity?"

This is why, contrary to some popular misunderstandings, cosmological arguments don't claim that everything needs a cause. They claim, rather, that contingent things need a cause. For instance, the kalam version of the argument, focusing on temporal causation, claims that everything that *begins to exist* needs a cause. The instinct at play here—to infer back from contingency to necessity—is an ancient one. Aristotle, for instance, who believed the universe is eternal, is famous for proposing an "unmoved Mover" (or the *uncaused Cause*).[18] The cosmological advances throughout the twentieth century have simply drawn this more widespread human intuition—that necessity is the appropriate context in which to understand contingency—into contact with the issue of *time*.

For this reason, the argument is actually not dependent on the claim that the universe began. The crucial issue is not just what caused our world but what could account for any and all finite, contingent reality. As Matthew Levering points out, responding to various secular criticisms of the cosmological argument, "Even if we discovered that the universe was produced by another universe, this problem—the inability of contingent being to account for its own existence—would remain in full force."[19] The whole point of the cosmological argument is to point to the need for a different kind of reality altogether—a cause from "outside the system." Thus, if we conceive of God as simply a prior cause within the chain of being, some kind of first or most powerful cause among the other causes, we have missed the force of the

---

18. For an overview, see Joe Sachs, *Aristotle's Metaphysics* (Santa Fe, NM: Green Lion, 1999), 231–52.

19. Matthew Levering, *Proofs of God: Classical Arguments from Tertullian to Barth* (Grand Rapids: Baker Academic, 2016), 209. Cf. also 1–3.

argument. What is needed to explain the existence of a book is not a first sentence but an author: what is needed to explain the existence of contingent reality is not prior contingent reality but a necessary reality.

In this respect, the first three of Thomas Aquinas's famous "five ways" of proving God in the *Summa Theologica* (often classified as cosmological arguments) have an advantage in helping us grasp the real issue, for these arguments do not require a temporal beginning. The first argument (an argument from motion) suggests a first mover who is himself unmoved by anything else; the second (an argument from causality) suggests a first cause that is itself uncaused; the third (an argument from contingency) suggests a necessary being whose necessity comes from himself.[20] What is crucial to see is the ontological vision entailed by such arguments, for they all require two fundamentally distinct kinds of being. In the first argument, there are things in motion, and they possess actuality and potentiality variously; and then there is the first mover who is *pure* actuality.[21] In the second argument, there are things within the causal chain, related to intermediate and ultimate causes; and then there is the first cause, which exists outside of this causal chain. In the third argument, there are contingent things that might not have been and are perishable; and then there is that which exists necessarily and eternally.

None of these arguments require that time began. The second argument might seem that way, but Aquinas is not thinking of the "first cause" merely in the sense of what happened before

20. Thomas Aquinas, *Summa Theologica* I, q. 2, a. 3, trans. Fathers of the English Dominican Province (Notre Dame, IN: Christian Classics, 1948), 13.

21. As Levering (*Proofs of God*, 211) puts it, "The real crux of Thomas's argumentation is how to account for motion/change in beings in which there is an evident admixture of potency and act, for which reason they cannot account for their own actuality. This is why, for Thomas, essentially ordered causal chains come to rest not just in a first mover but in a first mover who is 'put in motion by no other,' that is to say Pure Act." For a discussion of the distinction between act and potency, see Edward Feser, *Scholastic Metaphysics: A Contemporary Introduction*, Editiones Scholasticae 39 (Piscataway, NJ: Transaction Books, 2019), 36–38.

everything else. As Frederick Copleston puts it: "When Aquinas talks about an 'order' of efficient causes he is not talking of a series stretching back into the past, but of a hierarchy of causes, in which a subordinate member is here and now dependent on the causal activity of a higher member. . . . We have to imagine, not a lineal or horizontal series, so to speak, but a vertical hierarchy, in which a lower member depends here and now on the present causal activity of the member above it."[22]

Francis Beckwith and Shawn Floyd use the metaphor of a light from a lamp being causally related to the wires, cables, and pylons that supply the needed electricity, which in turn are dependent upon transformers, which in turn are dependent upon power plants, which in turn are dependent on the conversion of natural resources, and on and on we might go. There is a "causal order of dependency," but the causes within that order do not necessarily work sequentially.[23]

What emerges from Thomas's three arguments is a particular way of thinking about the nature of existence: everything that exists does so in one of two ways, either as (a) necessary and infinite and eternal or (b) contingent and finite and perishable.[24] You have a kind of primal anchor; and then there is everything else that emanates out from it. Without the first cause, the rest of the causal system becomes arbitrary. This is why this idea of an "uncaused cause" (a distinct kind of being, as Shakespeare is distinct from Hamlet) has come into philosophical consideration—not as an arbitrary preference or an exception to the rules, but as a way to try to make sense of the world we live in. It's a way of accounting

22. F. C. Copleston, *Aquinas: An Introduction to the Life and Work of the Great Medieval Thinker* (1955; repr., New York: Penguin, 1991), 122–23.

23. Francis J. Beckwith and Shawn Floyd, "Saint Thomas Aquinas: Defending Faith and Reason," in *The History of Apologetics: A Biographical and Methodological Introduction*, ed. Benjamin K. Forrest, Joshua D. Chatraw, and Alister E. McGrath (Grand Rapids: Zondervan Academic, 2020), 240.

24. For further discussion of Aquinas's metaphysics, focusing on his distinctions between substance and accident, matter and form, and existence and essence, see Copleston, *Aquinas*, 80–108.

for the deepest question of philosophy: Why does something exist rather than nothing?

Whether these kinds of cosmological arguments are right or wrong, one thing is sure: they cannot be adequately analyzed without sensitivity to this vision of ontological duality. One could, of course, provide an argument for ontological monism: one could insist, for some reason or another, that everything must exist on the same ontological plane. But if one goes no further than asking, "What caused God?" one has simply *assumed* this alternative ontology. The question fails to grasp the distinction between a "first cause" and an ontologically distinct *uncaused* first cause, and thus falls short of engaging the actual proposal at hand (let alone settling it).

Historically, when the question "Who made God?" came into view, it was utilized to demonstrate precisely this point. The seventh-century Eastern theologian John of Damascus, for example, argued that because our world is mutable it must be created. He then reasoned: "The maker cannot have been created. For *if he had been created*, he also must surely have been created by some one, and so on till we arrive at something uncreated."[25] In other words, John is saying that so long as we are dealing with anything created or caused, we are still working back on the chain of causation: we have not yet arrived at the source. Therefore, whatever is itself caused is automatically excluded from being the first cause. The whole goal is to arrive at some kind of uncreated cause that could explain all other reality. Only a very particular kind of entity—something beginningless and uncaused—could possibly

25. John of Damascus, *An Exact Exposition of the Orthodox Faith* 1.3, in *Nicene and Post-Nicene Fathers*, Series 2, vol. 9, *Hilary of Poitiers, John of Damascus*, ed. Philip Schaff and Henry Wace (1899; repr., Peabody, MA: Hendrickson, 1994), 2 (italics added). John provides a unique and intriguing historical window into the task of apologetics, since his theological vocation involved summarizing the earlier church fathers while anticipating and responding to the challenge of Islam. For a summary of John's contribution to the task of apologetics, see Daniel J. Janosik, "John of Damascus: Preparing Christians for the Coming Age of Islam," in Forrest, Chatraw, and McGrath, *The History of Apologetics*, 163–78.

meet the metaphysical need at hand. To be up for consideration as a candidate for this role, the thing in question *must* be uncaused. This is also why the cosmological argument is not a "god of the gaps" appeal, in which we invoke God as the cause of the universe simply because we do yet know of another cause.[26] The need for a ground of being is not a *gap*. For even if we possessed an exhaustive understanding of every physical event, such that no gaps in our knowledge remained, we would still not have explained where the *world itself* came from. Thinking that scientific advance will remove the need for a meta-cause is like getting two-thirds of the way through Hamlet and thinking that the final third will somehow replace the need for Shakespeare.

I will never forget the moment at which this consideration was impressed upon me: while reading Stephen Hawking's *A Brief History of Time*. At the very end of this book, after outlining the search for a grand unified theory that explains the entire universe, he writes: "Even if there is only one possible unified theory, it is just a set of rules and equations. What is it that breathes fire into the equations and makes a universe for them to describe? The usual approach of science of constructing a mathematical model cannot answer the questions of why there should be a universe for the model to describe. Why does the universe go to the bother of existing?"[27] This passage captures what is at the heart of the challenge presented by the big bang: Why is the universe here? Whatever laws could possibly explain it, how did *they* get here? Ludwig Wittgenstein expressed this intuition succinctly: "Not *how* the world, is the mystical, but *that* it is."[28]

26. Carl Sagan used to speak often of "god of the gaps" arguments. As he put it: "As science advances, there seems to be less and less for God to do. . . . Whatever it is we cannot explain lately is attributed to God. . . . And then, after a while, we explain it, and so that's no longer God's realm." Carl Sagan, *The Varieties of Scientific Experience: A Personal View of the Search for God*, ed. Ann Druyan (New York: Penguin, 2006), 64.

27. Stephen Hawking, *A Brief History of Time*, updated and expanded 10th anniv. ed. (New York: Bantam, 1998), 190.

28. Ludwig Wittgenstein, *Tractatus Logico-Philosophicus* 6.44 (New York: Harcourt, Brace, 1922), 187 (my translation and italics). For an insightful analysis of

So to return to the main point: If you don't like the hypothesis of "God" as the explanation of the big bang, you have a range of possibilities at your disposal, which we will consider next. But the one thing that cannot be done is to ask what *caused* God. Because—unless you insert your own private definition of the word "God"—the question is tantamount to: "What is the cause of the uncaused?" This question fares no better than "Who is older than eternity?"

Could the Universe Be a "Self-Starter"?

If the "What caused God?" objection is not the best response to cosmological arguments, what are the other options? One is to allow for the standard cosmological picture but simply deny that the beginning of the universe needs a cause. Several decades ago the philosopher J. L. Mackie rejected the cosmological argument along these lines. Because the cosmological argument relies on the principle of sufficient reason, he asserted, the argument "expresses a demand that things should be intelligible *through and through.* The simple reply . . . is that there is nothing that justifies this demand."[29] Mackie concluded that "we have no good ground for an *a priori* certainty that there could not have been a sheer unexplained beginning of things."[30]

It is difficult to out-argue such a line of resistance. How could one prove, without any remainder of doubt, that causality does not work differently at the singularity represented at the big bang?

Still, this is not a very popular view, since most people don't find it very satisfying to regard the big bang as a kind of brute fact requiring no explanation. Such a proposal runs contrary to

---

Wittgenstein's intriguing relevance to theology, see Fergus Kerr, *Theology after Wittgenstein*, 2nd ed. (London: SPCK, 1997).

29. J. L. Mackie, *The Miracle of Theism: Arguments for and against the Existence of God* (Oxford: Oxford University Press, 1982), 85 (italics original).

30. Mackie, *The Miracle of Theism*, 94.

our deepest intuitions and our every observation of how the world works.[31] Nonetheless, if you are inclined toward Mackie's "sheer unexplained beginning of things," I will not say a word against it—all I say is, congratulations, you have just inherited the most mysterious worldview ever.

The more common way of responding to arguments based on the big bang is to opt for some kind of nonstandard cosmology. Scientists continue to propose new models in which the universe had no beginning of time or in which the beginning of time is explained internally by the model itself. Among more recent models, some have a kind of science fiction feel to them. For instance, one theory proposes that the universe created itself through some kind of time loop. I won't spend much time on this one, but if you want to explore it, google "closed timelike curves" (and have your aspirin at hand for the headache that follows!).[32] One of the older hypotheses is the oscillating universe, in which the universe expands from a singularity, collapses back on itself, and then repeats this process indefinitely. This view has faced various challenges and is less common today, though new versions of it keep cropping up.[33]

A more widely considered model in recent decades draws from the observation that the universe went through a period of ex-

31. As William Lane Craig and James D. Sinclair note, even the skeptic David Hume asserted, "I have never asserted so absurd a principle as that anything might arise without a cause." Craig and Sinclair, "The *Kalam* Cosmological Argument," in *The Blackwell Companion to Natural Theology*, ed. William Lane Craig and J. P. Moreland (Malden, MA: Wiley-Blackwell, 2020), 190.

32. See J. Richard Gott and Li-Xin Li, "Can the Universe Create Itself?," *Physical Review D* 58, no. 2 (1998).

33. Many scientists believe there are good reasons to think that the universe will not contract but instead continue to expand indefinitely. There are also concerns as to whether it is physically possible for a collapsing universe to bounce back to expansion, as opposed to simply ending in a "crunch," since there are no known physics by which such a "bounce" could occur. A further challenge involves the likelihood that entropy would be carried over from one expansion to another, so that even if the oscillating model is correct, the universe would still have had a beginning. For more on the oscillating universe model, see William Lane Craig, "The Ultimate Question of Origins: God and the Beginning of the Universe," *Astrophysics and Space Science* 269–270 (1999): 723–40.

tremely rapid inflation immediately after the big bang.[34] According to the theory of "eternal inflation," this inflation lasts forever in at least some regions of the universe, as inflating regions reproduce themselves by creating new universes ("bubble universes") in the process. At the risk of oversimplifying, here's a way to picture it (though if you want to pursue this further, google "repulsive gravity" and keep the aspirin ready): Imagine a region of space inflating at an exponential rate. Within this region, new bubble universes come into being, and to each bubble universe, its own beginning *looks* like a "big bang" because the surrounding material is unobservable as it inflates more rapidly. New bubble universes continually come into being and the inflation never stops. The result is an eternally inflating, infinite multiverse. Pretty cool idea, right?

One of the potential consequences of eternal inflation is that it raises challenges for considering the big bang as an absolute beginning. Alan Guth, one of the model's architects, puts it like this: "Since our own pocket universe would be equally likely to lie anywhere on the infinite tree of universes produced by eternal inflation, we would expect to find ourselves arbitrarily far from the beginning."[35] But does eternal inflation entail an infinite past or just an infinite future? It turns out that Guth himself thinks that the multiverse likely still did have a beginning and that inflation is eternal only into the future, not into the past.[36] Thus, even if eternal inflation is correct, it does not necessarily remove the need for some kind of beginning.[37] We'll say a bit more about the relevance of the multiverse proposal in the next chapter.

34. This was understood to explain several anomalies in previous cosmological models, such as the flatness of the universe. Originally, inflation was held to occur immediately after the big bang, but some current models hold that it is what provides the initial conditions for the big bang.
35. Alan H. Guth, "Eternal Inflation," *Annals of the New York Academy of Sciences* 950, no. 1 (2001): 79.
36. See Alan H. Guth, "Eternal Inflation and Its Implications," *Journal of Physics A: Mathematical and Theoretical* 40, no. 25 (2007): 6811–26.
37. For further discussion of eternal inflation, see Craig and Sinclair, "The *Kalam* Cosmological Argument," 136–42.

Probably the most popular alternative models to the standard view of the big bang involve applying the principles of quantum mechanics to the origins of the universe. Quantum mechanics and general relativity are two of the great discoveries of twentieth-century physics: the former describes the universe at a very small scale; the latter describes the universe at a very large scale. The standard model of the big bang, based on the theorems of Hawking and Penrose, assumed the validity of general relativity. But what if the initial singularity should be understood in terms of quantum mechanics rather than general relativity?

Perhaps the most famous effort in this vein, published in 1983, is Stephen Hawking and James Hartle's "no boundary proposal," according to which time is finite and yet without a boundary.[38] On this proposal, if we could go back in time, as we approached the beginning of the universe we would at some point reach a state at which time as we know it ceases to exist and at which it is impossible to measure events. If the standard model pictures the origins of the universe like a cone, this model sees it like a shuttlecock (see fig. 1). Various other proposals avoiding an initial singularity or boundary conditions surfaced around this time, such as Alexander Vilenkin's "tunneling from nothing" theory, which also came out in the early 1980s.[39]

In a more recent work, Stephen Hawking and Leonard Mlodinow popularized the idea that the universe could have created itself from nothing.[40] They note that if the energy of a particular material object (say, a star) were negative, it could be created in a state of motion such that its positive energy and negative energy were exactly balanced. In such a situation, empty space would be

38. James B. Hartle and Stephen W. Hawking, "Wave Function of the Universe," *Physical Review D* 28 (1983): 2960–75.

39. Alexander Vilenkin, "Creation of Universes from Nothing," *Physics Letters B* 117 (1982): 25–28.

40. Stephen Hawking and Leonard Mlodinow, *The Grand Design* (New York: Bantam, 2010).

FIGURE 1

Shuttlecock Model for the Origins of the Universe

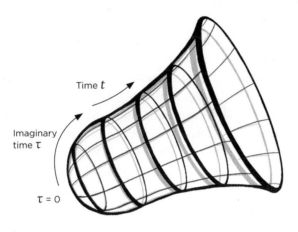

unstable—things could simply pop into being.[41] We don't observe things popping into existence from nothing, however, because the energy of the universe is constant. Thus, at the local level, empty space is stable because material things have more positive energy than negative energy. However, Hawking and Mlodinow propose that, because gravitational energy is negative, the law of gravity can shape space-time such that it is "locally stable but globally unstable."[42] Thus, while particular material bodies (say, stars) cannot pop into existence from nothing, the universe in its entirety can: "Because there is a law like gravity, the universe can and will create itself from nothing."[43]

Hawking and Mlodinow don't hesitate to draw out the philosophical implications of this proposal: "Spontaneous creation is the reason there is something rather than nothing, why the universe exists, why we exist. It is not necessary to invoke God to light the blue touch paper and set the universe going."[44] As fascinating

41. Hawking and Mlodinow, *The Grand Design*, 179.
42. Hawking and Mlodinow, *The Grand Design*, 180.
43. Hawking and Mlodinow, *The Grand Design*, 180.
44. Hawking and Mlodinow, *The Grand Design*, 180.

as this possibility is, we cannot help but notice here an antecedent condition for the universe's self-creation: the law of gravity. This, of course, raises the question, "Where did the law of gravity come from?" Thus, even if "spontaneous creation" were a completely accurate proposal, it does not explain why there is something instead of nothing, as it is purported to do. For the law of gravity is not nothing. More on this in a moment.

Two years after Hawking and Mlodinow's work, Lawrence Krauss published *A Universe from Nothing: Why There Is Something Rather Than Nothing*. Building on Vilenkin's "tunneling from nothing" model, Krauss argued that in a flat universe in which average Newtonian gravitational energy is ultimately zero, the universe will create itself from nothing.[45] It's worth engaging Krauss's book a bit, since it is sometimes claimed as a way out of the implications of the standard model. For example, in his afterword to the book, Richard Dawkins refers to Krauss's work as "the knockout blow" among various other antitheistic arguments. Dawkins concludes his afterword as follows: "If *On the Origin of Species* was biology's deadliest blow to supernaturalism, we may come to see *A Universe from Nothing* as the equivalent from cosmology. The title means exactly what it says. And what it says is devastating."[46]

But *does* the title mean "exactly" what it says? *Nothing*—used in both the title and subtitle of the book—is a tricky word, and trying to define it takes us into a cardinal difficulty at the intersection of cosmology and philosophy. In his *New York Times* review of Krauss's book, David Albert objects to the way Krauss defines "nothing" as a vacuum state containing no particles in a relativistic quantum field: "The fact that particles can pop in and out of existence, over time, as those fields rearrange themselves, is not a whit more mysterious than the fact that fists can pop in and out of existence, over time, as my fingers rearrange themselves. And

---

45. Krauss, *A Universe from Nothing*, 152. For further explanation of the meaning of a "flat universe," see 34–35, 75.
46. Richard Dawkins, afterword to Krauss, *A Universe from Nothing*, 191.

none of these poppings—if you look at them aright—amount to anything even remotely in the neighborhood of a creation from nothing."[47]

In a new preface to his book, Krauss acknowledges criticisms like this and delimits the question of his book to how space and time can come into being, as well as "perhaps" to how the laws of the universe come into being.[48] He recognizes that this simply leaves open the deeper question about why there is not "absolute nothingness." His response to this question is telling: "I take a rather flippant attitude toward this concern, because I don't think it adds anything to the productive discussion, which is 'What questions are actually answerable by probing the universe?' I have discounted this philosophical issue . . . because I think it bypasses the really interesting and answerable physical questions associated with the origin and evolution of our universe."[49]

But why discount the philosophical question of absolute nothingness simply because it cannot be answered by science? This judgment reflects a particular mentality, one that apparently sees only physical questions, answerable by science, as "productive" or "interesting." This is itself, ironically, a *philosophy*—for such a mentality does not depend on any empirical observations of physical reality.

In the actual procedure of the book, Krauss spends the greater portion of space surveying and reflecting on physics from Einstein to the present day. As the book finally climaxes into its implications in the last three chapters, Krauss offers three distinct definitions of

47. David Albert, "On the Origin of Everything," Review of *A Universe from Nothing*, *New York Times*, March 23, 2012, https://www.nytimes.com/2012/03/25 /books/review/a-universe-from-nothing-by-lawrence-m-krauss.html.

48. Krauss, *A Universe from Nothing*, xvi.

49. Krauss, *A Universe from Nothing*, xvii. It is not clear why Krauss's preferred way of limiting the question should be followed. To return to the abductive approach: Which way of thinking about "nothing" seems more open-minded and responsive to the data? Which seems more interdisciplinary and sensitive to alternative ways of thinking? Or, to put the question another way: Which seems more true to the investigative spirit of science?

"nothing." First, he proposes the "simplest definition of nothing, namely empty space."[50] Krauss thinks that this empty space is both endowed with energy and governed by physical laws. Even Krauss admits that this definition of nothing is not really nothing: "It would be disingenuous to suggest that empty space endowed with energy, which drives inflation, is really *nothing*."[51] That is why, to his credit, Krauss will frequently qualify the word "nothing" when it is being used in this sense, speaking of "empty space—what formerly could have passed for nothing,"[52] or "what is essentially nothingness,"[53] or what is "almost nothing."[54]

But since Krauss has not titled his book *A Universe from *Almost* Nothing*, we have to get further than this.[55] So Krauss asserts a second definition of "nothing," suggesting that "once we allow for the merging of quantum mechanics and general relativity, we can extend this argument to the case where space itself is forced into existence."[56] Here Krauss's argument is more tentative; he admits that it does not strictly *prove* a beginning from nothing.[57] But even so, there is a problem: quantum mechanics and general relativity are not nothing; they are particular laws that are observed in relation to the space-time universe. So we still have not answered the fundamental question that stands behind Krauss's subtitle: *Why There Is Something Rather Than Nothing*.

Krauss recognizes this concern, and he addresses it in the book's final chapter. It is here, at last, in treating this third sense of the

50. Krauss, *A Universe from Nothing*, 149.
51. Krauss, *A Universe from Nothing*, 152 (italics original).
52. Krauss, *A Universe from Nothing*, 183.
53. Krauss, *A Universe from Nothing*, 151.
54. Krauss, *A Universe from Nothing*, 148.
55. Krauss, *A Universe from Nothing*, 149, mistakenly thinks that this is how philosophers and theologians classically defined "nothing": "I suspect that, at the times of Plato and Aquinas, when they pondered why there was something rather than nothing, empty space with nothing in it was probably a good approximation of what there were thinking about."
56. Krauss, *A Universe from Nothing*, 161.
57. Krauss, *A Universe from Nothing*, 170.

term "nothing," that Krauss's proposal becomes relevant to the subtitle of his book. He opens the chapter by acknowledging the difficulty of the question at hand: "The central problem with the notion of creation is that it appears to require some externality, something outside of the system itself, to preexist, in order to create the conditions necessary for the system to come into being."[58] Krauss spends several pages reiterating the "What caused God?" objection and questioning the validity of the philosophical principle "Out of nothing, nothing comes."[59] Then he proposes his own solution, a combination of two tenets we will consider more in the next chapter: (1) the multiverse theory (which holds that there are many, possibly infinite, universes, each of which may be governed by different physical laws) and (2) the anthropic principle (which holds that the universe appears to us the way it does because of our location within it). From these two principles Krauss concludes the following: "In a multiverse of any of the types that have been discussed, there could be an infinite number of regions, potentially infinitely big or infinitesimally small, in which there is simply 'nothing,' and there could be regions where there is 'something.' In this case, the response to why there is something rather than nothing becomes almost trite: there is something simply because if there were nothing, we wouldn't find ourselves living there!"[60]

Krauss acknowledges the frustration inherent in this answer but observes that the history of science teaches us that the universe is counterintuitive and truth does not conform to our wishes or expectations. He then concludes by seeming to divert attention from the question itself: "Why is there something rather than nothing? Ultimately, this question may be no more significant or profound than asking why some flowers are red and some are

---

58. Krauss, *A Universe from Nothing*, 171.
59. Krauss, *A Universe from Nothing*, 171–74.
60. Krauss, *A Universe from Nothing*, 177. We will discuss the anthropic principle more in the next chapter.

blue. 'Something' may always come from nothing. It may be required, independent of the underlying nature of reality. Or perhaps 'something' may not be very special or even very common in the multiverse. Either way, what is really useful is not pondering this question, but rather participating in the exciting voyage of discovery that may reveal specifically how the universe in which we live evolved and is evolving."[61]

And that's it. That's the end of the argument. Except another one and a half pages to note that the universe will eventually return to nothing. Then the book concludes with a brief epilogue.

I can recall my surprise and dismay at this point of the book, having persevered so far to reach it. The dismay resulted partly from the thoroughly speculative nature of Krauss's hypothesis. It resulted partly from Krauss's downplaying of the significance of the question that his subtitle purported to answer (as though the question is like asking why some flowers are red and others are blue).[62] It resulted partly from the shining, resilient fact that a multiverse is not nothing. But mainly, it resulted from a sense of the rhetorical overreach of his project. Krauss himself summarizes the implications of his book as making it "possible to not believe in God" and making "religious belief . . . less and less necessary"[63] and as entailing that we live in "a universe without purpose or guidance."[64] The final sentence of the book sums it up: "God is unnecessary."[65] Elsewhere, he describes his hypothesis as doing to cosmology what Darwin did for biology: "Just as Darwin . . . removed the need for divine intervention in the evolution of the modern world, . . . our current understanding of the universe, its past, and its future makes it more plausible that

    61. Krauss, *A Universe from Nothing*, 178.
    62. This relates to Krauss's preference for asking *how* questions rather than *why* questions, which I do not share, and which recurs throughout *A Universe from Nothing* (see xiv, 144, 146, 178).
    63. Krauss, *A Universe from Nothing*, 183.
    64. Krauss, *A Universe from Nothing*, 181.
    65. Krauss, *A Universe from Nothing*, 185.

'something' can arise out of nothing without the need for any divine guidance."[66]

Now notice these final words: *without the need for any divine guidance.* As we observed, Krauss has acknowledged in his newer preface that he is not really dealing with pure nothingness; and when he treats this conception of nothing (his third definition), his proposal is speculative and inconclusive, downplaying the importance of the question. How, then, could the noninvolvement of God be legitimately inferred from such a proposal?

By presenting his proposal as removing the need for God and emptying the universe of purpose or guidance, Krauss has passed from the realm of physics into the territory of philosophy. Ironically, the very preference for scientific theories of how the universe developed rather than the ultimate philosophical issue of absolute nothingness is itself a philosophical outlook not required by any scientific evidence. The same is true of the bold claim with which Hawking and Mlodinow start off *The Grand Design*: "Philosophy is dead. . . . Scientists have become the bearers of the torch of discovery in our quest for knowledge."[67] There is no argument for this claim; it is just asserted. And again, it is itself a philosophical claim—it is not empirically verifiable in the way scientific theories are. So we must be clear: whatever else Hawking, Mlodinow, and Krauss are doing, and whether their models are correct are not, they are not replacing philosophy with physics; rather, they are using physics to offer to us their own (arguably less self-aware) philosophy.

To sum up, then, what shall we say about these various non-standard cosmological models? It is hugely difficult to *disprove* them. For one thing, many of them are exceedingly difficult to evaluate or even conceptualize. Some of the options seem about as intelligible as the "flux capacitor" that Dr. Emmett Brown uses to make the DeLorean travel through time in *Back to the Future*.

66. Krauss, *A Universe from Nothing*, 147.
67. Hawking and Mlodinow, *The Grand Design*, 5.

Furthermore, the field of cosmology is still developing, which alerts us to the possibility of future theories complicating or changing the conversation. In addition, as we have said, the subject matter is so difficult: the further we go back in time toward the beginning of the universe, the less we have experimental handles by which to make measurements and judgments, and the more we are dealing with matters that are extremely far removed from our ordinary reasoning and observation. The first moments immediately following the big bang are so alien to anything we experience that it's intimidating to even be confident in the vocabulary we use to describe it.

So what do we do in the meantime? A reasonable approach is to opt for the view that we believe is most likely and best supported by the available evidence and then place a proportionate amount of confidence in this choice based on *how much* more likely we think it is. This is a somewhat limited and provisional conclusion, but it is not irrelevant in the quest for truth. It might move the needle a few notches in one direction or another while we continue to assess other evidence.

For two reasons, I think positing some kind of antecedent cause to the universe remains the best hypothesis. First, the standard model of the big bang remains the most widely affirmed, and it is reasonable to regard it as the *best* currently available option. Second, it is not clear that the nonstandard models remove the need for a cause. For one thing, many of them still posit a beginning (Guth's eternal inflation theory, for instance—this is one of the more popular nonstandard models).[68] As long as there is a beginning, there remains the seemingly intractable question: *Why* did it begin? Moreover, as we have seen, even in a beginningless

---

68. Even if the "no boundary proposal" were right, this would not prove that the universe did not begin. It would, perhaps, blunt the confidence with which we propose a beginning. But to say it had no beginning requires a further extrapolation from the data of a philosophical nature, for the proposal explicitly tells us that it is impossible to measure events in the state in which time has broken down.

universe we still have to account for existence itself: Why is there any contingent, finite being? The best alternative would perhaps be some kind of infinite multiverse that is defined as, in some way, a "necessary being." But it's not easy to slap the label "necessary being" onto a physical realm that is defined by its own set of highly particular laws and characteristics. A necessary being is one that could not not exist; one of the great wonders that our universe almost invariably inspires is precisely why it *does* exist. We can quite easily imagine that it (and us) should not be here at all. As Hawking asked, "Why does the universe go to the bother of existing?"[69]

Drawing from both of these points, if we were to aim to restrict ourselves to the most modest conclusion possible, we might simply say that *it seems more likely than not that our physical world (universe/multiverse) has a cause, and therefore it seems a distinct possibility that our physical world is not all that exists (since whatever caused it would exist independently of it, as its cause).*

Supposing this were right, and there were some kind of transcendent Cause behind the universe—some kind of *Supernature*, if you will—what kind of thing would this Supernature be? Strictly on the basis of the cosmological argument, it is difficult to say. Certainly some kind of theism or deism may initially seem a natural candidate. Many have argued, for example, that personal agents have causal powers that impersonal things lack.[70] It certainly seems reasonable that the kinds of causes *that we know about* that would be capable of something like

---

69. Hawking, *A Brief History of Time*, 190.

70. Philosophers often speak of "agent causation" as a distinct kind of causation that can produce a new causal chain without prior effects. J. P. Moreland argues that this kind of cause can better account for the beginning of time: "The only way for the first event to arise spontaneously from a timeless, changeless, spaceless state of affairs, and at the same time to be caused, is this—the event resulted from the free act of a person or agent." J. P. Moreland, "The Kalam Cosmological Argument," in *Philosophy of Religion: Selected Readings*, ed. Michael Peterson, William Hasker, Bruce Reichenbach, and David Basinger (New York: Oxford University Press, 1996), 188.

the creation of the universe would be personal agents. If the cause is personal, this might also help answer some of the classic difficulties with the notion of the creation of time, such as the seeming incongruity involved in an eternal cause and a temporal effect.[71]

Nonetheless, it is difficult to be dogmatic about what the first cause must be like. The question is just so difficult and remote. I find theism a powerful explanatory framework for accounting for the existence of our world, but I admit that it seems easier to detect a first cause than to deduce what it must be like.

And yet, granting this restriction, what we still seem to be left with is a universe that doesn't very naturally account for its own existence. It looks suspiciously like Something else stands behind it. It appears less like a brute fact and more like an echo or consequence of Something prior. We may not know quite what this Something prior is just yet, but whatever else it may also be, the one thing it *must* be is *able to cause the universe*. It is therefore likely to be Something very powerful and intriguing (you may notice how I keep capitalizing the Thing in question)—perhaps even the Necessity itself that must stand apart from all causal chains.

Suppose for the sake of argument that there is indeed a so-called Supernature behind the universe: what effect might such a discovery have on our philosophical outlook? For many of us, such a possibility is deeply intriguing and evocative. In comparison, naturalism seems somewhat cramped and restricted. Why is this? What kinds of metaphysical possibilities open up if we allow for some kind of Supernature? Let's probe this way of thinking a bit more to explore the implications at stake.

71. This concern is often brought up in relation to Kant's first antinomy, and in particular its assertion that prior to the existence of time no moment has any more condition of existence than any other moment. See the discussion in Craig, *The Kalām Cosmological Argument*, 149–50. For three arguments in favor of the personality of the first cause, see also William Lane Craig, *Reasonable Faith: Christian Truth and Apologetics*, 3rd ed. (Wheaton: Crossway, 2008), 152–53.

Why a Supernature Makes Reality More Interesting

There are various ways we might envision a Supernature, but for the moment let us conceive of it as not merely older than the physical universe but as possessing a different and superlative kind of existence altogether (hence: *Super*nature). Such an idea is plausible insofar as we are talking about what could function as the first cause of the universe, and an effect is not generally greater than the cause. Moreover, as we have said, it is difficult to explain the existence of contingent things solely by means of other contingent things. A Supernature opens the door to the possibility of a noncontingent (necessary) being. Indeed, it could even itself *be* the necessary being: the ultimate terminus that explains the enigma of existence. On such a view, everything in our world, from rocks to quasars to the number eleven, would all trace back to one primal source that itself is a qualitatively greater *kind* of reality.

It is sometimes difficult to imagine such possibilities, because most of us are accustomed to thinking in terms of one fundamental *kind* of being, in all its different variations. Supergiant stars, mushrooms, protons, and lava are all very different from one another; nonetheless, they all inhabit the same fundamental plane of reality. When we talk about the Supernature, however, we are dealing with something of an entirely different realm of being.

We might be helped by considering our recurring metaphor of an author's creation of a story. Consider, for example, C. S. Lewis's Chronicles of Narnia. If you are familiar with these stories, you recall that when Lucy steps through a wardrobe in England, she finds herself in an altogether different world called Narnia. Narnia is not merely a different place but a different world. It can be accessed only by magic, not travel; time there passes differently; it is filled with talking animals; and so forth. There are other worlds as well, like Charn, and even a sort of transit world between the various worlds.

If there is a Supernature, its relation to nature should be envisioned as more like the relation between Narnia and England than the relation between any two locations in our universe. We are dealing with the possibility of a different world altogether, not just a different place in the world. Some people, of course, reject such a possibility out of hand. It feels like going down the rabbit hole in *Alice in Wonderland*. Such a rejection is not a scientific discovery, however, but a philosophical outlook. There is no conclusive evidence against the possibility of separate worlds; in fact, it may be the case that there *couldn't* be (what could ever constitute such evidence?).

Moreover, provocative as the idea of an alternate realm is, the fact that the physical universe we inhabit does not appear self-explanatory may encourage us to consider such possibilities. There is a significant body of philosophical thought that supposes this is the best way, perhaps even the only way, to explain the mystery of existence. David Bentley Hart outlines how this way of thinking has worked itself out in, for instance, the Christian tradition:

> [No philosopher] has ever succeeded at overcoming the perplexity that the enigma of our existence occasions in us, in those moments of wonder that we all from time to time experience and that are (according to Plato and Aristotle) the beginning of all true philosophy. In the terms of Thomas Aquinas, a finite thing's essence (*what* it is) entirely fails to account for its existence (*that* it is); and there is a very venerable and coherent Christian tradition of reflection that holds that this failure, when considered with adequate rigor, points toward an infinite and infinitely simple actuality transcendent of all material, composite, or finite causes and contingencies . . . in whom essence and existence are identical.[72]

Thus, with regard to the great question of metaphysics—Why is there something rather than nothing?—the one who believes in

72. David Bentley Hart, *Atheist Delusions: The Christian Revolution and Its Fashionable Enemies* (New Haven: Yale University Press, 2009), 104.

a Supernature believes that the mystery of existence ultimately terminates in Something that not only enjoys existence but also somehow *possesses* existence. One way to put it: the Supernature (or at least one part of the Supernature)[73] is not simply real but is reality itself. It is not one thing among others but is the ground of reality itself. This one, necessary, infinite reality *has always been here*. Indeed, it *could never not* have been here.

This way of thinking about the Supernature—an infinite, necessary, eternal Reality in which all other reality swims—is somewhat bracing when you are first considering it. It's almost hard to even grasp it at first. It runs counter to so many instincts of modern thought. As I have noted, many swiftly recoil against it. For others, it has a kind of elegance and intrigue, suggesting a more mystical, enchanted world. Here I propose that, in two ways, supernaturalism suggests a more interesting and evocative world than the one pictured by naturalism.

In the first place, the existence of a Supernature means reality is larger and grander. Peter Kreeft expresses the contrast in this way: on supernaturalism, there are more things in reality than in thought; on naturalism, there are more things in thought that in reality. He describes the first of these options as "the philosophy of the poet and of the happy man, for whom nature is a fullness, a moreness, and therefore wonderful." Naturalism, by contrast, is "the philosophy of the unhappy man, the cynic, the pessimist."[74] Kreeft notes that basically all premodern cultures were of the happy view, and you can hardly ever find the cynical one until the modern era.

What difference do these views make? Kreeft summarizes:

> It makes a total difference, a difference to absolutely every single thing in your life. It colors everything. For if you believe the first

---

73. Again, it could of course be the case that other contingent realities exist within the Supernature or in relation to the Supernature in some manner. But in order to ground being, the Supernature would need to contain more than *only* contingent realities.

74. Kreeft, *The Philosophy of Tolkien*, 33.

philosophy, . . . then your fundamental attitude toward all reality is wonder and humility. You are like a small child in a large house. As Tolkien said in one of his letters, "You are inside a very great story." You expect mysteries, you expect moreness: terrors to stop your heart and joys to break it. Reality is *big*. . . . In this big world there may be not only things like dragons, but even heroes.[75]

This metaphor of a child inside a large house is a poignant way of capturing the sense of mystery and wonder that the prospect of a Supernature holds. But is this entirely fair? Someone might say that even if the universe is all there is, it's still so immense as to inspire humility and wonder.

It is certainly true that the physical universe itself inspires wonder and humility. But the question at hand is, Which is *more* mysterious, *more* humbling? Here the answer seems clear. The possibility of a Supernature is a potentially infinite addition to reality, and the emotional impact of such an idea is profound and decisive. It feels as though we have spent all our lives living in the basement, with no conception of what "outside" means—only one day to happen upon a hidden staircase leading upward into the unknown, with sunlight streaming down through the cracks in the doorway at the top. Can you imagine the thrill of such a discovery? *Anything* could be up there.

Speaking for myself, supernaturalism is exciting in exactly this way, and it enhances and expands the experience of this world indescribably. To give just one example: on supernaturalism, there is the possibility that learning will never end. If indeed the Supernature turns out to be infinite, as is the case with theism, then we find ourselves in a world in which there will always be more to discover. For all eternity, our orientation toward reality can remain in the manner of exploration.

In a finite universe, by contrast, we can (eventually) run out of things to learn. Back in the early twentieth century, Bertrand

75. Kreeft, *The Philosophy of Tolkien*, 33.

Russell claimed that "physical science is thus approaching the stage when it will be complete, and therefore uninteresting."[76] Whether you agree with his optimism regarding the progress of science or not, his interpretation of the result of this perceived progress as "uninteresting" makes a certain kind of sense. Once everything were known, reality would become like a video game you have already beaten or a novel you have already finished. You can beat it or read it again, I suppose, but it seems more possible to get bored.

It is in relation to these kinds of sentiments that G. K. Chesterton claimed, "If the cosmos of the materialist is the real cosmos, it is not much of a cosmos. The thing has shrunk. . . . The whole of life is something much more grey, narrow, and trivial than many separate aspects of it. The parts seem greater than the whole."[77] Chesterton's claim that "the parts seem greater than the whole" is a point we will return to in the next chapter, when we consider what a naturalistic worldview entails for such "parts" as meaning, love, music, and so forth.

There is a second way that supernaturalism makes the world more interesting: it means that reality is thicker and more complicated than we thought. For not only is there something more than physical reality but physical reality *itself* becomes more enigmatic and mysterious—it apparently exists in a kind of interlocked relationship with some other, nonphysical reality. There is not only something beyond what we can see and measure, but something, so to speak, *behind* it.

Granted, this is not the only way a Supernature could be understood. But it is one plausible view, and certainly the theistic way of looking at things. Theists in the Western tradition, for example, have always correlated the *creation* of physical reality with the *sustenance* and *preservation* of physical reality. Sometimes this latter idea, called providence, is even spoke of as a kind of continuous

76. Russell, *Why I Am Not a Christian*, 49.
77. G. K. Chesterton, *Orthodoxy* (Peabody, MA: Hendrickson, 2006), 19.

creation.[78] (This idea is not at odds, of course, with finding physical causes for events; it simply holds that there is a deeper kind of explanation that lies beyond the physical causes.)

One way to put it is that physical objects share, or *participate*, in a deeper spiritual reality of which they are a part. Theologians have often described the ontology entailed by theism as a *sacramental* ontology, which theologian Hans Boersma describes like this: "According to the sacramental ontology of much of the Christian tradition, the created order was more than just an external or nominal symbol. Instead, it was a sign (*signum*) that pointed to and participated in a greater reality (*res*). . . . The reason for the mysterious character of the world—on the understanding of the Great Tradition, at least—is that it participates in some greater reality, from which it derives its being and its value."[79]

Theologian Thomas Torrance describes scientific progress as accessing rather than surpassing spiritual reality, and he speaks of "an ascending gradient of meaning" in which the spiritual realm is the ultimate animating cause of the material.[80] This vision of the interrelation of the spiritual and physical realms is a classical Christian instinct.[81] For the naturalist, by contrast, physical reality has a sense of inherent limitation. For instance, Lawrence Krauss emphasizes how in his model, since physical reality emerged from nothing, not only will it eventually return to nothing but in some sense it already *is* nothing. As he puts it, we live in a universe where "the very distinction between nothing and something has begun to

78. This is a complicated point that has often been considered throughout the history of Christian theology; see the discussion in G. C. Berkouwer, *The Providence of God*, trans. Lewis Smedes (Grand Rapids: Eerdmans, 1952), 60–67.

79. Hans Boersma, *Heavenly Participation: The Weaving of a Sacramental Tapestry* (Grand Rapids: Eerdmans, 2011), 23–24.

80. Cf. Alister McGrath, *T. F. Torrance: An Intellectual Biography* (Edinburgh: T&T Clark, 1999), 232–33.

81. It was not at all odd for major theologians like Augustine and Thomas Aquinas to exert enormous energy considering the relation of angels to physical phenomena such as stars (we will say more about this in the next chapter).

disappear."[82] This is why Krauss concludes his book considering various scenarios of the end of the universe, concluding from them that the answer to the question "Why is there something rather than nothing?" is simply "There won't be for long."[83]

The possibility of a Supernature enhances physical nature; it is no longer "almost nothing." We might summarize the difference that such a possibility makes like this: On naturalism, physical reality is like a cement wall; it ultimately encloses us such that we cannot penetrate beyond it. On supernaturalism, physical reality may function more like a screen door or window; it has a kind of interwoven or porous relation to something else, such that the more we understand it, the more we find ourselves simultaneously enmeshed with Something beyond.

Some might think of this latter outlook as an explicitly religious point of view, and that is certainly the case. But interestingly, it is also the outlook that many scientists adopt in connection with their study of the physical universe. Albert Einstein provides a good example. Consider, as an example of this quality of his thought, the following anecdote as recounted in Walter Isaacson's biography of Einstein:

> One evening in Berlin, Einstein and his wife were at a dinner party when a guest expressed a belief in astrology. Einstein ridiculed the notion as pure superstition. Another guest stepped in and similarly disparaged religion. Belief in God, he insisted, was likewise a superstition.
>
> At this point the host tried to silence him by invoking the fact that even Einstein harbored religious beliefs.
>
> "It isn't possible!" the skeptical guest said, turning to Einstein to ask if he was, in fact, religious.
>
> "Yes, you can call it that," Einstein replied calmly. "Try and penetrate with our limited means the secrets of nature and you will

82. Krauss, A Universe from Nothing, 182–83.
83. Krauss, A Universe from Nothing, 180.

find that, behind all the discernible laws and connections, there remains something subtle, intangible and inexplicable. Veneration for this force beyond anything that we can comprehend is my religion. To that extent I am, in fact, religious."[84]

Now, Einstein could be very critical of organized religion, and he certainly did not profess belief in a personal God. But he was equally (if not more) critical of aggressive atheism, and he often spoke in almost religious terms of the sense of humility and wonder that the world impresses upon us. For Einstein, the more one penetrates into an understanding of the physical universe, the more one is left with this lingering sense of Something else, Something beyond. He did not hesitate to speak of this Something with religious associations.

Once, when a little girl asked Einstein if scientists pray, Einstein included within his answer this assertion: "Everyone who is seriously involved in the pursuit of science becomes convinced that a spirit is manifest in the laws of the Universe—a spirit vastly superior to that of man, and one in the face of which we with our modest powers must feel humble."[85] In an interview with George Viereck just before Einstein's fiftieth birthday, Einstein was asked if he believed in God. His answer emphasized the difficulty of the question:

> I'm not an atheist. The problem involved is too vast for our limited minds. We are in the position of a little child entering a huge library filled with books in many languages. The child knows someone must have written those books. It does not know how. It does not understand the languages in which they are written. The child dimly suspects a mysterious order in the arrangement of the books but doesn't know what it is. That, it seems to me, is the attitude of even the most intelligent human being toward God. We see the

84. Walter Isaacson, *Einstein: His Life and Universe* (New York: Simon & Schuster, 2007), 384–85.
85. Isaacson, *Einstein*, 388.

universe marvelously arranged and obeying certain laws but only
dimly understand these laws.[86]

Einstein's views are very far away from the "science has replaced
religion" mentality so typical among the new atheists. Indeed,
Einstein's words have a kind of mystical and supernaturalistic
aura about them. Just think about this sentence for a moment:
The child knows someone must have written those books.

The difference between Einstein and some kind of super-
naturalist (say, for example, a deist) seems to involve not the
degree of likelihood of a Supernature but rather the sheer difficulty of understanding it. The metaphor he uses here is, in fact,
similar to one Kreeft used earlier to describe a supernaturalistic
worldview: a child in a house. Except that Einstein speaks not
of a house but of a *library*: for he wishes to emphasize not
merely the magnitude of the external world but also its order and
arrangement.

Einstein's metaphor conveys a more complicated view of physical reality than many secular alternatives (and, for that matter,
many religious alternatives as well). It is as though the more we
press into physical reality, the more we gather the impression of
something alluringly supra-physical. In the next chapter we will
consider how various characteristics and properties of the physical
universe might further encourage consideration of a Supernature.
For now we simply observe that theism, in particular, has much
resonance with Einstein's caution. Any theologian worth her salt
will agree unhesitatingly that, left to ourselves, we are indeed like
the child in the library trying to decipher foreign books. This
metaphor powerfully conveys the vastness of the God question
and our smallness in relation to it.

But there still remains one tiny possibility, to which we will
return in chapter 4: What if the author who wrote the books is

86. Isaacson, *Einstein*, 386.

still around? What if he is, in fact, also the Librarian—ready to help the child learn how to read?

Conclusion

This has been a modest chapter with a modest goal. We've suggested two things: (1) it looks more like the universe has a cause than not; (2) such a probability produces some exciting metaphysical implications.

I conclude on a personal note. The broad intuition of this chapter—that contingency suggests necessity, nature suggests Supernature—has been a resource to me in many poignant moments. It has functioned like a handrail on a steep staircase—something solid I can cling to that does not yield. I go back to it again and again and again and again, and it is there every time, constant and reliable—this inescapable impression that *this world does not seem to explain itself.*

I remember the first time it really hit me. I was a sophomore at the University of Georgia, wrestling with angst about my faith. One night I was up late in the dorm's computer lab, turning things over and over in my mind. If you have ever experienced a time of genuine doubt, you know the dizzying, terrible feeling it can be—like when an earthquake begins and what always felt solid is now shaking all around you, or when you watch *The Sixth Sense* for the first time, or when circumstances suddenly require you to question whether a good friend is trustworthy. It's a particularly painful, jarring kind of confusion.

In the throes of it, I had a breakthrough in the consideration of this argument. I went up to my dorm and wrote the following in my journal. It is a passage I have gone back to many times, and I include it here as a summation of the spirit of this chapter.

Why does anything exist at all? This is the great mystery, says Wittgenstein. Why is there something rather than nothing? Where did the universe come from? What is the Beginning which stands behind all other beginnings, the Reality which gives ground to all other realities? At every level, at every angle, we find ourselves confronted with the necessity of what Barth calls "the Wholly Other." The very fact that we are here to ponder the question is already the greatest miracle, the greatest improbability. Unless theism is presupposed, all thought and action become absurd—without purpose and suspended over nothingness. Unless the infinite exists, the finite would never have come to be. What sense does the painting make unless there is paper on which it is drawn? God is the great truth; we are his dream.

Or, as Einstein put it: the child knows someone must have written those books.

2

The Meaning of the World

*Why Things like Math, Music, and Love
Make More Sense If There Is a God*

This chapter suggests that it is more plausible to affirm an overarching, transcendent meaning behind the universe than the alternative; and then, secondly, that such an affirmation leads to a more elegant vision of the universe. Thus, not only is the possibility of a transcendent meaning behind the world reasonable, but it also enriches our experience of the world.

What do I mean by "transcendent meaning"? I mean something external to the physical world by which it is ordered and from which it—along with everything in it, including ourselves—receives significance, value, and purpose. Or, a shorter way to get at it: transcendent meaning is what a book has because there is an author. The book has a *meaning* because the author has intentions for writing it; and that meaning is *transcendent* because the author is outside the book (rather than a character within it). This is one way to look at the world—one of the ways we are considering in this book—that the world is rather like a story that Someone is writing.

For the sake of argument, suppose you reject this. Suppose you believe that the universe is ultimately without any final significance or interpretation. There is nothing transcendent that anchors what the world means: it is interpreted only in relation to itself, and therefore there is nothing it's *supposed* to be. Thus, while we can create meaning for our lives and our place within the world, we don't discover meaning. And, since it doesn't look like our species will be around forever (for example, once the "Big Chill" sets in), whatever meaning we invent looks rather flimsy in the long run.[1] There are other ways you might think about this, of course, but suppose just for now that this is your view.

Now suppose, again for the sake of your argument, that you come to change your mind. You now think that someone or something put our world here for a reason. You come to think of our own life, therefore, as Tolkien described it: "You are inside a very great story."[2] What especially interests me in this chapter is this: What difference does such a change make?

Speaking from my own experiences, embracing transcendent meaning feels like moving from a drab, artless apartment into an old mansion that is full of historical artifacts, elegant furniture, and libraries with books that smell the wonderful way an old book smells. It feels like the drama and excitement of being drawn into new friendships, new societies, new battles. It feels like the wonder a child has in getting lost in a good novel, when heroes and mysteries and adventures and danger are very real and somehow the world seems larger and richer.

1. The "Big Chill" is one common theory regarding the ultimate future of the universe. It proposes that the universe will continue to expand indefinitely, eventually making life impossible (this has sometimes been referred to as the "heat death" of the universe).

2. Quoted in Peter J. Kreeft, *The Philosophy of Tolkien: The Worldview behind "The Lord of the Rings"* (San Francisco: Ignatius, 2005), 33.

To me, transcendent meaning makes this decisive difference. It affects everything. Not one blade of grass can be looked at in the same way. Even the way you do geometry or listen to a symphony will be different. Life becomes as Brother Lippo Lippi described it in Robert Browning's poem "Fra Lippo Lippi":

> This world's no blot for us,
> Nor blank; it means intensely, and means good:
> To find its meaning is my meat and drink.[3]

So here we consider several particular aspects of our world— math, music, and love—to argue for transcendent meaning but also to draw out its implications. But first, we should situate these three arguments in relation to the broader intuition of which they are a part—namely, the powerful impression of design or purpose that our world conveys.

Moving beyond Fine-Tuning Arguments

Whittaker Chambers, a Soviet spy who defected and became a critic of communism, describes how the turning point in his life away from atheism and toward belief in God came from considering the intricacy of his daughter's ears:

> I was sitting in our apartment on St. Paul Street in Baltimore. . . .
> My daughter was in her high chair. I was watching her eat. She was
> the most miraculous thing that had ever happened in my life. . . .
> My eye came to rest on the delicate convolutions of her ear—those
> intricate, perfect ears. The thought passed through my mind: "No,
> those ears were not created by any chance coming together of atoms
> in nature (the Communist view). They could have been created only

3. Robert Browning, "Fra Lippo Lippi," lines 313–15, in *The Major Victorian Poets: Tennyson, Browning, Arnold*, ed. William E. Buckler (Boston: Houghton Mifflin, 1973), 272.

by immense design." The thought was involuntary and unwanted.
I crowded it out of my mind. But I never wholly forgot it or the
occasion. I had to crowd it out of my mind. If I had completed it,
I should have had to say: Design presupposes God. I did not then
know that, at that moment, the finger of God was first laid upon
my forehead.[4]

This impression of design in our world is among the most powerful and intuitive sources of belief in a Creator, and arguments
along these lines have been developed all throughout history. The
fourth century Cappadocian theologian Gregory of Nazianzus argued that the orderliness of the universe points to God's existence,
comparing our world to an elaborately constructed lyre: "No one
seeing a beautifully elaborated lyre with all its harmonious, orderly
arrangement, and hearing the lyre's music will fail to form a notion
of its craftsman-player, to recur to him in thought though ignorant
of him by sight."[5] Gregory's lyre metaphor differs from William
Paley's more famous watch metaphor in two respects: first, it is less
mechanical; second, it is less autonomous. A lyre is orderly not only
in its construction (creation) but also in being played (providence).

This imagery has a broad appeal. When we look up at the sky
on a summer night, observing the moon, the stars, the sounds of
insects and owls, the smells, and so on, we can appreciate Gregory's
metaphor: it feels like music. Many of us, like Chambers, have
moments where the intricacy and order of the universe we inhabit
compels us to think instinctively, "This cannot all be an accident!"
Such experiences are generally not dependent on having a science
degree. They are common and come in the midst of everyday life
from a variety of sources—while watching a *Planet Earth* docu-
mentary, for instance, or visiting Niagara Falls, or seeing an ultra-
sound picture of your baby growing in the womb. Lots of design

---

4. Whittaker Chambers, *Witness* (New York: Random House, 1952), 16.
5. St. Gregory of Nazianzus, *Second Oration* 28.6, in *On God and Christ: The Five Theological Orations*, trans. Frederick Williams and Lionel Wickham (Crestwood, NY: St. Vladimir's Seminary Press, 2002), 41.

arguments play on this perception, without appealing to technical knowledge (sometimes called "naïve teleological arguments"[6]).

But in the modern era this popular-level perception of design was widely perceived as discredited by various objections raised by David Hume and then by evolutionary science. It is only recently that design arguments have been revitalized in relation to current scientific knowledge, particularly from the realm of physics. What might be called the cutting edge of design arguments appeals to the fine-tuning of the laws of nature, the initial conditions of the universe, and physical constants like the speed of light, the cosmological constant, the gravitational constant, and many others.[7] Unless these were set in exactly the way that they are, with *unimaginable* precision, the universe could not sustain life in the way that it does.[8] Yet these values do not seem to be physically necessary. We can quite easily imagine our universe being different and thus nonpermitting of life. So the question is, *Why* are all these constants exactly right? Did we just get lucky?

Scientific discoveries throughout the twentieth and early twenty-first centuries have thus reinforced the common intuition, viewed more skeptically during earlier periods of modernity, that our world is designed. Even some settled atheists have been convinced by these revitalized design arguments.[9] It is not hard to find scientists without religious commitments marveling at the intricacy and exquisite calibration of the world we inhabit, particularly as understood

6. See C. Stephen Evans, "A Naïve Teleological Argument: An Argument from Design for Ordinary People," in *Two Dozen (or So) Arguments for God*, ed. Jerry L. Walls and Trent Dougherty (Oxford: Oxford University Press, 2018), 108–22.

7. For an up-to-date presentation of this argument, see Robin Collins, "The Teleological Argument," in *The Blackwell Companion to Natural Theology*, ed. William Lane Craig and J. P. Moreland (Malden, MA: Wiley-Blackwell, 2020), 211–22.

8. For an influential account of some of these constants, see John D. Barrow and Frank J. Tipler, *The Anthropic Cosmological Principle* (New York: Oxford University Press, 1986).

9. E.g., it was significant in the conversion of Antony Flew to deism late in his life, as recounted in Antony Flew and Roy Abraham Varghese, *There Is a God: How the World's Most Notorious Atheist Changed His Mind* (New York: HarperOne, 2007).

from the standpoint of modern science. The atheist astronomer Fred Hoyle put it memorably in an often repeated quote: "A common sense interpretation of the facts suggests that a superintellect has monkeyed with physics, as well as with chemistry and biology, and that there are no blind forces worth speaking about in nature. The numbers one calculates from the facts seem to me so overwhelming as to put this conclusion almost beyond question."[10]

Paul Davies, an agnostic physicist, has also reflected at great length on the apparent fine-tuning of the universe. He acknowledges his disinclination to believe in the supernatural but describes how his scientific work has influenced him away from a purely naturalistic way of looking at the world: "I belong to the group of scientists who do not subscribe to a conventional religion but nevertheless deny that the universe is a purposeless accident. Through my scientific work I have come to believe more and more strongly that the physical universe is put together with an ingenuity so astonishing that I cannot accept it merely as brute fact. There must, it seems to me, be a deeper level of explanation. Whether one wishes to call that deeper level 'God' is a matter of taste and definition."[11] Elsewhere he confesses, "There is for me powerful evidence that there is 'something going on' behind it all. The impression of design is overwhelming."[12]

Testimonies like these (and many others that could be cited) can be very powerful. But believers sometimes cite them and then move on too quickly. We need to be careful. In the first place, the views of those being quoted are often more complicated and less friendly to religion than a quote here or there may suggest. More basically, our intuitions about probability and design need to be subjected to greater self-criticism. In addition to challenges from

---

10. Fred Hoyle, "The Universe: Past and Present Reflections," *Engineering and Science* (November 1981): 12.

11. Paul Davies, *The Mind of God: The Scientific Basis for a Rational World* (New York: Simon & Schuster, 1992), 16.

12. Paul Davies, *The Cosmic Blueprint: New Discoveries in Nature's Creative Ability to Order Universe* (New York: Simon & Schuster, 1988), 203.

evolutionary psychology,[13] there is the problem of selection bias. While the apparent fine-tuning of our universe seems improbable, how do we know that this doesn't simply reflect the point of view from which we are considering the question? *Any* set of circumstances will seem improbable in relation to what could have occurred. For instance, if you spin a wheel that has one hundred thousand notches around it, whatever it lands on, you can always look back and say, "Wow, there was only a one-in-one-hundred-thousand chance this would happen!"

In the context of cosmological design arguments, considerations of this sort are often raised in relation to the so-called anthropic principle, which recognizes that whatever we observe about the physical universe is necessarily filtered by the fact that it is compatible with our existence as observers. Thus, our perception of the improbability of the conditions that allow for our existence may be a reflection of biases and limitations inherent to our point of reference. Nick Bostrom uses a fishing analogy to describe this danger: "How big is the smallest fish in the pond? You catch one hundred fishes, all of which are greater than six inches. Does this evidence support the hypothesis that no fish in the pond is much less than six inches long? Not if your net can't catch smaller fish."[14] Other metaphors can be used to make the same point: we see a universe that looks like it was furnished so perfectly to house us because it's the only thing we *could* see from the angle at which we are looking at it. Bostrom notes the possibility, for example, that there are huge regions of space-time that have different fundamental constants and values and are simply not the regions of space-time we can observe.[15]

13. A naturalistic worldview involves the claim that our capacities for detecting design have been shaped by our evolutionary past and thus are not invariably coordinated toward truth (for instance, it is frequently pointed out that false positives tend to be less threatening to survival than false negatives). Thus, we cannot assume at the outset that our amazement at improbabilities is always a reliable guide. This point will be considered more in our treatment of music and love below.
14. Nick Bostrom, *Anthropic Bias: Observation Selection Effects in Science and Philosophy* (New York: Routledge, 2002), 1.
15. Bostrom, *Anthropic Bias*, 4.

In its stronger variation, the anthropic principle faces the challenge of arbitrariness. For we have not spun a wheel with one hundred thousand notches and then happened upon just any old number. We have hit the exact number that needed to be hit for life to occur (and to accurately reflect just how *fine* the fine-tuning of our universe is, we'd need a number much larger than one hundred thousand). There is no obvious reason why the universe *must* be such that life can evolve in this way. Richard Swinburne illustrates this point with the parable of a man standing before a firing squad of twelve expert marksmen, each of whom fire twelve shots. The order is given, everyone fires, and yet somehow all 144 bullets miss, and the man survives. How should we explain such an event?[16] You are unlikely to satisfy the surviving man by telling him, "Of course you are surprised to be alive—if you were shot, you wouldn't be around to be surprised." After all, the fact that surprise would not occur in different circumstances does not mean that it needs no explanation in the circumstance we are in. As the atheist J. L. Mackie conceded, the apparent fine-tuning of our universe "is not made less surprising by the fact that if it had not been so, no one would have been here to be surprised."[17] Richard Dawkins admits this as well, suggesting that the man surviving this firing squad could "forgivably wonder why they all missed, and toy with the hypothesis that they were bribed, or drunk."[18]

Nonetheless, perhaps the weaker version of the anthropic principle can be maintained by the appeal to a multiverse, which suggests that there are countless universes and we just happen to be living in the one that is calibrated to be friendly to life.[19] If

16. Richard Swinburne, *The Existence of God*, rev. ed. (Oxford: Clarendon, 1991), 313. This is a variation of an often quoted illustration from John Leslie.
17. J. L. Mackie, *The Miracle of Theism: Arguments for and against the Existence of God* (Oxford: Oxford University Press, 1982), 141.
18. Richard Dawkins, *The God Delusion* (New York: Houghton Mifflin, 2006), 145.
19. The "weak anthropic principle," as expounded by Branden Carter, asserts that "we must be prepared to take account of the fact that our location in the universe is *necessarily* privileged to the extent of being compatible with our existence

there are enough universes, and many or all of them have varying characteristics, then surely *some* of them will be friendly to life. So maybe we are struck by the improbability of our existence because we happen to live in the right universe. This possibility is sometimes buttressed by an appeal to "cosmological Darwinism," in which the principles of natural selection are applied to the creation of new universes.[20] There are a number of challenges leveled against the attempt to apply Darwinian principles from biology to cosmology—for instance, it is disputed whether information can transfer from a parent to a daughter universe through a black hole, as is sometimes proposed.[21] Additionally, it is unclear whether cosmological Darwinism removes the need for design, since the fundamental laws that allow for universes to exist and reproduce still require an explanation.[22] Nonetheless, *some* kind of multiverse hypothesis is currently the primary alternative explanation for the fine-tuning of our universe.[23]

---

as observers." Brandon Carter, "Large Number Coincidences and the Anthropic Principle in Cosmology," in *Confrontation of Cosmological Theory with Astronomical Data*, ed. M. S. Longair (Dordrecht: Reidel, 1974), 291–98, quoted in Karlina Leksono-Supelli, "Cosmology and the Quest for Meaning," in *Science and Religion in a Post-Colonial World: Interfaith Perspectives*, ed. Zainal Abidin Bagir (Hindmarsh, Australia: ATF, 2005), 125.

20. Lee Smolin, *The Life of the Cosmos* (Oxford: Oxford University Press, 1997), hypothesizes that daughter universes (created by the collapsing of black holes) take on certain characteristics of their parent universes, with slight variation, ultimately favoring universes more friendly to life.

21. In a significant debate between Smolin and the physicist Leonard Susskind, Susskind argued that the current "consensus" among scientists requires that information cannot pass through the "infinitely violent singularity at the center of a black hole," and therefore "if such a thing as a baby universe makes any sense at all, the baby will have no special resemblance to the mother. Given that, the idea of an evolutionary history that led, by natural selection, to our universe, makes no sense." "Smolin vs. Susskind: The Anthropic Principle," *Edge*, August 18, 2004, https://www.edge.org/conversation/lee_smolin-leonard_susskind-smolin-vs-susskind-the-anthropic-principle.

22. Cf. Davies, *The Mind of God*, 222.

23. Explanations for fine-tuning are typically broken down into three kinds of explanation: (1) multiverse, (2) accident, or (3) design, with the most credible options being (1) and (3). See Francis Collins, *The Language of God: A Scientist Presents Evidence for Belief* (New York: Free Press, 2006), 74–75.

Is the multiverse hypothesis a compelling alternative? One challenge it faces is a lack of any clear proof. Though it is sometimes claimed that quantum mechanics implies other universes, the fact remains that we have no access to alternate universes: their existence is a speculative hypothesis. It is not clear that we ever *could* have scientific confirmation of them, as the subject matter in question pushes the boundaries of what is in the purview of science. Accordingly, among scientists the multiverse hypothesis is often regarded as unscientific.[24] (The anthropic principle is controversial among scientists as well, regarded by some as a kind of deus ex machina that simply reverses cause and effect.)[25] On the other hand, the existence of parallel universes cannot be *disproven*, either. Perhaps the subject matter is sufficiently complex and distant that we need to be more open-minded about all the various possibilities. So it seems reasonable to ask the question: Which of the available explanations of the apparent fine-tuning of the constants of our universe is *most likely*?

In *The God Delusion* Richard Dawkins relies upon the multiverse hypothesis to counter the fine-tuning argument.[26] He anticipates the objection that positing such a fanciful hypothesis without evidence is a "profligate luxury" that is at least equally as ad hoc as theism.[27] This is a concern that many have raised. J. Budziszewski, for example, objects that to posit countless un-

---

24. John Horgon, "Multiverse Theories Are Bad for Science," *Scientific American* (blog), November 25, 2019, https://blogs.scientificamerican.com/cross-check/multiverse-theories-are-bad-for-science.

25. Roger Penrose, *The Emperor's New Mind: Concerning Computers, Minds, and the Laws of Physics* (Oxford: Oxford University Press, 1989), 561, argues that the strong anthropic principle has a "dubious character" and that it "tends to be invoked by theorists whenever they do not have a good enough theory to explain the observed facts." For Stephen Jay Gould, even the weak anthropic principle is "utterly trivial." See Robert Ross, *Stephen Jay Gould: Reflections on His View of Life* (Oxford: Oxford University Press, 2008), 177.

26. Dawkins, *The God Delusion*, 145–46, considers classical multiverse models like that of Martin Rees, as well as Lee Smolin's more "Darwinian" conjecture of parent-daughter universes.

27. Dawkins, *The God Delusion*, 146.

known worlds just to explain the one we are in turns Occam's razor into Occam's beard: "multiply entities unnecessarily."[28] But Dawkins maintains that the multiverse is much simpler than God, because although it posits a vast number of universes, they all share the same basic laws. God, by contrast—or any personal, intelligent designer—is the most complex answer possible, and as such "is going to need a mammoth explanation in its own right."[29]

But this depends upon the criteria by which we determine simplicity. Which is simpler: an infinite number of worlds or an infinite person behind the world? The answer to this is not obvious, as it relates to intuitions that we bring to the question regarding size, personhood, physicality, natural laws, and so on. To sort this out requires *philosophical* reasoning, particularly concerning the nature of ontology (being).[30] Dawkins's own reasons for finding the multiverse simpler than God seem to be based not upon scientific conclusions but upon a philosophical outlook—indeed, given his obvious irritation with theism as an explanatory hypothesis, one might say a philosophical *bias*. As we saw in the last chapter, Dawkins seems to have little patience for considering the metaphysical possibilities that are involved in the notion of classical theism. Theists in the Abrahamic tradition have always held that God is *by definition* an ontologically simple entity. In fact, in developing the classical Western conception of God, Jewish, Muslim, and Christian theologians have historically been motivated, in part, by precisely the concern that the first cause of the world must be *simple* in order to function in that role. The whole point is, you need One primal thing that explains everything else.

Dawkins really dislikes this explanation because he thinks God himself needs a cause (as we noted, he is apparently conceiving of "God" in a nontraditional sense of the word). Even

28. J. Budziszewski, *What We Can't Not Know: A Guide* (Dallas: Spence, 2003), 84.
29. Dawkins, *The God Delusion*, 149.
30. Swinburne, *The Existence of God*, 93–106, provides an overview of the ways in which theism is a simple hypothesis.

supposing this were right, however, does the multiverse theory fare any better? Is it capable of its own explanation? After all, Dawkins thinks of each parallel universe as governed by the same physical laws. Thus, the question arises: Where did the laws come from? For that matter, where did the multiverse *itself* come from? This is why the multiverse theory, even if accepted, drains very little of the sense of wonder to which design arguments generally appeal. Even if successful, it simply pivots from one source of mystery and marvel (*Look how intricately put together our world is!*) to another (*Look how elaborate is the multiverse, such that there can be a world as intricately put together as ours!*).

The supranatural character of the multiverse theory should, if nothing else, reduce the contempt that is sometimes leveled at the notion of a Creator. As Rebecca McLaughlin puts it, "The idea of a Creator God does not sound quite so crazy when you realize that the best current alternative for the apparent fine-tuning of the universe for life is the existence of an infinite number of parallel universes."[31]

Bearing this in mind makes it harder to complacently accept the common claim that all appeals to design amount to a "god of the gaps" argument, in which we don't know what causes something, so we simply attribute it to God. It is certainly true that some believers have argued in this way. However, the idea that *all* appearances of design result from a "gap" in our knowledge tends to assume a materialist picture of reality, which is the very point in question. Calling something a "gap" assumes that you have a sense of the whole. In this connection Thomas Nagel notes that secular alternatives to creationist views can easily slide into what he calls "the materialism and Darwinism of the gaps," which are no less dogmatic, and no less philosophical (rather than strictly scientific).[32] The truth is, no one knows in advance whether all future discoveries

---

31. Rebecca McLaughlin, *Confronting Christianity: 12 Hard Questions for the World's Largest Religion* (Wheaton: Crossway, 2019), 128.

32. Thomas Nagel, *Mind and Cosmos: Why the Materialist Neo-Darwinian Conception of Nature Is Almost Certainly False* (Oxford: Oxford University Press, 2012), 127.

will support design, multiverse, or something else. So it seems more generous and more careful to refrain from labeling all appearances of design as "gaps" in our knowledge. Maybe they are gaps and maybe they aren't. Let's not decide until we know.

This same feeling of the sheer wondrousness of our world arises in other areas of the design argument. For instance, when we move from physics into biology we encounter alien-seeding theories for the origin of life, which Dawkins also considers, and which are more common than you might expect. Francis Crick, for example, the famous molecular biologist and staunch atheist, found the origin of life to be "almost a miracle," suggesting the notion of "directed panspermia"—that is, that our planet was seeded with unicellular life by advanced extraterrestrials.[33] The question again arises: Is such a proposal less incredible than theism? Is there *any* explanation of the origin of life that doesn't tell a tale so improbable it's almost impossible to believe?

It is interesting that in Carl Sagan's review of Crick's book, he questioned Crick's hypothesis but nonetheless acknowledged that his own more "natural" alternative explanation (that life arises through the laws of physics and chemistry) still creates a sense of awe that borders on the religious: "It is very hard to approach the question of the origin of life without coming to grips with religious sentiments of one sort or another."[34] If we think evolution has displaced the need for God, whatever else we have done we have not transitioned from the mysterious to the nonmysterious, from the wild to the prosaic. No, we are in a deeply mysterious world any way we look at it.

It is true that much of the apparent design around us, particularly in the biological realm, has been challenged by evolutionary

33. Francis Crick, *Life Itself: Its Origins and Nature* (New York: Simon & Schuster, 1981), 88.
34. Carl Sagan, "Is There Life Elsewhere, and How Did It Come Here?," review of *Life Itself: Its Origin and Nature*, by Francis Crick, *New York Times*, November 29, 1981, https://www.nytimes.com/1981/11/29/books/is-there-life-elsewhere-and-did-it-come-here.html.

science. Darwin himself confessed, "The old argument of design in nature, as given by Paley, which formerly seemed to me so conclusive, fails, now that the law of natural selection has been discovered."[35] We might debate whether Darwinian (now, neo-Darwinian) mechanisms have the kind of exhaustive power that can account for *all* biological complexity; and I think the theist can be more open-minded when considering such questions, since evolution could be a part of the design, whereas the one who rejects design is confined to evolutionary explanations. But even if you accept the entire neo-Darwinian picture without a moment's hesitation, this does not account for nonbiological fine-tuning, such as the physical constants that allow for the wondrous improbability of a world in which evolution can occur.

The plain and resilient fact we all must reckon with is simply this: we live in an intricate and mysterious world, and *every possible explanation* for that fact evokes wonder and amazement. There is no worldview available on the market that is entirely rational and explicable in terms of observable physical causes. If you don't like God, you're probably stuck with zillions of parallel worlds, for which you lack any conclusive evidence. Things are metaphysically interesting, any way you slice them.

So what do we make of all this? For the sake of my purposes in this chapter, let me restrict myself to the following extremely modest conclusion: *Some kind of theism, broadly considered, is a reasonable hypothesis for the apparent fine-tuning of our universe—it's at least as reasonable as alternative hypotheses.* I myself think that theism is much better than the alternatives, but it is not necessary to establish that here. Even this more modest conclusion is enough to encourage a consideration of where I want to put the focus in this chapter: namely, three other features of our everyday world that give, in their own more subtle and distinctive ways, a powerful impression that the universe *means something*.

35. Charles Darwin, *On the Origin of Species*, ed. Joseph Carroll (Orchard Park, NY: Broadview, 2003), 431.

Entering the Platonic World: The Argument from Math

Most people take numbers for granted. But when you stop to think about it, numbers are very curious. What are they? Where did they come from? Why are they so useful? In their noted introductory text to math, Philip J. Davis and Reuben Hersh put it like this: "If you do mathematics every day, it seems the most natural thing in the world. If you stop to think about what you are doing and what it means, it seems one of the most mysterious."[36]

I will never forget the way this problem was impressed upon me while reading Thomas Nagel on a different but related topic, the problem of consciousness. Nagel, who is not a religious believer, is discussing the famous mind-body problem, and at the climax of his discussion he confesses that he does not believe that consciousness can be reducible to strictly material processes. This, for Nagel, makes it unlikely that physical science can explain the whole of reality.[37] In the context of this argument, he asserts: "There seem to be two very different kinds of things going on in the world: the things that belong to physical reality, which many different people can observe from the outside, and those other things that belong to mental reality, which each of us experiences from the inside in his own case."[38]

In other words, for Nagel, there are basically two kinds of things: *mental* and *material*. (Other philosophers have said similarly.)[39]

36. Philip J. Davis and Reuben Hersh, *The Mathematical Experience* (Brighton: Harvester, 1982), 318.
37. Thomas Nagel, *What Does It All Mean? A Very Short Introduction to Philosophy* (Oxford: Oxford University Press, 1987), 36–37.
38. Nagel, *What Does It All Mean?*, 36.
39. For instance, Richard Swinburne, "The Argument from Colors and Flavors: The Argument from Consciousness," in Walls and Dougherty, *Two Dozen (or So) Arguments for God*, 294: "The history of the world includes events of two kinds: physical events (including brain events) and mental events." Swinburne distinguishes these two kinds of events by suggesting that mental events are those to which the subject having them has a kind of "privileged access," while physical

When I first read this passage, the question immediately popped into my mind: If the physical universe is all there is, why should there be these two distinct realms? Why do mental things exist, rather than exclusively material things? The question applies not only to our own mental thoughts (what Nagel is highlighting) but also (where Nagel led me next) to the abstract truths that our minds can discover. This would potentially include not only numbers but also things like sets, functions, counterfactuals, logical laws, and so on—though here we will focus just on numbers.[40]

Philosophers have puzzled over this question, and some have suggested that the existence of mental truths is best accounted for by some kind of antecedent mind. Alvin Plantinga, speaking of numbers and sets, puts it like this: "Most people who have thought about the question, think it incredible that these objects should just exist, just *be* there, whether or not they are thought of by anyone. . . . It is therefore extremely tempting to think of abstract objects as ontologically dependent upon mental or intellectual activity in such a way that either they just are thoughts, or else at any rate couldn't exist if not thought of."[41]

The intuition at work here appears to be basically this: some features of the intellectual world appear less arbitrary if they are sustained by some kind of mental activity. At first glance, this whole way of thinking might seem like a stretch. Why should mental truths require a mind to think them? Why can't they just *be*? But before dismissing the argument, it's worth thinking about the nature of math a bit. It really is a mysterious, enigmatic thing. Three features of math, in particular, are curious from a naturalistic perspective: (1) its permanence and durability, (2) its elegance and beauty, and (3) its applicability and usefulness.

---

events are public events. Cf. also his earlier treatment in Swinburne, *The Existence of God*, 160–66.

40. For some interesting arguments for God from these other abstract entities, see Walls and Dougherty, *Two Dozen (or So) Arguments for God*, 11–136.

41. Alvin Plantinga, *Where the Conflict Really Lies: Science, Religion, and Naturalism* (Oxford: Oxford University Press, 2011), 288.

First, most people conceive of math as possessing a kind of permanence and durability. The classic view of math, tracing back to Pythagoras and Plato as well as Christian theologians like Augustine, holds that mathematical truths are eternal and necessary, ultimately rooted in some kind of metaphysical reality (often the mind of God). Plato, for instance, taught that geometry is the knowledge of eternal truths.[42] Augustine maintained that all numbers are fixed in the knowledge of God, since his understanding has no limit (Ps. 147:5)—even infinity, he held, is "in some ineffable way" made finite to God's comprehension.[43] In an 1857 lecture at the inauguration of Washington University in St. Louis, Edward Everett expressed this view colorfully from a theistic perspective: "In the pure mathematics we contemplate absolute truths, which existed in the Divine Mind before the morning stars sang together, and which will continue to exist there, when the last of their radiant host shall have fallen from heaven."[44]

There are different ways to construe the metaphysical underpinnings of math, however. Here we shall use the label "mathematical realism" to refer to core claim that *mathematical truths exist independently of human minds.*[45]

In the modern era, some philosophers of math reject such a view and adopt some kind of antirealist position. There are all kinds of varieties of nonrealist views, but they share the conviction that math lacks the kind of objective reality traditionally ascribed

42. Plato, *Republic* 7.527, in *Plato: Complete Works*, ed. John M. Cooper (Indianapolis: Hackett, 1997), 1143.

43. Saint Augustine, *The City of God* 12.18, trans. Marcus Dods (New York: Modern Library, 2000), 401.

44. As quoted in Daniel J. Cohen, *Equations from God: Pure Mathematics and Victorian Faith* (Baltimore: Johns Hopkins University Press, 2007), 8.

45. The term "mathematical Platonism" is often used in this context to denote a realist view, but it is probably better to think of mathematical Platonism as one species of realism. For a clarifying discussion of the diverse meanings of "Platonism" as distinct from realism, see William Lane Craig, *God over All: Divine Aseity and the Challenge of Platonism* (Oxford: Oxford University Press, 2016), 6–12.

to it. Yehuda Rav describes an antirealist position with a poem
by Antonio Machado:

> Walker, just your footsteps
> are the path and nothing more;
> walker, no path was there before,
> the path was made by act of walking.

On an antirealist view, doing math is more like invention than
discovery. Rav identifies evolutionary science as the cause of this
change: "No, there are no preordained, predetermined mathematical 'truths' that just lie out or up there. Evolutionary thinking
teaches us otherwise."[46]

Interestingly, although various species of antirealism have become fashionable since the nineteenth century, realism remains
the default position, and most contemporary practicing mathematicians are realists.[47] Realism is often described as the most
natural and intuitive view of math, since the objective existence of
mathematical truths is typically assumed in the development and
application of mathematical theories,[48] and since mathematical

46. Yehuda Rav, "Philosophical Problems in the Light of Evolutionary Episte-
mology," in *Math Worlds: Philosophical and Social Studies of Mathematics and
Mathematics Education*, ed. Sal Restivo, SUNY series in Science, Technology, and
Society (Albany: State University of New York Press, 1993), 100.

47. Reuben Hersh, *What Is Mathematics, Really?* (Oxford: Oxford University
Press, 1997), 7, contrasting Platonism and formalism (one of the more common kinds
of antirealism), observes, "Platonism is dominant, but it's hard to talk about it in
public. Formalism feels more respectable philosophically, but it's almost impossible
for a working mathematician to really believe it." Later he writes, "An inarticulate,
half-conscious Platonism is nearly universal among mathematicians" (7). Davis and
Hersh quote J. D. Monk's estimate that 65 percent of working mathematicians are
Platonists (i.e., realists), but suggest that in actual practice it is much more (*The
Mathematical Experience*, 322).

48. Among the more influential arguments for realism is that of Gottlob Frege,
which essentially turns on the intuition that the reality of mathematics is the best
explanation for its truth. For a defense of Frege's argument against various common
responses, see Mark Balaguer, *Platonism and Anti-Platonism in Mathematics* (New
York: Oxford University Press, 1998), 95–112.

truths *appear* to us as universally binding.[49] Davis and Hersh put
it humorously: "The typical working mathematician is a Platonist
on weekdays and a formalist on Sundays."[50]

For instance, many mathematicians speak of the powerful
sense of *discovery* involved in mathematical progress. The British physicist Roger Penrose, referencing the discovery (rather than
the invention) of a fractal called the Mandelbrot set, exclaims,
"Like Mount Everest, the Mandelbrot set is just *there!*"[51] Penrose
speaks of doing math as like being guided to eternal, self-existing
truths, of which we have only partial knowledge:

> How "real" are the objects of the mathematician's world? From
> one point of view it seems that there can be nothing real about
> them at all. . . . Can they be other than mere arbitrary construc-
> tions of the human mind? At the same time there often does
> appear to be some profound reality about these mathematical
> concepts, going quite beyond the mental deliberations of any
> particular mathematician. It is as though human thought is,
> instead, being guided towards some eternal external truth—a
> truth which has a reality of its own, and which is revealed only
> partially to us.[52]

In a follow-up book, Penrose suggests that there are three distinct realms of reality: the physical, the mental, and the Platonic
(see fig. 2).[53] He outlines the relationships between these worlds,
emphasizing the mysteriousness of their interaction with each
other and the primacy of the Platonic realm (which he thought
might contain not only numbers but also other ideas). He defends

49. Davis and Hersh, *The Mathematical Experience*, 362–74, point to a number
of specific mathematical hypotheses, each of which, they argue, "*forces* a recognition
of the objectivity of mathematical truth" (362 [italics original]).

50. Davis and Hersh, *The Mathematical Experience*, 321.

51. Penrose, *The Emperor's New Mind*, 125 (italics original).

52. Penrose, *The Emperor's New Mind*, 123–24.

53. Roger Penrose, *Shadows of the Mind* (Oxford: Oxford University Press, 1994),
411–21.

FIGURE 2

Three Realms of Reality

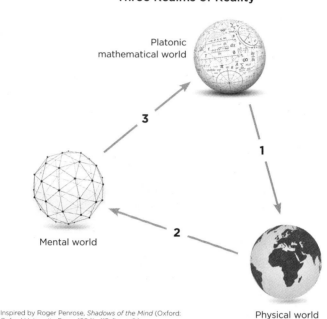

Platonic
mathematical world

3

1

2

Mental world

Physical world

Inspired by Roger Penrose, *Shadows of the Mind* (Oxford:
Oxford University Press, 1994), 415, figure 8.1.

the claim that the Platonic realm exists in the same sense as the
other two worlds:

> What right do we have to say that the Platonic world is actually a
> "world," that can "exist" in the same kind of sense in which the other
> two worlds exist? It may well seem to the reader to be just a rag-bag
> of abstract concepts that mathematicians have come up with from
> time to time. Yet its existence rests on the profound, timeless, and
> universal nature of these concepts, and on the fact that their laws
> are independent of those who discover them. The rag-bag—if indeed
> that is what it is—was not of our creation. The natural numbers were
> there before there were human beings, or indeed any other creature
> here on earth, and they will remain after all life has perished.[54]

54. Penrose, *Shadows of the Mind*, 413.

Different mathematicians have come up with various ways of expressing this sense of the independent reality of math. The mathematician Sylvain Cappell spoke of doing math as a kind of transit from one realm to another: "All mathematicians live in two different worlds. They live in a crystalline world of perfect platonic forms. An ice palace. But they also live in the common world where things are transient, ambiguous, subject to vicissitudes. Mathematicians go backward and forward from one world to another."[55] Penrose, likewise, spoke of discovering a mathematical truth as a kind of breaking into another world.[56] The mathematician Paul Erdős often referred to "the Book" in which God keeps the most elegant proof of each mathematical theorem. Thus, discovering a new proof is like God showing you a page of the book. Erdős dedicated the book to S. F. ("the Supreme Fascist")—his nickname for the Almighty.[57]

Now just think about what is entailed in these metaphors! To conceive of doing math as entering a distinctly different world (Cappell) or as discovering a page in a previously written book (Erdős)—these are provocative images for a realist vision of math. One can summarize such views by saying that doing math is less like being an *architect* who builds from scratch and more like being an *archaeologist* who excavates what is already there.[58]

55. Quoted in Sylvia Nasar, *A Beautiful Mind: The Life of Mathematical Genius and Nobel Laureate John Nash* (New York: Simon & Schuster, 1998), 99.

56. Penrose, *The Emperor's New Mind*, 554.

57. For an account of Erdős's life and approach to math, see Paul Hoffman, *The Man Who Loved Only Numbers: The Story of Paul Erdős and the Search for Mathematical Truth* (New York: Hyperion, 1998).

58. Some mathematicians have thus thought that the world we discover in math should be regarded with equal confidence as the world we discover with our physical senses. Kurt Gödel, the famous twentieth-century logician and mathematician, asserted that "the axioms force themselves upon us as being true. I don't see any reason why we should have less confidence in this kind of perception, i.e., in mathematical intuition, than in sense perception." Gödel, "What Is Cantor's Continuum Problem," quoted in David Bostock, *Philosophy of Mathematics: An Introduction* (Oxford: Wiley-Blackwell, 2009), 265. Gödel was a realist, and his incompleteness theorem is often interpreted as undermining nonrealist views of math. See, e.g., Penrose, *Shadows of the Mind*, 418; and Davies, *The Mind of God*, 100–102.

Most of us won't personally experience math in the same way that professional mathematicians like these do. Nonetheless, many of us might be able to appreciate how the clarity and precision of mathematical truth have a distinctly realist *feel*. Mathematical truths seem firm, boxy, metallic. When we are doing math, we seem to be engaging a different plane of reality than what exists on the coarser, more variegated realm of concrete objects. Math rises up around us like a vast, invisible castle—seemingly fixed and stable no matter where we look.

I like to use the following thought experiment to help people consider the problem: If the entire space-time universe were to collapse into nonbeing, would it still be the case that $2 + 3 = 5$? Many would answer, of course! What *else* could $2 + 3$ equal? But this means, of course, that the truth $2 + 3 = 5$ is somehow independent of physical reality. The question is, if physical reality is all that there is, where does it get this durability?

Suppose you're inclined to take a realist view of math. Whether anybody is around to know it or not, $2 + 3 = 5$. It just *is*. The question then arises: On naturalism, how might we explain this fact? Mathematical realism turns out to be a rather strange bedfellow to the broader metaphysical assumptions of naturalism. Specifically, it is difficult to explain why a finite space-time universe that is in constant flux should produce a mental realm characterized by apparently eternal, necessary truths. Where did this distinct realm come from? How did the temporal produce the permanent? Who wrote Erdős's book?

Many, of course, affirm the objective reality of mathematical truth without seeming to be bothered by these metaphysical oddities. Reuben Hersh comments on this situation: "Most mathematicians and philosophers of mathematics continue to believe in an independent, immaterial abstract world—a remnant of Plato's Heaven, attenuated, purified, bleached, with all entities but the mathematical expelled. Platonism without God is like the grin on Lewis Carroll's Cheshire cat. The cat had a grin. Gradually the cat disappeared, until all was gone—except the grin. The grin remained without the cat."[59] Comparing Platonism without God to a grin without the cat is a way of saying, really, that mathematics without God is contextless and mysterious. This is exactly Hersh's point: "The present trouble with the ontology of mathematics is an after-effect of the spread of atheism."[60]

On the other hand, if there is something beyond the universe, the nature of math may be less surprising. On theism, for instance, numbers have traditionally been understood, along with other abstract objects, as the ideas or thoughts of God.[61] Thus, the reason that mathematical truths are eternal and necessary is that they are sustained by an eternal mind. On such a view, discovering the existence of binding, thrillingly *objective* mathematical truths will be as natural as finding books in a library or food in the pantry. The question of the relation of God and abstract objects like numbers is a difficult one, and a variety of views on this point are contested among philosophers today.[62] But theism at least allows for such options, as other species of supernaturalism potentially do as well. On naturalism, it is difficult to see *any* solid foundation for a realist view of math.

The perception that eternal truths entail an eternal mind has long been asserted among theists. Gottfried Leibniz, for instance, put it like this: "If there were no eternal substance, there would be no eternal truths; and from this too God can be proved, who is the root of possibility, for his mind is the very region of ideas

---

59. Hersh, *What Is Mathematics, Really?*, 12. Hersh ultimately argues that math is constructed by human minds, though not arbitrarily (he calls this a "humanist" view). Recall here our previous discussions of the terms "Platonism" and "realism."

60. Hersh, *What Is Mathematics, Really?*, 126.

61. This is the general position of the premodern church and has been defended variously among contemporary Christians as well, e.g., Greg Welty, "Theistic Conceptual Realism," in *Beyond the Control of God? Six Views on the Problem of God and Abstract Objects*, ed. Paul M. Gould (London: Bloomsbury, 2014), 81–112. Cf. also Plantinga, *Where the Conflict Really Lies*, 290–91.

62. For an overview of several prominent positions, see Craig, *God over All*, esp. 1–12, 54–95, 144–205.

or truths."[63] In the ancient world as well, the identification of the Platonic realm of ideas with the thoughts of God was common, particularly in the interaction of Hellenistic philosophy and Jewish thought that blossomed in the era of Middle Platonism (roughly from the first century BC through the third century AD). Philo of Alexandria, for example, is well known for describing the world of ideas as a kind of archetypal plan existing in the Logos of God (just as any architect constructs a blueprint or model to work from before building).[64] The mathematician Nicomachus, who lived in the late first and early second centuries, claimed that arithmetic existed "in the mind of the creating God like some universal and exemplary plan, relying upon which as a design and archetypal example, the Creator of the universe sets in order his material creations and makes them attain their proper ends."[65]

In the Christian tradition, the nature of mathematical truth has been of special interest, since the doctrine of the Trinity entails that numbers are eternal in a special way: not only in the mind of God but also (in some sense) in the very being of God. For the trinitarian theist, reality is in some sense intrinsically numerical, since three-ness and oneness are predicated on what is first and more basic than space or time. More specifically, trinitarian theists consider mathematical truth to be ultimately rooted in the Word (Logos) of God, through whom all things, seen and unseen, were created (Col. 1:16; John 1:3). In classical Christian theology, the Second Member of the Trinity is associated with the thought, reason, and speech of God the Father, while also being himself fully divine.[66]

63. Quoted in Lorraine Juliano Keller, "The Argument from Intentionality (or Aboutness): Propositions Supernaturalized," in Walls and Dougherty, *Two Dozen (or So) Arguments for God*, 11.
64. See Philo, *On the Creation* 4.16–5.20, in *The Works of Philo: Complete and Unabridged*, trans. C. D. Yonge (Peabody, MA: Hendrickson, 1993), 4. For discussion of Philo's views in relation to divine aseity, see Craig, *God over All*, 18–24.
65. As quoted in Craig, *God over All*, 21.
66. For a good representation of this way of thinking, see Anselm, *Monologion* 29–48, in *Anselm: Basic Writings*, ed. and trans. Thomas Williams (Indianapolis: Hackett, 2007), 38–53.

Accordingly, following passages like John 1:3 and Colossians 1:16, Christians have spoken of the Son of God as the One in whom are the archetypal truths (such as math) with which the world was built. Joseph Cardinal Ratzinger (who later become Pope Benedict XVI), for example, addressing the church's use of music and liturgy, put it like this: "The mathematics of the universe does not exist by itself. . . . It has a deeper foundation: the mind of the Creator. It comes from the Logos, in whom, so to speak, the archetypes of the world's order are contained. The Logos, through the Spirit, fashions the material world according to these archetypes."[67]

How compelling you might find such a view will depend to a large degree on what you make of mathematical realism. If you find mathematical realism plausible, supernaturalism of some kind provides a kind of explanatory framework for that fact. However, there are other features of math that are less dependent on a realist view. A second feature of math that is curious on naturalism is its elegance and beauty.

The very fact that mathematical truth is accessible to us at all is striking. Many have wondered how abstract objects can have a causal relation with concrete objects. Why should it be that physical objects like brains and mental objects like numbers should interact? As Penrose put it, "How is it that subtly organized material objects can mysteriously conjure up mental entities from out of its material substance?"[68]

But it's not just that we can access mathematical truth—it's that what we discover when we do appears to us as beautiful. Mathematics is often seen, in fact, as the area in which two of the transcendentals, truth and beauty, converge. What is it, exactly, that makes a particular mathematical formula beautiful? Mathematicians often speak of proofs as beautiful when they are

<hr>

67. Joseph Cardinal Ratzinger, *The Spirit of the Liturgy*, trans. John Saward (San Francisco: Ignatius, 2000), 153, quoted in Stratford Caldecott, *Beauty for Truth's Sake: On the Re-enchantment of Education* (Grand Rapids: Brazos, 2009), 14–15.
68. Penrose, *Shadows of the Mind*, 413–14.

unusually simple or orderly or when they contain a surprisingly wide range of applicability, as does, for instance, the Pythagorean theorem ($a^2 + b^2 = c^2$). The Nobel Prize–winning astrophysicist Subrahmanyan Chandrasekhar notes that mathematical beauty is easier to recognize than define but suggests two criteria for determining the beauty of an idea: (1) it has the proper degree of strangeness; and (2) the conformity of its parts to one another and to the whole.[69] On the recognizability of mathematical beauty, he quotes the Austrian physicist Ludwig Boltzmann: "Even as a musician can recognize his Mozart, Beethoven, or Schubert after hearing the first few bars, so can a mathematician recognize his Cauchy, Gauss, Jacobi, Helmholtz, or Kirchhoff after the first few pages."[70]

It's not hard to find mathematicians who describe the discovery of mathematical truths as a kind of encounter with beauty. In *A Beautiful Mind*, the story of the mathematical genius John Nash, a fellow student is entranced by one of Nash's ideas not because of its possible applications but because of it elegance: "The mathematics was so beautiful. It was so right mathematically."[71] Bertrand Russell compares math to poetry, claiming that "mathematics, rightly viewed, possesses not only truth, but supreme beauty— a beauty cold and austere, like that of sculpture."[72] Paul Erdős considers the beauty so obvious as to need no explanation: "Why are numbers beautiful? It's like asking why is Beethoven's Ninth Symphony beautiful. If you don't see why, someone can't tell you. I know numbers are beautiful. If they aren't beautiful, nothing is."[73]

69. Subrahmanyan Chandrasekhar, *Truth and Beauty: Aesthetics and Motivations in Science* (Chicago: University of Chicago Press, 1987), 70. He derives this first criterion from Francis Bacon and the second from Werner Heisenberg.
70. Chandrasekhar, *Truth and Beauty*, 64.
71. Nasar, *A Beautiful Mind*, 95.
72. Bertrand Russell, *Contemplation and Action, 1902–14*, ed. Richard A. Rempel, Andrew Brink, and Margarat Moran, vol. 12 of *The Collected Papers of Bertrand Russsell* (New York: Routledge, 1993), 86.
73. As quoted in Keith Devlin, *The Math Gene: How Mathematical Thinking Evolved and Why Numbers Are Like Gossip* (New York: Basic Books, 2011), 140.

Many mathematicians have even valued beauty as a criterion for truth. Einstein's thoughts on this topic are often referenced. Paul Dirac, another influential twentieth-century theoretical physicist alongside Einstein, declares, "It is more important to have beauty in one's equations than to have them fit experiment. . . . If one is working from the point of view of getting beauty in one's equations, and if one has really a sound insight, one is on a sure line of progress."[74] Such a view is often challenged at the technical level, but it is undeniable that many professional mathematicians rely upon the intuition of beauty in their actual procedure.

Some mathematicians experience the beauty of math in terms of a kind of transcendence. Writing from a secular humanist perspective, Luc Ferry observes, "I can do nothing about it, 2 + 2 = 4, and this is not a matter of taste or subjective choice. The necessities of which I speak impose themselves upon me as if they come from elsewhere, and yet, it is inside myself that this transcendence is present, and palpably so."[75] The nineteenth-century French mathematician Gabriel Lamé spoke of getting goosebumps while reading about his fellow mathematician Charles Hermite's treatment of modular functions.[76] The twentieth-century British mathematician George Watson compared mathematical discovery to the thrill of seeing Michelangelo's sculptures.[77] Werner Heisenberg felt giddy while discovering quantum mechanics, expressing gratitude for its strange beauty.[78] Fred Hoyle and Richard Feynman spoke of a feeling of euphoria that lasted for days after a mathematical breakthrough.[79]

74. *Paul Dirac: The Man and His Work*, ed. Peter Goddard (Cambridge: Cambridge University Press, 1998), xi.

75. Luc Ferry, *A Brief History of Thought: A Philosophical Guide to Living*, trans. Theo Cuffe (New York: Harper Perennial, 2011), 237. Ferry explores not only math but also four areas—truth, beauty, justice, and love—that he calls "the fundamental values of human existence."

76. Chandrasekhar, *Truth and Beauty*, 61.

77. Chandrasekhar, *Truth and Beauty*, 61.

78. Chandrasekhar, *Truth and Beauty*, 64–65.

79. See Davies, *The Mind of God*, 229, where he also describes Hoyle's experience, while hiking in the Scottish Highlands, of a sudden insight into the mathematics

Why should this be? Why should math be so *exciting*? Perhaps math, as we will suggest also with music, is a genuine point of contact with Something beyond nature. Perhaps its beauty and intricacy are a reflection of the Beauty by which the world was made. Mystical as such a proposal might sound, it's not easy to think of alternate explanations that are any *less* mystical. Paul Davies put it like this: "If beauty is entirely biologically programmed, selected for its survival value alone, it is all the more surprising to see it re-emerge in the esoteric world of fundamental physics, which has no direct connection with biology. On the other hand, if beauty if more than mere biology at work, if our aesthetic appreciation stems from contact with something firmer and more pervasive, then it is surely a fact of major significance that the fundamental laws of the universe seem to reflect this 'something.'"[80]

But maybe you are not convinced by this. Maybe you are not sure what to make of mathematical realism (this is admittedly an abstruse topic), and maybe you have never liked math or found it beautiful (I feel your pain, as I myself never enjoyed doing math in school—I am only now developing an interest in the *philosophy* of math). There is, nevertheless, a third feature of math that is not dependent on mathematical realism or beauty and is curious for naturalism: that is, the applicability of math to the physical world.

Whatever else we make of numbers, we cannot deny that they are incredibly *useful*. Mathematical truths apply to the physical universe with amazing consistency, allowing us to make predictions with astonishing accuracy. Indeed, ideas and objects seem to fit together as perfectly as two puzzle pieces. On naturalism, why should this be so? It is one thing for physical reality to somehow generate a separate, mental reality; another for us to en-

---

involved in a cosmological theory of electromagnetism that felt "as if a huge brilliant light had suddenly been switched on."

80. Davies, *The Mind of God*, 176.

counter this reality as beautiful; but still something more that material and mental reality should then turn out to have such a tight interrelation.

In 1960, Eugene Wigner argued that "the enormous usefulness of mathematics in the natural sciences is something bordering on the mysterious and . . . there is no rational explanation for it."[81] In accordance with this, Wigner suggested that the uncanny usefulness of mathematical concepts raises questions about the uniqueness of physical theories: "We are in a position similar to that of a man who was provided with a bunch of keys and who, having to open several doors in succession, always hit on the right key on the first or second trial. He became skeptical concerning the uniqueness of the coordination between keys and doors."[82] For Wigner, the applicability of math to physics was a kind of miracle for which we should be grateful, but we cannot be confident that it will continue: "The miracle of the appropriateness of the language of mathematics for the formulation of the laws of physics is a wonderful gift which we neither understand nor deserve. We should be grateful for it and hope that it will remain valid in future research and that it will extend, for better or for worse, to our pleasure, even though perhaps also to our bafflement, to wide branches of learning."[83]

Wigner is not alone in perceiving math as a kind of miracle. Decades earlier, Albert Einstein delivered a lecture in which he marveled at the same issue: "An enigma presents itself which in all ages has agitated inquiring minds. How can it be that mathematics, being after all a product of human thought which is independent of experience, is so admirably appropriate to the objects of reality?"[84] Roger Penrose calls this "mathematical fruitfulness,"

81. Eugene Wigner, "The Unreasonable Effectiveness of Mathematics," *Communications on Pure and Applied Mathematics* 13 (1960): 2.

82. Wigner, "The Unreasonable Effectiveness of Mathematics," 2.

83. Wigner, "The Unreasonable Effectiveness of Mathematics," 14.

84. *Albert Einstein's Theory of General Relativity*, ed. Gerald E. Tauber (New York: Crown, 1979), 159.

emphasizing that the more you know about math, the more remarkable it is, and cites Einstein's theory of general relativity as
a prime example: "Einstein was not just 'noticing patterns' in the
behaviour of physical objects. He was discovering a profound
mathematical substructure that was already hidden in the very
workings of the world."[85]

The word "hidden" in this last sentence emphasizes that this remarkable congruence between math and physical reality becomes
more and more detectable as we learn more about both realms. It
also raises the question, of course, of how the math got there in
the first place. Many scientists speak of this mystery in religious
terms. Thus Paul Dirac: "God used advanced mathematics in constructing the universe."[86]

But of course, this doesn't require God per se. You could be a
nontheistic Platonist of some variety. Or, from a naturalistic point
of view, you could just say that it's an accident. Mary Leng, operating from a fictionalist (i.e., nonrealist) view of math, argues that
the predictive success of mathematical theories is, for nonrealists,
"a happy coincidence."[87] Is that it? Is it just a coincidence?

I don't know how we might absolutely disprove such a claim.
But it seems better to consider the alternatives than simply to accept a coincidence. If you believe in theism, in which a mind pre-
dates and constructed the world, you have a powerful explanatory
framework for the nature of math as we experience it. Other forms
of supernaturalism might provide a similar framework. If, on the
other hand, your worldview allows for nothing beyond nature,
mathematical truth becomes more mysterious and inexplicable.
Many, even among those who are not otherwise favorable to religious belief, find this fact to weaken the plausibility of naturalism.[88]

85. Penrose, *Shadows of the Mind*, 415.
86. Quoted in Plantinga, *Where the Conflict Really Lies*, 285–86.
87. Mary Leng, *Mathematics and Reality* (Oxford: Oxford University Press, 2010),
238–39.
88. Thomas Nagel, for instance, marvels at the intelligibility of the world that is
presupposed by all scientific endeavor, uncomfortable with the bare assertion that

We have only scratched the surface here. And we've been dealing mainly with common math. There is much more to be explored in advanced math. If you're interested in pursuing this further, read Hersh's *What Is Mathematics, Really?* It's fascinating. I do believe the deeper you go into mathematical truth, the more enigmatic it becomes. It really is like entering a different world or reading a mysterious book.

The Language of Angels: The Argument from Music

Before you read this section, I suggest you listen to Hans Zimmer's "Chevaliers de Sangreal" (a search on YouTube will bring it up). Really *listen*. Without doing anything else. If you have time and interest, do the same with Tomaso Albinoni's "Adagio in G Minor." Done? Okay, now read on.

In his highly acclaimed *A Secular Age*, Charles Taylor notes that in premodern cultures, art functioned as a kind of mimesis or imitation of reality. The poet or composer could rely upon "certain publicly available orders of meaning" shared by their audience.[89] For instance, in premodern cultures people more frequently operated with a sacramental view of nature, an understanding of human beings as image-bearers of God, a sense of progression in history, a presupposition of ontological coherence rooted in God as the source of all being, and so forth (these are my own examples). Starting in the Romantic period, however, and increasingly since then, as Taylor notes, art has been disembedded from these larger metaphysical assumptions. The result is that modern

---

"this is just how things are." *Mind and Cosmos*, 16–17. In consequence of this and other considerations, he affirms his conviction that "mind is not just an afterthought or an accident or an add-on, but a basic aspect of nature" (16).

89. Charles Taylor, *A Secular Age* (Cambridge, MA: Harvard University Press, 2007), 352–53.

appreciation of art involves a sense of loss and of uncertainty: "The Mozart G Minor Quintet gives us a powerful sense of being moved by something profound and archetypical, not trivial and passing, which is both immensely sad, but also beautiful, moving, and arresting. We could imagine being moved in some analogous kind of way by some beautiful story of star-crossed love, of loss or parting. But the story isn't there. We have something like the essence of the response, without the story."[90] Taylor characterizes music in secular contexts as fundamentally mysterious. Because it conveys transcendence and yet is divorced from any transcendent referent, music becomes a kind of "deception, play-acting."[91] And in actual experience it often proves difficult to disassociate the meaning conveyed in music from its transcendent object: "There are certain works of art—by Dante, Bach, the makers of Chartres Cathedral: the list is endless—whose power seems inseparable from their epiphanic, transcendent reference. Here the challenge is to the unbeliever, to find a nontheistic register in which to respond to them, without impoverishment."[92]

Secular people often give testimony to this kind of experience. In his memoir *Nothing to Be Frightened Of*, Julian Barnes describes, as an agnostic, "missing God." One area of life in which he particularly notices God's absence is the enjoyment of art: "Missing God for me is focused by missing the underlying sense of purpose and belief when confronted with religious art."[93] He describes the hollowed-out feeling of listening to Mozart's *Requiem*, for example, or experiencing a Giotto painting or a Donatello sculpture while no longer believing in the significance undergirding them. Even admiring the architecture of churches and cathedrals conveys a sense of loss and disadvantage.[94] What exactly is this loss? "[Religion] gave

90. Taylor, *A Secular Age*, 355.
91. Taylor, *A Secular Age*, 356.
92. Taylor, *A Secular Age*, 607.
93. Julian Barnes, *Nothing to Be Frightened Of* (London: Jonathan Cape, 2008), 54.
94. Barnes, *Nothing to Be Frightened Of*, 54.

human life a sense of context, and therefore seriousness. . . . Was it true? No. Then why miss it? Because it was a supreme fiction, and it is normal to feel bereft on closing a great novel."[95]

Music and the other arts remain among our chief sources of transcendence in Western culture. Probably all of us, whether we hold religious beliefs or not, can relate on a personal level to this association between music and transcendence. Think of the way you feel while listening to the soundtrack during the climax of your favorite movie.[96] Music *feels* important—it feels meaningful, grand, palatial—as though it were conveying to us something too poignant for words, some haunting beauty from another world. At the same time, this "transcendence" associated with the arts in secular contexts is a somewhat vague concept since, as Jeremy Begbie notes, it is usually unmoored from any traditional ontology or metaphysics.[97] So it's worth asking, Why do people still find music so powerful, so *spiritual*? What is this "transcendence" we experience through it?

For some, music points to God himself. This point often comes up in debates on the existence of God, and it is not uncommon to hear atheists treat arguments from music more seriously than any other argument.[98] Others speak (however metaphorically) of

95. Barnes, *Nothing to Be Frightened Of*, 57.

96. Kutter Callaway argues that our culture's interest in movies represents a kind of spiritual impulse. He explores how film music (e.g., in Pixar films or Paul Thomas Anderson films) conveys a sense of transcendence: "The more that the music disturbs us, the more we sense the presence of an immanent transcendence—an Other, who, from beyond the margins of our immanent frame, rushes back into the void, filling the spiritual gaps in both the film and in our own lives." *Scoring Transcendence: Contemporary Film Music as Religious Experience* (Waco: Baylor University Press, 2013), 146–47.

97. Jeremy Begbie, *Redeeming Transcendence in the Arts: Bearing Witness to the Triune God* (Grand Rapids: Eerdmans, 2018), 3–12. Begbie delivers a careful and penetrating account of how the arts witness to divine transcendence, highlighting ways they do so specifically with regard to divine otherness and uncontainability. See Begbie, *Redeeming Transcendence in the Arts*, esp. 127–82. Elsewhere he explores how music can contribute to theology. See Jeremy Begbie, *Theology, Music, and Time*, Cambridge Studies in Christian Doctrine (Cambridge: Cambridge University Press, 2000).

98. E.g., Philip Tallon notes, "In a debate with theist Jerry Walls about the problem of evil, Peter S. Fosl admitted that sometimes, listening to Cat Stevens' 'Morning Has Broken,' his deep agnosticism becomes much less certain." Tallon, "The Mozart

"finding God" in music. Albert Einstein once told a young violin prodigy, after hearing him play, "Now I know there is a God in heaven!"[99] Steve Jobs, after hearing Yo-Yo Ma play Bach on his 1733 Stradivarius while visiting Jobs's house, teared up and told him, "You playing is the best argument I've ever heard for the existence of God, because I don't really believe a human alone can do this."[100]

In *The Joy of Music*, the famous conductor Leonard Bernstein describes an imagined conversation between himself, his younger brother, and a British literary critic (L.P., "Lyric Poet") about his love of Beethoven.

L.B.

Rightness—that's the word! When you get the feeling that whatever note succeeds that last is the only possible note that can rightly happen at that instant, in that context, then chances are you're listening to Beethoven. Melodies, fugues, rhythms—leave them to the Chaikovskys and the Hindemiths and Ravels. Our boy has the real goods, the stuff from Heaven, the power to make you feel at the finish: *Something is right in the world. There is something that checks throughout, that follows its own law consistently: something we can trust, that will never let us down.*

L.P.

(Quietly): But that is almost a definition of God.

L.B.

I meant it to be.[101]

Argument and the Argument from Play and Enjoyment: The Theistic Argument from Beauty and Play," in Walls and Dougherty, *Two Dozen (or So) Arguments for God*, 338.

99. As quoted in Jim Howard, *The Miracle of Man: Evidence for God from Human Nature* (Eugene, OR: Resource, 2016), 100.

100. Walter Isaacson, *Steve Jobs* (New York: Simon & Schuster, 2011), 424–25.

101. Leonard Bernstein, *The Joy of Music* (Pompton Plains, NJ: Amadeus, 1959), 29 (italics original). Cf. the discussion in Tim Keller, *Making Sense of God: An Invitation to the Skeptical* (New York: Viking, 2016), 17.

These various examples may be speaking metaphorically of "God." Others, however, find their way to genuine faith with the help of music. Rebecca McLaughlin tells of an Iranian science professor and musician who described coming to Christ "through the ministry of J. S. Bach." By this he meant that in his musical practice he gradually came to see the Christian fabric undergirding Bach's works, and "when he first walked into a church a few years later, he sensed the same reality."[102] Philosopher Peter Kreeft gives an argument for God's existence from the same composer:

> There is the music of Johann Sebastian Bach.
> Therefore there must be a God.
> You either see this or you don't.[103]

Doubtless, Kreeft is being somewhat tongue-in-cheek here. But before we dismiss his point, and these various testimonies recounted above, let's ask the question: *Why* do so many experience a sense of the divine through music? What is the best explanation for this experience? Here we consider two alternatives.

First, from a naturalistic perspective, the power of music is explained in terms of our evolutionary history. Neuroscientists note that music affects the same part of our brains as sex and food. But unlike sex and food, it has no obvious survival function—so, from the standpoint of evolutionary psychology, why does it affect us so emotionally?

One older explanation emphasizes pattern recognition: the brain (unconsciously) anticipates what is coming next in music and gets dopamine when it's right.[104] Another hypothesis says that

102. McLaughlin, *Confronting Christianity*, 47.

103. Peter Kreeft and Ronald Tacelli, *Handbook of Christian Apologetics* (Downers Grove, IL: InterVarsity, 1994).

104. E.g., Leonard B. Meyer, *Emotion and Meaning in Music* (Chicago: University of Chicago Press, 1956). Obviously Meyer did not relate his general idea to the discussion in contemporary evolutionary psychology (e.g., he did not use the term "dopamine").

music mirrors speech and thus essentially fools our brains into reacting the way we react to speech (in which we often mirror the emotions of the person speaking).[105] Other explanations stress the social dimension of human life to account for our love of music, interpreting music along with dance, religion, and laughter "as aids to promoting the sense of group membership and mutual well-being that gives rise to . . . self-sacrificial emotions."[106]

We could multiply various theories like these from the field of evolutionary psychology, an area of study that is growing rapidly. Most commonly, explanations of music of this sort will rely on some combination of theories. But all such accounts of music, in the end, boil down to seeing music as what Stephen Jay Gould called an "evolutionary spandrel"—that is, the unintentional by-product of adaptive mechanisms that evolved for other reasons (in architecture, a spandrel is the triangular space necessarily created by the construction of an arch).[107] In other words, music's power upon us is a "spin-off" of the evolutionary process.

On such a view, our love for music is rooted in biological factors related to those that give power to drugs, alcohol, and rich desserts. Hence Steven Pinker's famous description of music, from the standpoint of evolutionary psychology, as "auditory cheesecake."[108] As Pinker puts it: "We enjoy strawberry cheesecake, but not because we evolved a taste for it. We evolved circuits that gave us trickles of enjoyment from the sweet taste of ripe fruit, the creamy mouth feel of fats and oils from nuts and meat, and the coolness of fresh water.

105. Brian Resnick, "The Scientific Mystery of Why Humans Love Music," *Vox*, February 4, 2016, https://www.vox.com/science-and-health/2016/2/4/10915492/why-do-we-like-music.

106. Mark Pagel, *Wired for Culture: Origins of the Human Social Mind* (New York: Norton, 2013), quoted in David Skeel, *True Paradox: How Christianity Makes Sense of Our Complex World* (Downers Grove, IL: InterVarsity, 2014), 68.

107. For an initial influential paper on the topic, see Stephen Jay Gould and Richard C. Lewontin, "The Spandrels of San Marco and the Panglossian Paradigm: A Critique of the Adaptationist Programme," *Proceedings of the Royal Society of London B* 205, no. 1161 (1979): 581–98.

108. Steven Pinker, *How the Mind Works* (New York: Norton, 1997), 534.

Cheesecake packs a sensual wallop unlike anything in the natural world because it is a brew of megadoses of agreeable stimuli which we concocted for the express purpose of pressing our pleasure buttons."[109] Pinker identifies two other examples where our brains are tricked by the evolutionary process into enjoying something that has no intrinsic reproductive value: pornography and art.[110]

Many people find such an explanation of music unsatisfying. In the first place, it feels inauthentic to the experience of music. It is difficult to enjoy music while realizing, *My brain is tricking me into the experience of transcendence as a result of the happenstance of evolutionary history. I enjoy this simply because it intersects with factors that helped animals survive.* It seems implausible that such richness of experience could emerge from such poverty of causation—almost like a story that is greater than the world in which it is written.[111] On considering such a view of music, most of us can relate to Julian Barnes's sense of loss and nostalgia. (If you don't feel the sting of this point, recall listening to Hans Zimmer.)

This is not to say, of course, that evolutionary factors have no explanatory power at all. Doubtless they are part of the equation. But if they are the sum total explanation—if, as Pinker would suggest, all art is reducible to psychology, and all psychology is reducible to biology—then it is difficult not to feel that the human experience has been dramatically impoverished. For such a view entails that our love of music is both accidental (we could have evolved such that music would be nothing more to us than white noise) and illusory (the sense of significance conveyed by music has no external reference or meaning).

Now consider the alternative: What if the transcendence associated with music is not deceptive but actually a clue about reality?

109. Pinker, *How the Mind Works*, 524–25.
110. Pinker, *How the Mind Works*, 525.
111. As Skeel, *True Paradox*, 71, puts it, purely evolutionary explanations of beauty "flatten out the complexity of beauty and describe something that most of us do not recognize as its essence."

From a theistic perspective, the world itself can be seen as a work of art or music—the free creation of a personal agent. In such a worldview, music is understood, like all beauty, as a reflection of the Creator himself. It is a faint echo of what preceded space-time: a little whisper of a World beyond the world. Thus, instead of being illusory, music gives us a glimpse into the very heart of reality: it is not a dream but a window.

For the Christian theist, for example, music (along with all beauty) is understood as a consequence of the love and joy forever pulsating between Father, Son, and Holy Spirit (the three persons in the Godhead). Thus, it is not surprising that Christians have often attributed metaphysical significance to music. In the creation account at the beginning of *The Silmarillion,* for example, J. R. R. Tolkien portrays the world's creation as, essentially, a work of music. In the first section of the book, called "The Music of the Ainur," the supreme being Eru Ilúvatar creates the Ainur—who are angel-like creatures in the metaphysics of his world—and gives them themes of music to play. For a long time the Ainur play music individually, or in small groups, while the rest listen. Then Ilúvatar summons them all together and declares, "I will now that ye make in harmony together a Great Music."[112]

The Ainur begin singing with "endless interchanging melodies woven in harmony," like that of many different instruments coming together, and Tolkien writes that "the music and the echo of the music went out into the Void, and it was not void."[113] Interestingly, it is this *harmonious* singing that produces the transition from the "Void" to "not void." In other words, music makes the world. This is how Tolkien summarizes it in the next section: "In this music the world was begun."[114] Related to this, Tolkien portrays the intrusion of evil as a kind of discord or disharmony. This occurs when the

112. J. R. R. Tolkien, *The Silmarillion,* 2nd ed., ed. Christopher Tolkien (New York: Houghton Mifflin, 2001), 15.
113. Tolkien, *The Silmarillion,* 15.
114. Tolkien, *The Silmarillion,* 25.

most powerful of the Ainur, Melkor, introduces his own music that contends with that of Ilúvatar. Melkor's music is ultimately distinctive for its lack of harmony: "It was loud, and vain, and endlessly repeated; and it had little harmony, but rather a clamorous unison as of many trumpets braving upon a few notes."[115]

In the Chronicles of Narnia, Tolkien's friend C. S. Lewis attached a similar significance to music in the creation of the world. Not only does Aslan, the Christ figure of that world, *sing* the world into being, but other voices join in harmony—and these voices appear to be the stars themselves:

> Then two wonders happened at the same moment. One was that the voice was suddenly joined by other voices; more voices than you could possibly count. They were in harmony with it, but far higher up the scale: cold, tingling, silvery voices. The second wonder was that the blackness overhead, all at once, was blazing with stars. They didn't come out gently one by one, as they do on a summer evening. One moment there had been nothing but darkness; next moment a thousand, thousand points of light leaped out—single stars, constellations, and planets, brighter and bigger than any in our world. There were no clouds. The new stars and the new voices began at exactly the same time. If you had seen and heard it, as Digory did, you would have felt quite certain that it was the stars themselves which were singing, and that it was the First Voice, the deep one, which had made them appear and made them sing.[116]

Thus, for both Tolkien and Lewis, not only does music play a role in creation, but it is particularly the harmonious music of angels (or angel-like creatures). This vision of music's role was not invented by Lewis and Tolkien: it is the literary expression of

---

115. Tolkien, *The Silmarillion*, 17.

116. C. S. Lewis, *The Magician's Nephew* (New York: Scholastic, 1995), 107. The Cabby's response to hearing this music is relevant to the argument here: "I'd ha' been a better man all my life if I'd known there were things like this."

various long-held features of Christian imagination.[117] This tradition of thought is rooted in God's speech in the book of Job, where he declares that when he laid the foundation of the earth, "the morning stars sang together and all the angels shouted for joy" (Job 38:7 NIV).

Now consider this view of music in contrast to the naturalistic alternative. The difference is stark. In one, music is an accidental product of nature; in the other, it is the deliberate producer of nature. In one, the power of music is a fleeting illusion; in the other, it is the creator of reality. So let's ask this question, and try to be a bit more specific in answering it: Which of these two options provides a more compelling explanatory framework for our experience of music? Suppose, for example, that you adopt the theistic view of music—what particular characteristics of music might such a worldview better position you to enjoy?

First, on theism, one has more categories by which to make sense of musical *meaning*. Music's power to convey meaning is frequently noted. For instance, even when music is not accompanied by words, it can be described in expressive terms like "triumphant" or "sad"; it can be interpreted; and it can be followed.[118] The dominant question in the philosophy of music for the last several centuries has concerned the role of emotion in musical meaning.[119] There are disputes about *how* music conveys meaning, but *that* it does so is difficult to deny. Many musicologists simply express

117. For a classic treatment of the role of angels in God's creation and government of the universe, particularly in relation to stars, see Augustine, *On Genesis: A Refutation of the Manichees,* . . . *The Literal Meaning of Genesis* 2.18.38, trans. Edmund Hill, ed. John E. Rotelle, The Works of Saint Augustine I/13 (Hyde Park, NY: New City, 2002), 214. Thomas Aquinas displayed a great deal of interest in these same questions throughout his *Summa Theologica.*

118. See the discussion of these three points in R. A. Sharpe, *Philosophy of Music: An Introduction* (Montreal: McGill-Queen's University Press, 2004), 168.

119. The question, divided between the so-called expressionists and formalists, concerns whether music can communicate emotions or is merely an art form whose beauty derives from its patterns. For an overview of some of these issues involved, see Sharpe, *Philosophy of Music,* 85–121.

uncertainty at how music conveys meaning, asserting that musical meaning is "real but ineffable."[120]

In some respects, musical meaning functions like nothing else we experience. For instance, Jeremy Begbie notes that music conveys meaning in a nonrepresentational manner, unlike our other forms of communication.[121] Thus, music's power of communication is unique: "Music is the least imitative of the arts, the least reducible to other things (certainly the least translatable into verbal discourse), the least dependent on preexisting things outside itself. Music is the closest we will get in this life to creating out of nothing."[122] Leonard Meyer notes that music utilizes no linguistic signs but instead "operates as a closed system—that is, it employs no signs or symbols referring to the non-musical world of objects, concepts, and human desires."[123] At the same time, Meyer notes that unlike the similarly "closed system" of mathematical truth, music is not entirely abstract but has the ability to convey concrete emotional and aesthetic meaning. This ability to bring together the human and the nonhuman, the abstract and the concrete, makes music, as he calls it, a "puzzling combination."[124]

It is in relation to these kinds of considerations that some, particularly Christians, have thought of music as its own kind of language. Peter Kreeft, for example, reflecting on the role of music in Tolkien's writings, surveyed just above, calls music "the most powerful and magical language" and "the original language."[125] Some regard the meaning conveyed by music as clearer than other forms of language. The composer Felix Mendelssohn famously

120. Roger Scruton, *The Aesthetics of Music* (Oxford: Oxford University Press, 1997), 159, uses this description for the positions of Benedetto Croce and Arthur Schopenhauer.

121. On this point, see Begbie, *Redeeming Transcendence in the Arts*, 30, 169.

122. Begbie, *Redeeming Transcendence in the Arts*, 32.

123. Meyer, *Emotion and Meaning in Music*, vii.

124. Meyer, *Emotion and Meaning in Music*, vii–viii.

125. Peter J. Kreeft, *The Philosophy of Tolkien: The Worldview behind "The Lord of the Rings"* (San Francisco: Ignatius, 2005), 161.

said, "To me music is still a more precise language than words and letters."[126]

One unique feature of musical meaning is its ability for harmony, which may create analogies for theological reflection. As Begbie notes, although two different objects cannot occupy the same *visual* space at the same time and remain distinct, two different tones can occupy the same *audible* space at the same time and remain distinct. He draws parallels (allowing for points of disanalogy as well) between this aspect of music and the nature of divine transcendence, as well as the Trinity.[127] Likewise Dietrich Bonhoeffer, in a letter near the end of his life, marveled at the polyphony of music, comparing this to the relation of divine and creaturely loves and ultimately to the divine and human natures of Christ.[128]

If our worldview allows for something beyond the physical realm, we are better positioned to accommodate the rich account of musical meaning that is implicit in these reflections. For instance, we are allowed to see music's unique powers of communication (the "closed system" of musical meaning) as a legitimate avenue by which divine transcendence touches and graces our lives. Instead of regarding its power as an accidental by-product of the evolutionary process, we can listen to it as a kind of ancient, primordial language. To put it simply: on supernaturalism, music is *telling us something*, and we can trust the message we hear.[129]

---

126. Letter to Eduard Devrient, March 10, 1832, quoted in J. Rigbie Turner, "Mendelssohn's Letters to Eduard Devrient: Filling in Some Gaps," in *Mendelssohn Studies*, ed. R. Larry Todd (Cambridge: Cambridge University Press, 1992), 217.

127. Begbie, *Redeeming Transcendence in the Arts*, 153–54. See also Jeremy Bebgie, "Room of One's Own? Music, Space, and Freedom," in Jeremy Begbie, *Music, Modernity, and God: Essays in Listening* (Oxford: Oxford University Press, 2013), 141–75.

128. Speaking of the *cantus firmus* and the counterpoint in a polyphonic music, Bonhoeffer claimed, "The two are 'undivided and yet distinct,' in the words of the Chalcedonian Definition, like Christ in his divine and human natures." Dietrich Bonhoeffer to Eberhard Bethge, May 20, 1944, in Dietrich Bonhoeffer, *Letters and Papers from Prison*, enlarged ed., ed. Eberhard Bethge (New York: Touchstone, 1997), 303.

129. Something of this worldview is implicit in the famous quip attributed to Johann Sebastian Bach: "I play the notes as they are written, but it is God who makes

Second, on theism, the beauty of music can be more naturally received with gratitude, as a gift. Almost everyone intuitively senses that music is beautiful. Music speaks straight to the heart. It does not work upon us through the medium of ideas but instead touches us at a visceral level.[130] As musical composer Benjamin Zander puts it, "Music doesn't go through the brain. It goes through the molecules."[131]

If you believe music reflects the world beyond nature, you have a greater context by which to receive the beauty of music with gratitude. It is an intentional gift, no less than a present wrapped under the tree on Christmas Day. But if music is an accident, it's difficult to know where to express your gratitude. I think it was Chesterton who said the worst moment for the skeptic is when he feels truly grateful but has no one to thank.

Finally, on theism, the transcendent longings that music provokes can be experienced in terms of hope for final happiness. Though there are exceptions, music frequently takes on a kind of narrative structure, moving toward complexity and ultimately denouement.[132] The power of music often lies in this pattern of tension and then release. Think of the musical soundtrack during the climax of the movie—and then how it feels right after. In this way, music has a kind of forward-looking, eschatological quality built into it. As Begbie puts it, the divine transcendence associated with music gives the impression that "things are not only what they

---

the music." This is an eloquent way of expressing a nonphysicalist view of music. It's more than the notes. It's something God is doing *through* the notes.

130. Begbie, *Redeeming Transcendence in the Arts*, 178.

131. "Benjamin Zander: How Does Music Transform Us?," *TED Radio Hour*, November 10, 2017, NPR, https://www.npr.org/transcripts/562884481. In his popular TED Talk on the power of classical music, Benjamin Zander energetically exclaimed, "Everyone loves classical music—they just haven't found out about it yet!" "The Transformative Power of Classical Music," YouTube video, 20:43, posted by TED, June 27, 2008, https://www.youtube.com/watch?v=r9LCwI5iErE.

132. It should be noted that this may be a feature more consistently of Western music, and even in Western music it is not universal, as noted by Sharpe, *Philosophy of Music*, 3.

are. . . . Things are more than they are at this particular moment in time: they are *on their way* to a future."[133]

My own interest in this topic began (unexpectedly) with a piercing longing for heaven that music provoked. I suspect I am not the only one for whom music creates the longing for heaven—for reunion with loved ones, for a lasting happiness, for an ultimate resolution to the world. In Herman Hesse's novel *Steppenwolf*, for example, the narrator is lonely and melancholy, reflecting on joys he has lost. But then he describes how attending a concert opened to him the door to "the other world," creating a kind of mystical experience that he forever longs to recover:

> After two or three notes of the piano the door was opened of a sudden to the other world. I sped through heaven and saw God at work. I suffered holy pains. I dropped all my defences and was afraid of nothing in the world. I accepted all things and to all things I gave up my heart. It did not last very long, a quarter of an hour perhaps; but it returned to me in a dream at night, and since, through all the barren days, I caught a glimpse of it now and then. Sometimes for a minute or two I saw it clearly, threading my life like a divine and golden track. But nearly always it was blurred in dirt and dust. Then again it gleamed out in golden sparks as though never to be lost again and yet was soon quite lost once more.[134]

This is somewhat like how C. S. Lewis experienced what he called *Sehnsucht*—that ravishing longing for God and heaven that, once experienced, becomes the dominant theme of life, the Desire that takes up all other desires into itself. Lewis called it "the stab, the pang, the inconsolable longing."[135] If you believe in a world beyond nature, with the possibility of heaven, music can be, instead of a trick fobbed off on us by the evolutionary process, one of the

133. Begbie, *Redeeming Transcendence in the Arts*, 139 (italics original).
134. Hermann Hesse, *Steppenwolf* (New York: Picador, 1927), 29–30.
135. C. S. Lewis, *Surprised by Joy: The Shape of My Early Life* (New York: Harcourt, Brace, Jovanovich, 1966), 72.

ways we experience a sense of connection to this realm. Think of it like this: the way a musical piece comes to an ultimate climax or resolution—*that is what will one day happen to the whole world.*

To conclude, we can make the contrast between a theistic and a naturalistic account of music as stark as possible by describing them in metaphor. On a naturalistic worldview, music is like an opiate for a dying man. It is pleasant in such a way as *distracts* us from reality. Music is pleasant and beautiful, but reality is ultimately chaotic and dark. Thus, we like music to the degree that it pulls us away from what things are *really* like.

On a theistic view, by contrast, music is like a window to an imprisoned man. It is pleasant insofar as it is a portal *into* ultimate reality. It is a little glimmer that there might be more out there. It is one avenue by which transcendence and ultimacy reach down to us, however drab our prison cell may be.

So, imagine a man locked away underground. It's dark. Stuffy. He has no clue what the outside world is like. He has never seen redwood trees soaring into the sky, or thundering cascading waterfalls, or the night sky lit up with countless stars. He knows nothing of this. But he can look up and see the light pouring in through the window and sense that *there must be something more.*

What if music, and the nostalgic stab of longing it provokes, is like that window? What if we are the man in the cellar?

Stronger than Death: The Argument from Love

I'll start this section with a confession: I love the music of *Frozen II*. (I have a five-year-old daughter, so at least I have a good excuse for having seen it so many times . . . I'm not telling how many.)

The song that is perhaps most poignant for me is "Do the Next Right Thing," which is sung by the character Anna right after her friend Olaf, the loveable snowman, dies in her arms. Earlier the

film had explored themes of transience and permanence in the
song "Some Things Never Change." Now, as Olaf lays dying,
Anna and Olaf have a conversation:

Olaf: "Hey Anna, I just thought of one thing that is permanent."
Anna: "What's that?"
Olaf: "Love."
Then they hug, and Anna says, "I love you," as Olaf melts away.[136]

The sentiment expressed in this scene is so common that it
probably doesn't inspire much philosophical reflection. The claim
that "Love never dies" or "Love is forever" is extremely common
in movies and literature, and it is also one of the greatest themes
in songs. But when you stop to think about it, the idea that *love
is permanent* is actually a fascinating idea. Is it true?

Paul Kalanithi was a brilliant neurosurgeon. He had degrees
from Stanford, Cambridge, and Yale, and a promising future lay
ahead of him. But he began to have health difficulties during his
last year of residency at Stanford. Eventually he was diagnosed
with terminal lung cancer and passed away in 2015. In his bestsell-
ing memoir, *When Breath Becomes Air*, he describes this whole
experience and his journey of faith through it all. During the
course of his education, he had moved away from the religion of
his upbringing:

> Although I had been raised in a devout Christian family, where
> prayer and Scripture readings were a nightly ritual, I, like most
> scientific types, came to believe in the possibility of a material
> conception of reality, an ultimately scientific worldview that
> would grant a complete metaphysics, minus outmoded con-
> cepts like souls, God, and bearded white men in robes. I spent a
> good chunk of my twenties trying to build a frame for such an
> endeavor.[137]

---

136. *Frozen II*, directed by Chris Buck and Jennifer Lee (Burbank, CA: Walt Disney Pictures, 2019).
137. Paul Kalanithi, *When Breath Becomes Air* (New York: Random House,
2016), 169.

Eventually, however, he came back to faith, having seen a vital difficulty for his naturalistic philosophy:

> The problem, however, eventually became evident: to make science the arbiter of metaphysics is to banish not only God from the world but also love, hate, meaning—to consider a world that is self-evidently *not* the world we live in. That's not to say that if you believe in meaning, you must also believe in God. It is to say, though, that if you believe that science provides no basis for God, then you are almost obligated to conclude that science provides no basis for meaning and, therefore, life itself doesn't have any.[138]

On first glace it might seem exaggerated to claim that a scientific, materialist worldview will necessarily banish love from existence once it has banished God. But think about it: on a naturalistic account of reality, the feeling of love has a similar status to the enjoyment of music. Love came about in the evolutionary process as a by-product of natural selection. It affects us the way it does because it helped our ancestors survive and pass on their genes. Love is therefore an accidental feature of reality, and the feeling of significance that accompanies it is your brain tricking you. Olaf's sentiment that "love is permanent" is therefore only true in the most poetic and limited of senses, if at all.

I don't mean to suggest that naturalism has no possible explanations for altruism or love. There are evolutionary explanations for why love came about. But they are just that—explanations. Edward O. Wilson's classic text on sociobiology, for example, opens by referencing "the central theoretical problem of sociobiology: how can altruism, which by definition reduces personal fitness, possibly evolve by natural selection?"[139] On a naturalistic worldview, love is a problem that must be accounted for, since it fits awkwardly with the ruthlessly selfish nature of biological life.

138. Kalanithi, *When Breath Becomes Air*, 169.
139. Edward O. Wilson, *Sociobiology: The New Synthesis*, 25th anniv. ed. (Cambridge, MA: Belknap, 2000), 3.

Many expressions of love are, accordingly, regarded as irrational. Richard Dawkins, for instance, thinks that polyamory is more rational than the "fanatically monogamous devotion to which we are susceptible," even considering the possibility that religion is the by-product of these irrational mechanisms in our brain that cause us to fall in love.[140]

By contrast, on a theistic worldview, particularly trinitarian theism, love is at the very core of reality. It is eternally shared among the members of the Godhead and was the motive for the creation of the world. The Bible even says, "God is love" (1 John 4:8, 16). On such a view, there is every reason to affirm Olaf's statement that "love is permanent" in an exactly literal sense.

We could sum up the differences between these two options in three ways:

Love in Naturalism	Love in Trinitarian Theism
Accidental: it very well could never have existed	*Essential*: it lies at the core of reality itself, eternally flowing between the Father, the Son, and the Spirit
Biological: it did not exist before animals, and will not exist after them	*Spiritual*: it is prior to the biological world, and even prior to the physical world—indeed, it is the very motive behind the existence of the physical world
Functional: it is a survival mechanism for animals, devoid of any deeper or abiding significance	*Purposeful*: it is both the cause and ultimate destination of the world

Thus, when it comes to explaining love, the difference between naturalistic and theistic worldviews is striking. Jerry Walls highlights the difference by comparing love and death in each view: "There is a divide of radical proportions between those who believe love is stronger than death, and those who believe death is stronger than love."[141] Almost all of us intuitively sense the decisive

---

140. Dawkins, *The God Delusion*, 184–85.
141. Jerry L. Walls, "The Argument from Love and the Argument from the Meaning of Life," in Walls and Dougherty, *Two Dozen (or So) Arguments for God*, 304.

importance of this contrast. Whichever of these alternatives turns out to be correct, it feels like a matter of despair versus infinite relief. But are things really so bad on naturalism? Someone might say, "Why does love need to be some big, eternal thing? So what if it won't exist forever? Right now, today, I can still love and be loved and enjoy the experience." It's true, of course, that you don't need to believe in an eternal love to experience love in the here and now. At the same time, what we ultimately believe about love typically affects our experience of it in the here and now. C. S. Lewis describes the experience of someone who embraces a thoroughly materialist view of the universe and then tries to get on with life as usual:

> You can't, except in the lowest animal sense, be in love with a girl if you know (and keep on remembering) that all the beauties both of her person and of her character are a momentary and accidental pattern produced by the collision of atoms, and that your own response to them is only a sort of psychic phosphorescence arising from the behavior of your genes. You can't go on getting very serious pleasure from music if you know and remember that its air of significance is a pure illusion, that you like it only because your nervous system is irrationally conditioned to like it. You may still, in the lowest sense, have a "good time"; but just in so far as it becomes very good, just in so far as it ever threatens to push you on from cold sensuality into real warmth and enthusiasm and joy, so far you will be forced to feel the hopeless disharmony between your own emotions and the universe in which you really live.[142]

Here Lewis threads together the experience of both music and love: both are equally impoverished on a naturalistic worldview, because one's enjoyment of them can only operate on a "lower level" (think of Barnes listening to Mozart's *Requiem*). Anyone

142. C. S. Lewis, "On Living in an Atomic Age," in *Present Concerns: A Compelling Collection of Timely, Journalistic Essays*, ed. Walter Hooper (San Diego: Harcourt Books, 2002), 76.

who has ever been in love—truly, achingly in love—may relate to Lewis's words here. When you love someone, it is like a transcendent experience. This is true of romantic love, or *eros*; but the same sentiment holds true for friendship love, what Lewis calls *philia*.[143] Love, in all its various manifestations, feels like getting caught up into something transcendent, something Good and Nourishing. To have to reinterpret such feelings as illusory is a bitter prospect to consider.[144]

Many of those writing from a secular perspective, of course, affirm that our experiences of love do have transcendent significance. Luc Ferry, for instance, advocates for a "humanism without metaphysics" in which we can retain the transcendence of these values, as opposed to those reductive materialist views that drain them of transcendence.[145] But the question is, How, on a purely naturalistic plane, can we do so? If "the strong devour the weak" is how we all got here, *why* sacrifice your good for the good of another? *Why* commit yourself to monogamy? *Why* put the needs of children or the elderly or the sick above your own comfort?

For in a world that is entirely explicable by the driving forces of natural selection, death is indeed stronger than love. All you have to do is wait, and love will cease to exist, as will every consequence or memory of love. Love is like an accidental glitch in the program that eventually gets worked out.

The atheist Bertrand Russell described what a world devoid of the supernatural ultimately entails, speaking of the world as without purpose or meaning, and concluding that the only option is an unyielding despair:

> Amid such a world, if anywhere, our ideals henceforward must find a home. That Man is the product of causes which had no prevision

143. C. S. Lewis, *The Four Loves* (New York: Harcourt, Brace, Jovanovich, 1960).
144. On this point, see also Josh Chatraw, *Telling a Better Story: How to Talk about God in a Skeptical Age* (Grand Rapids: Zondervan, 2020), 80–82.
145. Ferry, *A Brief History of Thought*, 236–37.

of the end they were achieving; that his origin, his growth, his hopes and fears, his loves and his beliefs, are but the outcome of accidental collocations of atoms; that no fire, no heroism, no intensity of thought and feeling, can preserve an individual life beyond the grave; that all the labours of the ages, all the devotion, all the inspiration, all the noonday brightness of human genius, are destined to extinction in the vast death of the solar system, and that the whole temple of Man's achievement must inevitably be buried beneath the debris of a universe in ruins—all these things, if not quite beyond dispute, are yet so nearly certain, that no philosophy which rejects them can hope to stand. Only within the scaffolding of these truths, only on the firm foundation of unyielding despair, can the soul's habitation henceforth be safely built.[146]

Such a worldview is pretty grim. Deep in our hearts, we both sense and hope that there is something more to it all than this. That is why we tell stories like *Beauty and the Beast*, and countless others, in which love somehow overcomes death. What if such stories are yet another clue of what the ultimate Story is like?

Looking for Other Clues

Math, music, and love are really just examples of a larger point: namely, *better sense can be made of human experience if there is some ultimate meaning undergirding our world*. Other qualities of the human condition, such as consciousness,[147] rationality,[148] and

146. Bertrand Russell, *Mysticism and Logic and Other Essays* (London: Longmans, Green, 1918), 47–48.
147. Philosopher Thomas Nagel (not himself a believer in God) finds various features of consciousness so problematic that they undermine the whole reductive materialist picture of the universe: "If the appearance of conscious organisms in the world is due to principles of development that are not derived from the timeless laws of physics, that may be a reason for pessimism about purely chemical explanations of the origin of life as well." *Mind and Cosmos*, 12.
148. As J. B. S. Haldane put it many years ago: "If my mental processes are determined wholly by the motions of atoms in my brain, I have no reason to suppose that my beliefs are true. . . . And hence I have no reason for supposing my brain to

free will,[149] could be referenced for similar purposes. Many have argued that these characteristics of life—our self-awareness, our ability to reason, and our sense of making meaningful choices—cohere more organically within a supernaturalistic worldview of some kind. For again, on naturalism, everything about our experience is the result of purposeless physical processes that preceded us, and therefore all these aspects of human psychology are reducible to evolutionary explanations. On such a worldview, it is difficult to avoid the conclusion that the human presumption of meaning, reflected in these various capacities, has no transcendent referent and is therefore in a vital sense illusory.

The loss of transcendent meaning is therefore devastating. It cuts into the very essence of our humanity. It brought the writer Leo Tolstoy to the verge of suicide as he wrestled with it, asking, "Is there any meaning in my life that the inevitable death awaiting me does not destroy?"[150] The existentialist philosopher Albert Camus describes human existence as "absurd" because of the loss of transcendent meaning. In *The Myth of Sisyphus*, Camus describes the absurdity of life as the divorce of humanity from our setting—we long for meaning in the face of a meaningless world, we long for happiness and perpetuity in the face of the total annihilation of death, and we long for coherence and unity in the face of chaos and disintegration.[151] At one point he compares

be composed of atoms." Quoted in Victor Reppert, *C. S. Lewis's Dangerous Idea: In Defense of the Argument from Reason* (Downers Grove, IL: InterVarsity, 2009), 50. Alvin Plantinga is perhaps the most prominent contemporary advocate of this argument. See, e.g., Alvin Plantinga, "Against Materialism," *Faith and Philosophy* 23 (2006): 11–32.

149. Bertrand Russell speculated about this point on various occasions, e.g., "If, when a man writes a poem or commits a murder, the bodily movements involved in his act result solely from physical causes, it would seem absurd to put up a statue to him in the one case and to hang him in the other." *Why I Am Not a Christian: And Other Essays on Religion and Related Subjects*, ed. Paul Edwards (New York: Simon & Schuster, 1957), 38. C. S. Lewis and many others have taken up the same point.

150. Leo Tolstoy, *A Confession* (New York: Charles Scribner's Sons, 1902), 33.

151. Albert Camus, *The Myth of Sisyphus and Other Essays* (New York: Vintage, 2012), 19, even applies this disintegration of meaning and coherence to our

the absurdity of our situation to "sin without God."[152] Earlier he describes the absurd as a kind of frustration of our basic human impulses of thought and appetite for life: "A stranger to myself and the world, armed solely with a thought that negates itself as soon as it asserts, what is this condition in which I can have peace only by refusing to know and to live, in which the appetite for conquest bumps into walls that defy its assault?"[153]

Camus compares the human plight to the character Sisyphus in Greek mythology, who was bound to eternally roll a stone up a hill only to watch it fall down repeatedly (hence the title of Camus's book). But Camus does not think that the meaninglessness of this situation entails suicide; absurdism is not nihilism.[154] On the contrary, he thinks Sisyphus's task is enough to occupy his energies and satisfy his heart: "Each atom of that stone, each mineral flake of that night-filled mountain, in itself forms a world. The struggle itself toward the heights is enough to fill a man's heart. One must imagine Sisyphus happy."[155]

It's difficult to accept such a worldview without a feeling of great loss and devastation. If absurdism is right, most of us would rather give in to it begrudgingly than, as Camus suggests, kiss it;

---

self-understanding: "Forever I shall be a stranger to myself. In psychology as well as in logic, there are truths but no truth." To be clear, Camus does not strictly deny that the world has a transcendent meaning; he simply asserts that such a meaning is unattainable to us: "I don't know whether this world has a meaning that transcends it. But I know that I do not know that meaning and that it is impossible for me just now to know it. What can a meaning outside my condition mean to me?" (51).

152. Camus, *The Myth of Sisyphus*, 40.

153. Camus, *The Myth of Sisyphus*, 20.

154. The driving question Camus pursues throughout *The Myth of Sisyphus* is the question of suicide: Since life is absurd, should we kill ourselves? Camus says no, and that the proper response to our condition is to "revolt" against the longing for meaning and to embrace the absurdity of life—as he colorfully puts it, to "kiss the absurd" (54). For Camus, we should embrace the freedom of our ability to construct our own meaning. There is, paradoxically, a kind of meaning in this choice, in which we embrace consciousness of hopelessness without yielding to despair: "Within the limits of nihilism it is possible to find the means to proceed beyond nihilism" (123).

155. Camus, *The Myth of Sisyphus*, 123.

and it's easier to think that Sisyphus is happy only to the extent that he is distracted from what he is actually doing.

What if there is an alternative that allows us to retain a transcendent meaning by which to orient human life? On the Christian view, for example, and some other theistic views as well, human beings are made in God's image. There are lots of different ways of developing what that means, but they all involve the fundamental idea that we are imbued with certain characteristics of the Creator himself. Such a view can offer a compelling account of why love feels the way it does, why our choices are meaningful, and why our reasoning can be geared toward truth and not merely survival. Beyond its potential explanatory power, such a view leads to a remarkably elegant vision of humanity.[156] We are not just an accidental offshoot of physical processes. We are, instead, the thing in all the universe that most closely mirrors its Creator.

One way to sum this up is to say that theism allows us to live within our humanity more comfortably. We need not distrust our deepest intuitions—our intuitions of love, of reason, of beauty.[157] We can relax into them. The fundamental feeling that this world—and our place within it—*means something* is not deceiving us. We

156. Throughout history Christians have frequently associated being made in God's image with rationality, resulting in a particularly dignified view of reason. Pascal, for example, spoke of man as a "thinking reed," maintaining that "all our dignity consists in thought." Peter Kreeft, *Christianity for Modern Pagans: Pascal's Pensées Edited, Outlined, and Explained* (San Francisco: Ignatius, 1993), 55. This vision of the dignity of thinking undergirds the Pascalian intuition that thought is greater than place, for thought can grasp reality while place is inevitably grasped by it. As Pascal put it, "Through space the universe grasps me and swallows me up like a speck; through thought I grasp it." Kreeft, *Christianity for Modern Pagans*, 57.

157. Intuition is generally taken as a valid form of knowledge, distinct from rational inference, and also not dependent on memory, testimony of others, or our sense experience. Most of us recognize that there are certain things that we know in a more immediate, intuitive way—for instance, certain mathematical, logical, moral, and philosophical truths. Of course, one can always simply deny the reliability of these intuitions. But it's difficult to function in the real world like that. For further discussion of the nature of intuition and its role in human knowledge and reasoning, see Robert C. Koons, "The General Argument from Intuition," in Walls and Dougherty, *Two Dozen (or So) Arguments for God*, 238–39.

are not "accidental collocations of atoms," as Russell put it—we are characters in the middle of the greatest story ever told. We are not rolling a boulder up a hill with Sisyphus—we are progressing dramatically toward the final chapter.

Conclusion

In chapter 1 we suggested that the origins of our world put "a foot in the door" for supernaturalistic worldviews, suggesting the possibility of some kind of transcendent source for the world. The considerations of this chapter extend and clarify this impression. For it looks like our world derives not only its *being* from some kind of transcendent foundation but also a kind of intricate *meaning* from it as well—much like a story derives meaning from an author. For in our world we discover truths (like math) and beauty (like music) that seem out of place within a strictly naturalistic conception of reality. Moreover, most of us live on the assumption of certain values (like love) and intuitions (like rationality) that are difficult to substantiate within the boundaries of pure naturalism. Where do these alluringly metaphysical qualities come from? Better sense can be made out of our world, and of our experience within it, on the hypothesis that it has been ordered or structured by something ulterior to itself.

What kind of entity might be responsible for imbuing the world with transcendent meaning? We still cannot yet say, but we can note that many of the features of our world give every impression of intelligence and beauty. Thus, when we consider who or what might be behind space-time, what might be the wraparound Reality that explains why there is anything at all, we get a provocative impression of something *personal*. The Source of our world is apparently the kind of thing that can produce equations and sonatas. It put together a universe in which Bach and Gödel (and, for that matter, Olaf) can do what they do. Such an entity seems less likely to be a raw, impersonal power.

After all, consider that the universe includes *us*—people who reason and love, who feel and imagine, who create and dream, who thirst for meaning and happiness. It's strange to think that the effect should be greater than the cause—that the personal should derive from the impersonal, that a universe devoid of meaning should produce creatures who cannot live without it.

In the next chapter we carry this intuition a bit further, turning to another clue that is deeply embedded within us, so much so that you have never seen a movie that is not telling us about it.

3

The Conflict of the World

*Why Good and Evil Shape the Plot
of Every Story You've Ever Heard*

This chapter is about morality. It envisions moral struggle
as the fundamental conflict of the world. Thus, if we are
thinking of our world as a kind of story, good versus evil
will be where the drama lies.

I will draw attention to two aspects of our moral experience:
first, our intuitive sense of the objective reality of moral values and
obligations[1] (what we will call "conscience"); second, our longing
for moral justice and moral hope (what we will call a "Happy Ending"). I propose that a worldview that allows for the supernatural
provides both a more plausible and a more meaningful explanatory

---

1. It is common to distinguish between moral values (relating to moral goodness)
and moral duties or obligations (relating to moral rightness). In speaking of morality
as "objective," I have in mind a broad moral realism, according to which moral values
and obligations have a robust independence from human opinion. For further analysis
of the nuances involved in defining moral realism, see David O. Brink, *Moral Realism and the Foundations of Ethics*, Cambridge Studies in Philosophy (Cambridge:
Cambridge University Press, 1989), 14–36.

framework for these two aspects of moral experience. Specifically, such a worldview can (1) ground objective moral reality and (2) offer moral hope. By contrast, the story that naturalism tells is a dreadful tale in which moral drama is fundamentally illusory, for conscience is deceiving us and no Happy Ending is coming.

To this end, I will walk through a series of examples from philosophy, movies, and literature to describe the nature of morality as we encounter it. The recurring question will be, Which worldview can better account for this reality: a supernaturalistic one or a naturalistic one? Throughout, but particularly in conclusion, I begin to consider *theism* more concretely, in contrast to other supernaturalistic alternatives.

The Power of Conscience

In a favorite scene of my favorite novel, *That Hideous Strength*, the character Mark Studdock is imprisoned and subjected to a kind of psychological torture. He is placed in a room in which the architecture is just a little bit (not too much) out of proportion. He notices dots on the ceiling of an *almost* orderly arrangement, apparently corresponding to dots on the floor and table—but not quite. The shape and features of the room are designed to disturb the mind, offering the impression of a purpose or pattern but continually frustrating that impression.

The room is also filled with paintings. Mark views them all one by one. Some are grotesque and bizarre: "There was a portrait of a young woman who held her mouth wide open to reveal the fact that the inside of it was thickly overgrown with hair. . . . There was a giant mantis playing a fiddle while being eaten by another mantis, and a man with corkscrews instead of arms bathing in a flat, sadly coloured sea beneath a summer sunset."[2] But most of the paintings are not so obviously disturbing. Most of them appear

2. C. S. Lewis, *That Hideous Strength: A Modern Fairy-Tale for Grown-Ups* (1945; repr., New York: Scribner, 2003), 295.

to be normal at first glance, only to reveal upon closer examination little discrepancies or oddities. For instance, there is a painting of the Last Supper, but with lots of beetles on the floor under the table. Oddly, many of the paintings have scriptural themes. The sheer weirdness of the room gives Mark the disturbing impression of *evil*—somewhat like the effect of a gross or bizarre scene in a horror film. In fact, the cumulative effect of the room as a whole gives Mark the feeling that he has come into contact with a deeper kind of evil than he had previously known: "Long ago Mark had read somewhere of 'things of that extreme evil which seem innocent to the uninitiate,' and had wondered what sort of things they might be. Now he felt he knew."[3]

The purpose of Mark's time in this room (we will call it the "crooked room") is a kind of psychological conditioning by which Mark's captors hope to impress upon him their own moral philosophy. This philosophy—called "objectivity" by one of Mark's captors—involves the claim that all human motives are simply instinctive reactions rooted in biological factors. There is no objective moral realm; all values, including moral values, are "merely animal, subjective epiphenomena."[4] To embrace this view, and to abandon all such conscious motives toward good or evil, is to obtain "objectivity." Mark knows that in order to kill natural human instincts and obtain objectivity, further tasks will be assigned to him—"the eating of abominable food, the dabbling in dirt and blood, the ritual performances of calculated obscenities."[5]

But staying in the crooked room has a different effect upon Mark than his captors intended:

> The built and painted perversity of this room had the effect of making him aware, as he had never been aware before, of this room's opposite. As the desert first teaches men to love water, or

3. Lewis, *That Hideous Strength*, 296.
4. Lewis, *That Hideous Strength*, 293.
5. Lewis, *That Hideous Strength*, 296.

as absence first reveals affection, there rose up against this background of the sour and the crooked some kind of vision of the sweet and the straight. Something else—something he vaguely called the "Normal"—apparently existed. He had never thought about it before. But there it was—solid, massive, with a shape of its own, almost like something you could touch, or eat, or fall in love with. It was all mixed up with Jane and fried eggs and soap and sunlight and the rooks cawing at Cure Hardy and the thought that, somewhere outside, daylight was going on at that moment. He was not thinking in moral terms at all; or else (what is much the same thing) he was having his first deeply moral experience.[6]

Several things are noteworthy about Lewis's depiction of moral experience here. First, Mark does not consciously experience goodness in moral categories. He does not call it "morality," or even "goodness." He calls it the "Normal." Related to this, it becomes apparent to him in aesthetic categories—through art. He comes to perceive evil through oddities of architecture and ugliness in paintings, just as he associates goodness with things like soap and daylight and fried eggs. All this suggests a more complex, variegated conception of goodness than is often conceptualized in discussions of the nature of morality.

Second, it is noteworthy that Mark does not have what Lewis calls "his first deeply moral experience" *until* he is in the crooked room. The realm of conscience appears to lie latent within him, unconsidered in more comfortable scenes of life, discovered only in the context of suffering. Earlier Lewis emphasizes that the moral philosophy of Mark's captors is the logical follow-through of his "modern" worldview—though he had never considered it till now.[7] This suggests an almost revelatory quality to morality—it is, in Lewis's vision, *discoverable*, rather than equally obvious to every person at every moment.

6. Lewis, *That Hideous Strength*, 296–97.
7. Lewis, *That Hideous Strength*, 293.

Third, the robustness and objectivity of moral goodness is emphasized here. It is "solid, massive, with a shape of its own." This aspect of the "Normal" is further drawn out as the training wears on and Mark is continually made to do seemingly obscene, meaningless tasks:

> Day by day, as the process went on, that idea of the Straight or the Normal grew stronger and more solid in his mind till it had become a kind of mountain. He had never before known what an Idea meant: he had always thought till now that they were things inside one's own head. But now, when his head was continually attacked and often completely filled with the clinging corruption of the training, this Idea towered up above him—something which obviously existed quite independently of himself and had hard rock surfaces which would not give, surfaces he could cling to.[8]

The comparison to a mountain and the references to "hard rock surfaces" here serve to emphasize the *practical* effect of objective morality. Because goodness exists outside of Mark's mind, completely independent of his thoughts, he can cling to it in the midst of his torment. When everything else is taken from him, it is still there, unmoved, untouched. It ultimately saves him.

Reflecting on this idea of the "Normal" is a way of getting at the central, metaethical question of this chapter: Is there such a thing?[9] That is, Is there some source and standard of goodness that exists objectively—independent of human judgment—like a solid mountain, with hard surfaces?

8. Lewis, *That Hideous Strength*, 307.
9. Whereas normative and applied ethics are concerned with what constitutes moral behavior, metaethics is the branch of moral philosophy concerned with the nature of morality itself. Metaethics is the more abstract and more foundational branch of the three. Using an analogy with football, Andrew Fisher compares applied ethicists to the players, normative ethicists to the referees, and metaethicists to the analysts or pundits. See Andrew Fisher, *Metaethics: An Introduction* (New York: Routledge, 2014), 1–2.

We are not yet in a position to answer this question. At the moment we are simply attempting to articulate the question as vividly as possible. Most of us can probably relate, in one way or another, to Mark's experience in this passage. Some of us have had our own crooked room—our own encounter with real evil, real darkness, real pain. We understand, in an intuitive way, why such a thing can be associated with grossness and disorder. Most of us can also understand Mark's longing for the sweet and the straight, for "soap and sunlight." We instinctively long for our lives to arrive upon not mere happiness but a kind of *rightness*. The question is, How do we best account for such feelings? In what kind of story do they make the most sense?

What Is Conscience, Precisely?

Before we attempt to interpret moral feelings, we might benefit from describing them a bit further, stemming from this scene in *That Hideous Strength*. Three characteristics are worth observing (though many more could be mentioned as well). First, moral feeling is instinctive. Morality is not some foreign concept that you gradually discover if you think about it long enough, like an obscure subject in school. It's inward and basic. We feel it as naturally as we feel happiness or hunger. Philosophers of natural law sometimes speak of "deep conscience" (as opposed to "surface conscience") to refer to this deeply interior realm where morality is not merely felt; it is *known*.[10] Accordingly, we generally don't argue *for* this knowledge; we argue *from* it.

This instinctive awareness of morality appears to be universal, or nearly universal (even psychopaths understand on some level what morality is—and we all recognize that their lack of feeling it is a deficit or aberration). A sense of moral reality has been

---

10. See the discussion in J. Budziszewksi, *What We Can't Not Know: A Guide* (Dallas: Spence, 2003), 79–81. This does not entail, however, that our moral knowledge is unaffected by the will: the realm of conscience can be ignored, suppressed, and/or abused.

foundational to all civilizations throughout human history. Some have supposed that as the modern West grows more secular, it will become more tolerant and mild with respect to the realm of conscience—but on the contrary, our culture appears to be rapidly escalating in moral outrage and tribalism. The social psychologist Jonathan Haidt has put a great deal of reflection into the moral psychology reflected in our current divisions.[11] In the modern West, our moral framework is primarily grounded in considerations of harm, whereas virtually all other cultures have developed their moral vision from a variety of other criteria, such as care, fairness, loyalty, authority, and sanctity.[12] Thus, morality plays out a bit differently in the modern West—but it is very far from disappearing! The far-left secularist and the far-right fundamentalist disagree about what the right morality is, but neither side has to convince the other that *there are such things as good and evil, and they are a big deal*. We all already seem to know this somehow. It is hardwired into our nature. As Haidt puts it, "Human nature is not just intrinsically moral, it's also intrinsically moralistic, critical, and judgmental. . . . An obsession with righteousness (leading inevitably to self-righteousness) is the normal human condition."[13] This helps explain why human beings so frequently divide into hostile groups, with each side certain that their opponents are wrong.[14]

11. Jonathan Haidt, *The Righteous Mind: Why Good People Are Divided by Politics and Religion* (New York: Vintage, 2012), 3–108, argues that intuitions shape our moral thinking more than reasoning does, and that different ideological tribes are functioning with different moral intuitions.
12. Haidt, *The Righteous Mind*, 150–79. Haidt accordingly argues that conservatives and liberals often talk past one another because they don't take into account their differing intuitions about the nature of morality. We therefore need to be slower to dismiss others simply because we can refute their arguments and more discerning of the role our moral convictions are playing in us. As he puts it, "Morality binds and blinds. It binds us into ideological teams that fight each other as though the fate of the world depended on our side winning each battle. It blinds us to the fact that each team is composed of good people who have something important to say" (366).
13. Haidt, *The Righteous Mind*, xix–xx.
14. Aleksandr Solzhenitsyn's observation points to a more realistic and penetrating way to view the distinction between good and evil: "Gradually it was disclosed

Second, moral feeling has a kind of transcendent *importance* associated with it. To the extent that we have contact with the realm of conscience, we have the impression of something possessing lasting, vital significance. We sense that it matters, and matters deeply, whether good or evil shall win. Accordingly, questions of morality are closely related to questions of meaning and happiness, and morality plays a foundational role in government and law.

At the individual level, we all intuitively sense the importance bound up with moral feelings. Morality produces some of the fiercest human emotions, like shame, pride, and rage. When we see a young boy comforting and standing up for his friend who is being bullied, we feel admiration. When we learn of rich businessmen remorselessly stealing from poor families, we experience indignation. When we consider a man who comes to realize that he has wounded and betrayed his own family, we understand his regret. When we hear about a selfish teenager who, in becoming a father and loving his daughter, learns how to put others first, we respect this process of redemption.

As I type this sentence, it is June 1, 2020. The world is languishing in many different ways (I hope by the time you read this, it will be better). Among the many other sources of grief reverberating through the world right now, particularly gripping for me is the painful and ugly reality of racial prejudice and injustice. I will never forget what it felt like to watch the video of George Floyd's death. How do you describe the darkness and agony of what injustice *feels* like? There are no words that fully capture it, but unless you have had an unusually peaceable life, you likely know what I mean. As we have said, many of us have had our own crooked rooms.

---

to me that the line separating good and evil passes not through states, nor between classes, nor between political parties either—but right through every human heart." Solzhenitsyn, *The Gulag Archipelago*, quoted in Daniel J. Mahoney, *Aleksandr Solzhenitsyn: The Ascent from Ideology* (Lanham, MD: Roman & Littlefield, 2001), 50.

Again, we are not yet interpreting the feeling of significance associated with morality. All we are saying thus far is that such moral feelings exist in the human heart and they at least *feel* very significant to us.

But moral feelings feel significant to us in a very particular kind of way. A third characteristic of moral feeling, closely related to the second, is that it has a kind of *authoritative* quality to it. It impresses itself upon us, not merely as an inspiration or motivation, but as a kind of law. It makes demands of us. As David Baggett puts it, "Moral obligations are not mere suggestions, cautionary ideals, means of avoiding trouble, or sage pieces of advice."[15] Rather, when we speak of "moral obligations," we have in mind something exacting, something that binds us and others, something like a set of laws or rules. We all sense this law deep within. It is as though there is a whole judicial system within the heart of every human being.

Elizabeth Anscombe has emphasized this binding, legal quality of morality, arguing that when we speak of a moral obligation, we are speaking of something that ought to be done for reasons more than mere flourishing or happiness.[16] Rather, moral obligation functions like a verdict, passing a sentence for or against a particular action.[17] Thus, moral obligation is not merely a reason to do something in the sense that it is expedient or reasonable to do so (e.g., you should brush your teeth so that you don't get

---

15. David Baggett, "An Abductive Moral Argument for God," in *Two Dozen (or So) Arguments for God*, ed. Jerry L. Walls and Trent Dougherty (Oxford: Oxford University Press, 2018), 268.

16. G. E. M. Anscombe distinguishes Aristotle from modern philosophy on this point. "Modern Moral Philosophy," in *The Collected Philosophical Papers of G. E. M. Anscombe*, vol. 3, *Ethics, Religion, and Politics* (Minneapolis: University of Minnesota Press, 1981), 26. For Anscombe, the lawlike character of morality suggests a lawgiver. C. Stephen Evans, *God and Moral Obligation* (Oxford: Oxford University Press, 2013), 16–19, qualifies Anscombe's point by distinguishing between an ontological and an epistemological dependence of morality on God (thus, Socrates, for example, had a keen sense of moral obligation, apart from any specifically Christian or theistic influence). As we will discuss, our interest in this chapter is on the ontological relation of God and morality more than the epistemological.

17. Anscombe, "Modern Moral Philosophy," 32.

cavities, and cavities are not conducive to human flourishing). It is a particular *kind* of reason, deriving its power from some kind of law (e.g., you should not cheat on your test, because it is wrong to do so *whether or not* you pass the class). C. Stephen Evans calls the set of characteristics involved in moral obligation the "Anscombe intuition," summarizing it by simply noting that "moral obligations have a law-like character."[18]

Again, we are not yet in a position to judge whether morality is, in fact, authoritative. We are merely observing that it *feels* that way. All of this thus far is simply to better inform the question, How shall we best understand moral experience—what do these instinctive, important, and authoritative feelings *mean*? We consider naturalism first.

Can Morality Live without God? The New Atheists versus the Old

To consider how we might understand morality from an naturalistic viewpoint, it will be useful to canvas how this question has been approached historically in secular or atheistic contexts. Atheism is a tradition of thought like any other (though some contemporary atheists, like many believers, do not read well in their own tradition); and it would be careless to ignore the contributions of earlier generations.[19]

As an entry point, we consider a (now famous) 1979 article in the *Duke Law Journal* by Arthur Leff, which poignantly describes the relation of morality and God. Throughout the article he wrestles

18. Evans, *God and Moral Obligation*, 16.
19. Here I'm using the term "atheist" in a broad way, rather than in hard distinction from, say, various species of agnosticism. For instance, what I am envisioning with this term in what follows would incorporate both what Antony Flew calls "negative atheism" (the lack of belief in God, without certainty that he does not exist) as well as "positive atheism" (the explicit assertion that there is no God). See Antony Flew, *The Presumption of Atheism and Other Philosophical Essays on God, Freedom, and Immortality* (New York: Barnes & Noble, 1976).

with a tension between our need for a transcendent moral order, on the one hand, and the terrible freedom that results from realizing it may not be out there, on the other hand. He realizes the loss of God is vital: "A God-grounded system has no analogues. Either God exists or He does not, but if He does not, nothing and no one else can take His place."[20] He explores various efforts to determine an ontological basis for morality other than God, but points out that they all suffer from the "Grand Sez Who" problem—that is, there does not appear to be any ultimate criterion or referee by which to adjudicate competing claims. Thus, the death of God turns out to be not merely *his* funeral but the loss of any objective, coherent ethical or legal system.[21] With no "brooding omnipresence in the sky," as Leff puts it, it's up to us.[22]

Toward the end of the article, Leff sums up the situation and then concludes with a kind of poem:

> All I can say is this: it looks as if we are all we have. Given what we know about ourselves and each other, this is an extraordinarily unappetizing prospect; looking around the world, it appears that if all men are brothers, the ruling model is Cain and Abel. . . . As things now stand, everything is up for grabs.
> Nevertheless:
> Napalming babies is bad.
> Starving the poor is wicked.
> Buying and selling each other is depraved.
> Those who stood up to and died resisting Hitler, Stalin, Amin, and Pol Pot—and General Custer too—have earned salvation. Those who acquiesced deserve to be damned.
> There is in the world such a thing as evil.
> [All together now:] Sez who?
> God help us.[23]

20. Arthur Allen Leff, "Unspeakable Ethics, Unnatural Law," *Duke Law Journal* 6 (1979): 1231.
21. Leff, "Unspeakable Ethics, Unnatural Law," 1232.
22. Leff, "Unspeakable Ethics, Unnatural Law," 1233.
23. Leff, "Unspeakable Ethics, Unnatural Law," 1249.

Is Leff's worry here warranted? Does the absence of God leave us unable to condemn Stalin?

Many of the "new atheists" dispute this correlation, wanting to do away with God and religion while retaining values like individual human rights. Sam Harris, for example, thinks we can ground morality in human reason: "We are the final judges of what is good, just as we remain the final judges of what is logical. . . . There need be no scheme of rewards and punishments transcending this life to justify our moral intuitions."[24] Harris denies that morality is subjective, distinguishing his approach from that of other secularists.[25] He thinks that morality can be objectively grounded in science, and he links moral goodness with the well-being of conscious creatures.[26] Harris is representative of the general new-atheist claim that God and religion are not only unnecessary for this aim—they are impediments.[27]

Within the purview of "well-being" (and thus moral goodness), Harris envisions values like compassion, tolerance, and generosity. For example, in one section of *The Moral Landscape*, Harris describes what he calls "The Good Life," and he includes not only prosperity and happiness in the description but generosity and charity to others: "One of your greatest sources of happiness has been to find creative ways to help people who have not had your good fortune in life. In fact, you have just won a billion-dollar grant to benefit children in the developing world. If asked, you would say that you could not imagine how your time on earth could be better spent."[28]

24. Sam Harris, *The End of Faith: Religion, Terror, and the Future of Reason* (New York: Norton, 2004), 226.

25. Baggett, "An Abductive Moral Argument for God," 261–76, analyzes other attempts by contemporary secularists to ground morality apart from God, such as that of Erik Wielenberg (265–65) and Philip Kitcher (272–73). As he notes, such perspectives struggle to account particularly for moral obligations.

26. Sam Harris, *The Moral Landscape: How Science Can Determine Human Values* (New York: Free Press, 2011), 1–3; Harris, *The End of Faith*, 170–203.

27. E.g., Harris, *The End of Faith*, 225.

28. Harris, *The Moral Landscape*, 15–16.

It is wonderful to envision such a life and to hope for it. But then a worry enters in: What is the basis or ground for these values? Some people will find it personally meaningful to be generous, to be sure. But others will not. Within the limits of a secular worldview, stripped of any supernatural referent, what is the *objective basis* for valuing generosity over greed? This is a different question than asking how we *know* that generosity is good (the epistemological question). It is a different question than asking whether religious people are, in actual practice, more generous than secular people (a sociological question). It is the deeper, ontological question: Why is it not merely desirable or fulfilling but actually *moral* to care for the needy? How would such a value acquire the lawlike quality that Anscombe detected, or the mountain-like stature that Mark Studdock experienced?

Such questions draw attention to the tenuousness of Harris's definition of morality in terms of "well-being." Consider when a gazelle is eaten by a crocodile: we understand that something painful is occurring, but we do not regard it as immoral. The gazelle has lost its "well-being," but the crocodile is not thereby guilty of any injustice. If there is nothing beyond the natural order, and the evolutionary history is the sum total explanation of our existence, why is human well-being a moral good while the well-being of the gazelle is not? Why can a crocodile merely kill while a human being can murder? At what point in the development of animal evolution did such moral capabilities come into being?

On Harris's view, it is not easy to know how to answer this question. It is also far from obvious, contrary to Harris's imagination, that the rejection of religious beliefs will result in a happy, rational, scientific mentality in which individual rights and tolerance and democracy are privileged. Such values have a history and context.[29] They are not the universal dream of humanity and

29. We take the goodness of individual freedom or compassion for granted today; but on naturalistic grounds, why should we? As David Bentley Hart puts it, "We live in the long twilight of a civilization formed by beliefs that, however obvious or

certainly not well grounded in our nonhuman, evolutionary history. So where do values like tolerance and equality come from? The answer cannot be science: science can help us understand and pursue certain values, but it cannot tell us why they are values in the first place.[30] Moreover, the authority of science *itself* requires some kind of explanation. If the strong devouring the weak is the paradigm by which we all got here, why should truth have intrinsic (as opposed to merely instrumental) value, and why should we trust our ability to arrive at it through experimentation and observation?

Worries like these are often raised against Harris from a variety of corners.[31] But intriguingly, perhaps his fiercest opposition comes from historic atheism itself. Harris represents a common contemporary way of thinking, but it is rarer among classic atheists. In fact, it is striking how many among older generations of atheists shared Leff's anxiety that the loss of God means the loss of intelligible values.

Perhaps the most obvious example is Friedrich Nietzsche, whose philosophy is sometimes summarized as the courageous outworking of a consistently atheistic position.[32] Nietzsche was a kind of

---

trite they may seem to us, entered ancient society rather like a meteor from a clear sky." *Atheist Delusions: The Christian Revolution and Its Fashionable Enemies* (New Haven: Yale University Press, 2009), 169; cf. 171–74, 213–15. History may bear this worry out, as well—as we will discuss more in the next chapter, the events of the twentieth century make it difficult to share Harris's expectation that atheism will be so nice and accommodating.

30. For an interesting discussion of this point, see Jürgen Habermas et al., *An Awareness of What Is Missing: Faith and Reason in a Post-Secular Age* (Cambridge: Polity Press, 2010).

31. Jordan Peterson, for example, has repeatedly argued that Enlightenment values like reason and tolerance cannot be abstracted from the metaphysical structures in which they arose and suggests that Harris, in affirming these values, is actually functioning with unconscious theistic instincts. See, for instance, their discussion in Vancouver, June 23, 2018, moderated by Bret Weinstein, "Sam Harris & Jordan Peterson—Vancouver—1," YouTube video, 2:06:37, posted by Pangburn, August 31, 2018, https://www.youtube.com/watch?v=jey_CzIOfYE.

32. This is the description of George A. Morgan as referenced by Walter Kaufmann, *Nietzsche: Philosopher, Psychologist, Antichrist*, 4th ed. (Princeton: Princeton Univer-

moral nihilist, denying the existence of moral facts and regarding moral judgments as absurd. As he put it:

> My demand upon the philosopher is known, that he take his stand *beyond* good and evil and leave the illusion of moral judgment beneath himself. This demand follows from an insight which I was the first to formulate: that *there are altogether no moral facts.* Moral judgments agree with religious ones in believing in realities which are no realities. Morality is merely an interpretation of certain phenomena—more precisely, a misinterpretation. Moral judgments, like religious ones, belong to a stage of ignorance at which the very concept of the real, and the distinction between what is real and imaginary, are still lacking; thus "truth," at this stage, designates all sorts of things which we today call "imaginings." Moral judgments are therefore never to be taken literally: so understood, they always contain mere absurdity.[33]

It is striking that Nietzsche here links his skepticism of morality with his skepticism of religion; and it is indeed the case that his moral nihilism derives more generally from his atheism.[34] Its general feel can be conveyed in the famous parable of the "madman" in *The Gay Science*, where he articulates the sense of the chaos that he thinks is unleashed in the loss of God, by which Nietzsche is mainly thinking of developments in Western civilization.[35] The madman (generally regarded as representing Nietzsche) runs to the marketplace and cries out:

sity Press, 1974), 99: "Beyond question the major premise of Nietzsche's philosophy is atheism."

33. Friedrich Nietzsche, *Twilight of the Idols*, in *The Portable Nietzsche*, trans. Walter Kaufmann (New York: Penguin, 1954), 463.

34. We might further call Nietzsche a nihilist in that he does not believe that there is *anything* in the world that has value—though this point is sometimes qualified or disputed. See the discussion in Nadeem J. Z. Hussain, "Honest Illusion: Valuing for Nietzsche's Free Spirits," in *Nietzsche and Morality*, ed. Brian Leiter and Neil Sinhababu (Oxford: Oxford University Press, 2007), 157–91.

35. Kaufmann, *Nietzsche*, 100, refers to the "death of God" in this passage as "an attempt at a diagnosis of contemporary civilization, not a metaphysical speculation about ultimate reality."

"Whither is God?" he cried; "I will tell you. We have killed him—
you and I. All of us are his murderers. But how did we do this?
How could we drink up the sea? Who gave us the sponge to wipe
away the entire horizon? What were we doing when we unchained
this earth from its sun? Whither is it moving now? Whither are
we moving? Away from all suns? Are we not plunging continually?
Backward, sideward, forward, in all directions? Is there still any up
or down? Are we not straying, as through an infinite nothing? Do
we not feel the breath of empty space? Has it not become colder?
Is not night continually closing in on us? Do we not need to light
lanterns in the morning? Do we hear nothing as yet of the noise
of the gravediggers who are burying God? Do we smell nothing
as yet of the divine decomposition? Gods, too, decompose. God
is dead. God remains dead. And we have killed him.

"How shall we comfort ourselves, the murderers of all murderers? What was holiest and mightiest of all that the world has yet
owned has bled to death under our knives: who will wipe this blood
off us? What water is there for us to clean ourselves? What festivals
of atonement, what sacred games shall we have to invent? Is not
the greatness of this deed too great for us? Must we ourselves not
become gods simply to appear worthy of it? There has never been
a greater deed; and whoever is born after us—for the sake of this
deed he will belong to a higher history than all history hitherto."[36]

There is no question in this passage as to the totality of the chaos
and ruin that is involved in the loss of God. Metaphors like wiping
away the horizon or unchaining the earth from the sun make the
point vividly. For Nietzsche, the situation introduced by atheism
is well captured by his words: "Is there still any up or down?"
Provocatively, the passages stress the magnitude of this upheaval
in *moral* terms: "Who will wipe this blood off us?" Losing God is
some great, unforgivable sin, requiring atonement. It is a matter
of guilt. This passage also emphasizes the finality of this event.

36. Friedrich Nietzsche, *The Gay Science*, as quoted in R. J. Hollingdale, *Nietzsche: The Man and His Philosophy* (Cambridge: Cambridge University Press, 2001), 139.

Humanity has been decisively altered. Those born after the death
of God "belong to a higher history than all history hitherto."

Nietzsche should not be read as though he thought the collapse of Christian morality in Western civilization was a pure
tragedy. Elsewhere he spoke contemptuously of the despair of
the modern man as a kind of weakness,[37] and it is clear that he
regarded Christian morals to be a kind of corruption, enshrouded
in hypocrisy and contemptible frailty.[38] In *Thus Spoke Zarathustra*,
he rails against "preachers of equality" not simply because of his
opposition to equality but, more deeply, because of their "secret
ambitions to be tyrants."[39] Nonetheless, it remains the case that
for Nietzsche the loss of belief in God was of colossal significance
for morality. It is impossible to know, and very sad to wonder,
about the relation of the philosophy espoused by "the madman"
to Nietzsche's own mental descent.[40]

Nietzsche's atheism is interesting as a point of reference or contrast to the more upbeat quality of Sam Harris's. For Harris, it is
simply obvious that "The Good Life" will involve compassion and
generosity. Nietzsche, by contrast, regarded pity with contempt,

37. Friedrich Nietzsche, *The Antichrist*, trans. Anthony M. Ludovici (Amherst,
NY: Prometheus, 2000), 3.

38. Kaufmann, *Nietzsche*, 113, describes Nietzsche's concept of the revaluation
(or transvaluation) of values as the "discovery that our morality is, *by its own stan-
dards*, poisonously immoral: that Christian love is the mimicry of impotent hatred;
that most unselfishness is but a particularly vicious form of selfishness; and that
ressentiment is at the core of our morals" (italics original).

39. As quoted in Kaufmann, *Nietzsche*, 373. It is also the case that Nietzsche's
rejection of Christian morality was inextricably bound up with his own dedication
to the will to power. See the discussion in Kaufmann, *Nietzsche*, 420–23.

40. The details of Nietzsche's mental collapse in early 1889 are disputed, but one
common story is that as he walked the street in Turin, Italy, he saw a horse being
whipped by its owner. Distraught at the sight, Nietzsche rushed to the animal and
threw his arms around its neck to protect it, only to collapse on the ground soon after.
For an analysis of Nietzsche's health and the cause of his mental collapse, as well
as an overview of historical interpretations of this event, see Charlie Huenemann,
"Nietzsche's Illness," in *The Oxford Handbook of Nietzsche*, ed. Ken Gemes and
John Richardson (Oxford: Oxford University Press, 2013), 63–82. For a portrait of
Nietzsche's time in Turin leading up to and including his mental collapse, see Lesley
Chamberlain, *Nietzsche in Turin: An Intimate Biography* (New York: Picador, 1998).

seeing it as Christianity's great sin: "Christianity is called the religion of pity. Pity is opposed to the tonic passions which enhance the energy of the feeling of life: its action is depressing. A man loses power when he pities."[41] He likewise regarded love as the greatest delusion.[42]

Nietzsche and Harris can be taken to stand for two starkly different strands of atheism, what we will call the "new atheists" and the "old atheists." Of course, there were many optimistic atheists in the nineteenth century and there are many nihilistic ones in the twenty-first. It is not a neat or consistent categorization. Moreover, there is a spectrum of varieties of atheism/agnosticism not perfectly represented by either view. Nonetheless, it is not entirely misleading to set up a general contrast along these lines: an instinct among older atheists that tended toward moral despair (represented by Nietzsche), and a more confidant, even superior, moral outlook among the newer atheists (represented by Harris).

Another iconic example of the older, more ruthless brand of atheism, though involving a different range of nuances, is the existentialist philosophy of Jean-Paul Sartre. In his influential treatment of existentialism, Sartre defined his existentialist philosophy as simply the results of a consistent atheism: "Existentialism is nothing else but an attempt to draw the full conclusions from a consistently atheistic position."[43] Thus, Sartre's famous definition

41. Nietzsche, *The Antichrist*, 7. He proceeds to compare pity to a germ or disease, and states that his business in life is like the doctor who removes it (cf. 9).
42. Nietzsche, *The Antichrist*, 29.
43. Jean-Paul Sartre, "Existentialism Is a Humanism," in *Existentialism from Dostoevsky to Sartre*, rev. ed., ed. Walter Kaufmann (New York: Plume, 2004), 369. I use this famous lecture of Sartre's for its eloquence and historical influence, though recognizing its limitations in providing a full account of Sartre's thought or existentialist philosophy more generally. As Walter Kaufmann notes, it is "only an occasional lecture which, though brilliant and vivid in places and unquestionably worthy of attention, bears the stamp of the moment." Kaufmann, "Existentialism from Dostoevsky to Sartre," in Kaufmann, *Existentialism from Dostoevsky to Sartre*, 45. A fuller portrait of Sartre's moral philosophy can be found in his *Being and Nothingness: An Essay on Phenomenological Ontology*, trans. Hazel E. Barnes (New York: Citadel, 1956).

of "existentialism"—*existence precedes essence*—derives from atheism because the category of "essence" becomes destabilized apart from God. Thus, with regard to human beings, "there is no human nature, because there is no God to have a conception of it. Man simply is."[44] For Sartre, the loss of God entails that things no longer have an inherent nature or purpose.

In this lecture Sartre used the terms "anguish," "abandonment," and "despair" to describe the existentialist dilemma. Of these, the second term, abandonment, is the application of existentialist principles to the moral realm. By this term Sartre essentially means that we cannot have traditional morality apart from God. Sartre describes how, beginning in the 1880s, French philosophers had sought to develop a "secular morality," disposing of God but maintaining certain a priori moral values for the sake of the good of society. Sartre rejected this effort categorically, maintaining that God and a priori moral values are inextricably linked: "The existentialist finds it extremely embarrassing that God does not exist, for there disappears with him all possibility of finding values in an intelligible heaven. There can no longer be any good *a priori*, since there is no infinite and perfect consciousness to think it." Sartre approvingly quotes Dostoevsky's famous dictum, "If God did not exist, everything would be permitted," claiming that this truth is, for the existentialist, the "starting point."[45]

This is not to say that Sartre is a moral nihilist to the same degree as Nietzsche. For instance, Sartre is sometimes read as locating moral value in the affirmation of freedom, which comes subsequent to the contradiction of the simultaneous necessity and impossibility of value, and uniquely providing the means of existing within this contradictory status.[46] Despite this possible

44. Sartre, "Existentialism Is a Humanism," 349.
45. Sartre, "Existentialism Is a Humanism," 353.
46. Sebastian Gardner, "Sartre," in *The Cambridge History of Moral Philosophy*, ed. Sacha Golob and Jens Timmermann (Cambridge: Cambridge University Press, 2017), 636–52, combats a common interpretation of Sartre as a moral nihilist along these lines.

solution, the fundamental problem of the loss of any external moral domain remains. Later Sartre compared morality with art: "There is this in common between art and morality, that in both we have to do with creation and invention."[47] Sartre acknowledges that such a view comes at great cost, and he takes seriously various objections that the loss of objective morality is devastating for human life and society. But he thinks that there remains a kind of meaning and freedom in selecting our own morality. To those who object that self-constructed values are not really *serious* values, Sartre's response is blunt yet honest: "I am very sorry that it should be so; but if I have excluded God the Father, there must be somebody to invent values."[48]

Sartre's conception of morality as malleable to human construction may seem initially attractive, particularly when we are envisioning moral choices that are more respectable (e.g., in his essay Sartre discusses the difference between marrying or not marrying). But its full significance becomes visible when we think of moral atrocities—think about the horrors inflicted by Nazi Germany, for instance (of which Sartre himself was a victim). Think about those who steal from the vulnerable, who torture without compassion, who abduct and harm children. Almost no one can accept that such atrocities are objectionable only in the sense that bad art is objectionable. We feel deep in our bones that there must be more to it than that. We recall Mark's revulsion in the crooked room, which we understand instinctively. Yet if naturalism is the metanarrative—if the strong devouring the weak is the ultimate story of biological existence, if there is no "intelligible heaven" to ground morality—then we can perhaps understand how Sartre could be driven to a malleable, constructible morality.

An important influence on both Sartre or Nietzsche, despite not sharing their religious outlook, is Fyodor Dostoevsky, whose novels have such historical significance and psychological depth that

47. Sartre, "Existentialism Is a Humanism," 364.
48. Sartre, "Existentialism Is a Humanism," 367.

they cannot be ignored in a historical discussion of morality and atheism. We just referenced Sartre's quotation of Dostoevsky's famous assertion "If God did not exist, all things are permitted." A variant of this phrase occurs four times in Nietzsche's writings (though always in quotation marks);[49] and Nietzsche stated that Dostoevsky was the only psychologist from whom he had learned something, and also identified several of the characters in Dostoevsky's novels as Übermensch (such as Rodion Raskolnikov, the protagonist in *Crime and Punishment*).[50] This quoted statement, asserted by the character Ivan in *The Brothers Karamazov*, should not be identified strictly with Nietzsche's own philosophy;[51] but it nonetheless is a good encapsulation of the general worry that we have identified as representative of the old atheists.

It is sometimes erroneously claimed that this maxim—"If God did not exist, all things are permitted"—does not actually occur in *The Brothers Karamazov*. On the contrary, there are numerous places where the phrase "everything is permitted" is used to denote a moral anarchy entailed by the nonexistence of God;[52] and the exploration of this sentiment can arguably be regarded as one of the novel's great themes, according to Dostoevsky himself.[53] One

49. See Geoff Waite, "Nietzsche—Rhetoric—Nihilism: 'Every Name in History'—'Every Style'—'Everything is Permitted' (A Political Philology of the Last Letter)," in *Nietzsche, Nihilism, and the Philosophy of the Future*, ed. Jeffrey Metzger (New York: Continuum, 2009), 67. The phrase as it appears in Nietzsche's writings is "Nothing is true, everything is permitted."

50. For discussion of this point and Dostoevsky's general influence on Nietzsche, see *Nietzsche and Dostoevsky: Philosophy, Morality, Tragedy*, ed. Jeff Love and Jeffrey Metzger (Evanston, IL: Northwestern University Press, 2016), 1–12.

51. Paolo Stellino, *Nietzsche and Dostoevsky: On the Verge of Nihilism* (Bern: Peter Lang, 2015), argues for points of disanalogy between Nietzsche's moral philosophy and that of Ivan Karamazov.

52. E.g., in the famous chapter "The Grand Inquisitor," Alyosha and Ivan discuss the phrase "everything is lawful" as a description of Ivan's rejection of God and acceptance of debauchery, picking up on earlier usage of this phrase in the book. See Fyodor Dostoevsky, *The Brothers Karamazov*, trans. Constance Garnett (New York: Signet, 1958), 256.

53. Dostoevsky wrote in a letter to a friend concerning *The Brothers Karamazov*: "The chief problem dealt with throughout this particular work is the very one which

important passage comes with the impassioned speech of Dmitri (Mitya) to Alyosha in part 4, book 11, chapter 4, "A Hymn and a Secret," where he references his earlier statement to Alyosha's companion Rakitin: "'But what will become of men then,' I asked him, 'without God and immortal life? *All things are lawful then*, they can do what they like?'"[54] Just a bit later in this same dialogue, Dmitri extends this claim, worrying that the absence of God entails not only moral relativism but also a kind of moral anarchy and disorder:

> It's God that's worrying me. That's the only thing that's worrying me. What if He doesn't exist? What if Rakitin's right—that it's an idea made up by men? Then if He doesn't exist, man is the chief of the earth, of the universe. Magnificent! Only how is he going to be good without God? That's the question. I always come back to that. For whom is man going to love then? To whom will he be thankful? To whom will he sing the hymn? Rakitin laughs. Rakitin says that one can love humanity without God. Well, only a sniveling idiot can maintain that. I can't understand it.[55]

Perhaps the most provocative engagement with this theme comes earlier in the novel from Dmitri's brother Ivan, who is the rationalist and skeptic among the brothers.[56] Ivan's words to Alyosha in part 2,

---

has, my whole life long, tormented my conscious and subconscious being: The question of the existence of God." Quoted in Manuel Komroff, foreword to Dostoevsky, *The Brothers Karamazov*, xv.

54. Dostoevsky, *The Brothers Karamazov*, 557 (italics added).

55. Dostoevsky, *The Brothers Karamazov*, 561.

56. Ivan's views are somewhat complicated. His appeal to Alyosha in these chapters is something other than a strict atheism, since he doesn't explicitly deny God's existence. Michael Martin, *Atheism: A Philosophical Justification* (Philadelphia: Temple University Press, 1990), 466, suggests the term "alienated theism" for Ivan's outlook, comparing it to Sartre's assertion that even if God exists, he is irrelevant to the fundamental existential question, the choice of freedom. The most famous expression of this aspect of Ivan's perspective comes just later in this dialogue with Alyosha: "It's not God that I don't accept, Alyosha, only I most respectfully return the ticket to Him." Dostoevsky, *The Brothers Karamazov*, 238. On the other hand, there are passages in which Ivan does appear to explicitly deny God's existence. For

book 5, chapters 3–5 constitute, for me, the most heartrending articulation of the problem of evil I have ever read. As a father of young children, it is frankly difficult for me to read them. Part of what makes Ivan's speech so poignant is that he is aware of, and even to some degree accepts, traditional responses given by believers for the problem of suffering. For instance, he begins by professing that suffering will be made up for in heaven, but rejects it nonetheless:

> It's not that I don't accept God, you must understand, it's the world created by Him I don't and cannot accept. Let me make it plain. I believe like a child that suffering will be healed and made up for, that all the humiliating absurdity of human contradictions will vanish like a pitiful mirage, like the despicable fabrication of the impotent and infinitely small Euclidian mind of man, that in the world's finale, at the moment of eternal harmony, something so precious will come to pass that it will suffice for all hearts, for the comforting of all resentments, for the atonement of all the crimes of humanity, of all the blood they've shed; that it will make it not only possible to forgive but to justify all that has happened with men—but though all that may come to pass, I don't accept it. I won't accept it.[57]

As he proceeds, Ivan recounts various unspeakable atrocities committed by human beings to one another, and especially to women and children, marveling at the evil of which people are capable. "People talk sometimes of bestial cruelty, but that's a great injustice and insult to the beasts," says Ivan. "A beast can never be so cruel as a man, so artistically cruel. The tiger only tears and gnaws, that's all he can do."[58] Throughout the dialogue Ivan focuses especially on the suffering of children. He seems especially burdened by the suffering of children because of their innocence,

---

a discussion of the nuances of Ivan's view, see Bernard Schweizer, "Literature," in *The Oxford Handbook of Atheism*, ed. Michael Ruse and Stephen Bullivant (Oxford: Oxford University Press, 2013), 688–89.

57. Dostoevsky, *The Brothers Karamazov*, 229.

58. Dostoevsky, *The Brothers Karamazov*, 231–32.

which seems to remove some of the explanations given for adult suffering.[59] After cataloging one particularly disgusting and vile act of cruelty committed against an innocent five-year-old girl, Ivan accosts his brother:

> Can you understand why a little creature, who can't even understand what's done to her, should beat her little aching heart with her tiny fist in the dark and the cold, and weep her meek unresentful tears to dear, kind God to protect her? Do you understand that, friend and brother, you pious and humble novice? Do you understand why this infamy must be and is permitted? Without it, I am told, man could not have existed on earth, for he could not have known good and evil. Why should he know that diabolical good and evil when it costs so much? Why, the whole world of knowledge is not worth that child's prayer to "dear, kind God"! I say nothing of the sufferings of grown-up people, they have eaten the apple, damn them, and the devil take them all! But these little ones![60]

If Ivan earlier anticipated a kind of "greater goods" theodicy, here he envisions something like a "free-will" defense, or perhaps a "soul-making" theodicy, which emphasizes the necessity of suffering for the moral development as human beings.[61] His answer is direct and pungent: it's not worth it. The suffering of that one child outweighs the whole world.

This sentiment is expressed so forcefully and perceptively throughout this dialogue, and with no answer whatsoever from

59. E.g., Dostoevsky, *The Brothers Karamazov*, 237: "If all must suffer to pay for the eternal harmony, what have children to do with it, tell me, please? It's beyond all comprehension why they should suffer, and why they should pay for the harmony. Why should they, too, furnish material to enrich the soil for the harmony of the future? I understand solidarity in sin among men. I understand solidarity in retribution, too; but there can be no such solidarity with children."

60. Dostoevsky, *The Brothers Karamazov*, 235.

61. For a discussion of theodicy in *The Brothers Karamazov*, and direction to further literature on this point, see Victor Terras, *A Karamazov Companion: Commentary on the Genesis, Language, and Style of Dostoevsky's Novel* (Madison: University of Wisconsin Press, 1981), 47–50.

Alyosha, that one wonders if Ivan's philosophy is Dostoevsky's own outlook, shining through Ivan's words. Plausibility is added to this possibility by the fact that Dostoevsky's writing of the novel was interrupted in May 1878 by the death of his three-year-old son—whose name was . . . *Alyosha*. This is what I wondered when I first read through the novel and got to these passages, which culminate in the famous "The Grand Inquisitor" chapter—that in Ivan's words we are getting Dostoevsky's message.

But I kept reading. It eventually occurred to me that although Ivan's arguments against God are so powerfully articulated, and although they receive no counterargument throughout the book, the *events* of the story undermine Ivan's words (because the character Smerdyakov justifies his murder of their father on the basis of Ivan's philosophy). Ivan, in coming to terms with his indirect complicity in his own father's murder, has a mental breakdown, while redemption in the end comes with Alyosha, through his simple love for others and faith in God.[62] Thus, the rejection of Ivan's nihilism and despair seems to come not through argument but through the unfolding narrative. It is a testimony to the realism and genius of Dostoevsky's writing that he can so capably expound the atheistic view and leave it hanging before the reader without answer. One gets the impression that Dostoevsky is not incapable of sympathizing with this outlook.

I read Dostoevsky's novel during a season in which my wife and I lived in a little studio apartment on Capitol Hill in Washington, DC. When I (finally) finished it, I walked home from the park and sat down at my desk. I was alone. I sat in silence for a while. It was among the greatest moments of intellectual and emotional clarity in my life. I felt neither hopeful nor sad, simply calm. Then I got up and scribbled a single sentence inside the back cover of my copy of the book: *However difficult faith in God may be when faced with the terrible reality of suffering in the world, its only alternative is an un-livable despair.*

62. For instance, the novel ends with Alyosha being cheered by the boys at Ilyusha's funeral (Dostoevsky, *The Brothers Karamazov*, 729).

Is that right? Do Dostoevsky, Sartre, and Nietzsche represent the real implications of the loss of God, or is there the possibility of a more hopeful atheism, like that envisioned by Sam Harris? We argue next that, on naturalism, the old atheism is indeed more authentic than its newer counterparts. Dostoevsky, Sartre, and Nietzsche saw into the heart of the matter.

The Naturalistic Story about Conscience: Evolutionary Psychology

The naturalistic explanation for our moral faculties comes from evolutionary psychology, like the naturalistic explanation for music and love, which we touched on in the last chapter. In a naturalistic worldview, our moral instincts are the epiphenomenal by-product of the evolutionary process—they function as they do because of the winnowing effect of unimaginable eons of natural selection. Passing on our genes has determined everything. The conscience exists, ultimately, because it helped animals survive.

On such a view, at least two things follow: first, morality is illusory; second, morality is arbitrary. Morality is, first of all, *illusory* because the feelings of significance, guilt, and obligation that accompany moral feelings (remember Anscombe's intuition) are not grounded in anything metaphysically stable. It *feels* significant that Batman should defeat the Joker rather than the Joker defeat Batman; it *feels* wrong that your neighbor slashed your car tires with a knife because you were playing music too loudly; we *feel* that we ought not to rob a bank when we cannot pay for our child's college tuition. But such feelings are reductively explainable by factors involved in the evolutionary process, and the evolutionary process is interested in survival, not truth. As Mark Linville puts it, "The mechanisms responsible for our moral beliefs appear to be *fitness*-aimed, and such an account of those mechanisms seems not to require our thinking that they also be truth-aimed."[63] So on naturalism, we have no reason to trust that our conscience isn't telling us a false tale. Figuring out ultimate metaphysical truths is something our brains simply are not equipped to do. As Steven Pinker explains, "Given that the mind is a product of natural se-lection, it should not have a miraculous ability to commune with all truths; it should have a mere ability to solve problems that are sufficiently similar to the mundane survival challenges of our ancestors. . . . Religion and philosophy are in part the application of mental tools to problems they were not designed to solve."[64]

Thus, on naturalism, morality works, fundamentally, by de-ceiving us. Michael Ruse and Edward Wilson articulate this view clearly: "Morality, or more strictly our belief in morality, is merely an adaptation put in place to further our reproductive ends. Hence the basis of ethics does not lie in God's will—or in the metaphori-cal roots of evolution or any other part of the framework of the Universe. In an important sense, ethics as we understand it is an illusion fobbed off on us by our genes to get us to cooperate. It is without external grounding."[65]

Ruse and Wilson deny that an evolutionary accounting of morality leads to moral relativism, and they attempt to ground ethics in the shared qualities of human nature that enable us to survive.[66] It is important to stress this point, because a naturalistic interpretation of morality is sometimes too quickly dismissed as leading to a kind of moral anarchy. Yet most of those advo-cating for such a view are very concerned about the important role our moral feelings must play—they may be fictions, but they are *useful* fictions. For instance, Daniel Dennett says that from a

63. Mark Linville, "The Moral Argument," in *The Blackwell Companion to Natural Theology*, ed. William Lane Craig and J. P. Moreland (Malden, MA: Wiley-Blackwell, 2020), 404 (italics original).
64. Steven Pinker, *How the Mind Works* (New York: Norton, 1997), 525.
65. Michael Ruse and Edward O. Wilson, "The Evolution of Ethics," *New Sci-entist* 17 (1985): 51–52.
66. Ruse and Wilson, "The Evolution of Ethics," 52.

Darwinian perspective the notion of individual rights is "nonsense
on stilts"—but adds that it's a *good* nonsense because it helps us
not destroy each other.[67]

We must also distinguish between a naturalistic account of morality per se and an evolutionary account broadly conceived. It
is entirely possible to resist a naturalistic view of morality while
nonetheless accepting the broad claim that our moral intuitions
are shaped by our evolutionary history (for my purposes in this
book, I allow for this view and refrain from questioning evolutionary science in general).[68] For this reason it is illegitimate for Ruse
and Wilson to infer from the evolutionary data the *non*involvement of God or any other agent not inherent in the evolutionary
process. This inference can be seen in their description of ethics as "without external grounding" and in their conclusion that
"the basis of ethics does not lie in God's will." This follows only
if one rules out the possibility of God or another agent working *through* the evolutionary process. Even if our morality could
be exhaustively explained from an evolutionary standpoint, this
would not require that it has no external basis beyond the biological realm. To assume otherwise is to commit the genetic fallacy,
which evaluates the validity of a particular claim on the basis of
its origins and/or history. The question of how our moral instincts
developed in history is a separate issue from the *ontological basis*
for our moral beliefs.

What excludes God from consideration is not evolutionary explanations but *naturalistic* explanations—and naturalism is by no
means a requirement of evolution. Jerry Walls and David Baggett
point out that evolution can, at most, tell us things about the
knowledge of morality (the order of knowing), not about morality

67. See the discussion in Linville, "The Moral Argument," 411.

68. Mainly because I don't think I need to oppose evolutionary science to make
the relevant point. I consider the question of evolution in my *Retrieving Augustine's
Doctrine of Creation: Ancient Wisdom for Current Controversy* (Downers Grove,
IL: IVP Academic, 2020), 183–239.

itself (the order of being). As they put it, "An evolutionary account of *feelings of* or *beliefs in*, say, moral obligation is certainly possible, but how would naturalism explain obligation itself?"[69]

Thus, the broader question is this: However the conscience came to be, does it have any objective referent in the nonhuman world? Is there anything like Mark Studdock's "the Normal" out there, independent of any process, evolutionary or other, by which we could come to know it? It's difficult to see, on naturalism, what it could be. For our moral instincts are simply an offshoot of the evolutionary process, without any ultimate or transcendent grounding. The feeling of transcendence and authority invested in moral struggle is ultimately illusory.

On such a worldview, morality also becomes *arbitrary*. That is to say, if the evolutionary process had gone differently, we could have had completely different moral intuitions—for instance, we might have regarded mariticide, siblicide, and infanticide as not only morally acceptable but morally obligatory under certain conditions (as they are throughout the animal kingdom). Scenarios like this are sometimes called "Darwinian counterfactuals," and they are a provocative way of drawing out the precariousness of our moral sensibilities on naturalism. For instance, sexual cannibalism, in which the creature eats its sexual partner, is common among animals like praying mantises, octopuses, and various kinds of spiders and scorpions. We find such behavior repugnant—but if we were to rewind the tape of evolutionary history and things played out differently, could we not have evolved to find it noble and dutiful?

This worry goes back to Darwin himself, who in *The Descent of Man* speculated that animals could have evolved a different morality than ours, just as different animals have evolved different kinds of sensitivity to beauty: "In the same manner as various animals have some sense of beauty, though they admire widely

69. David Baggett and Jerry L. Walls, *Good God: The Theistic Foundations of Morality* (Oxford: Oxford University Press, 2011), 11 (italics original).

different objects, so they might have a sense of right and wrong, though led by it to follow widely different lines of conduct. If, for example, to take an extreme case, men were reared under precisely the same conditions as hive-bees, there can hardly be a doubt that our unmarried females would, like the worker-bees, think it a sacred duty to kill their brothers, and mothers would strive to kill their fertile daughters, and no one would think of interfering."[70]

Darwin proceeded to speculate that in the evolutionary process, the bee would develop a conscience, such that amid competing impulses "an inward monitor would tell the animal that it would have been better to have followed the one impulse rather than the other."[71] Ruse and Wilson make the same point, more recently, with a different comparison: "If, like the termites, we needed to dwell in darkness, eat each other's faeces and cannibalise the dead, our epigenetic rules would be very different from what they are now. Our minds would be strongly prone to extol such acts as beautiful and moral."[72] Or we might consider the cruelty of alien species, such as the creature "Calvin" in the 2017 film *Life*, who lacks any compassion and is endlessly ruthless. Might we not have evolved such that we would see no goodness in compassion? Such thoughts are horrifying to consider. But what is our escape? That is the very point: on naturalism, there is nothing outside the evolutionary process to pass judgment on which direction it goes.

These comparisons between animal and human behavior allow us to see the stakes of a naturalistic account of morality more clearly. If all morality is reducible to our biology, then what the Nazis did to the Jewish people is difficult to qualitatively differentiate from a shark eating a seal or a Venus flytrap liquidating a bug. Those with power exploit those without. That is simply how

70. Charles Darwin, *The Descent of Man, and Selection in Relation to Sex*, 2nd ed. (New York: D. Appleton, 1876), 99.
71. Darwin, *The Descent of Man*, 100.
72. Ruse and Wilson, "The Evolution of Ethics," 52.

the biological world works. It's how we all got here. There is no particularly obvious reason why the rules should suddenly change when it comes to our particular animal species, *Homo sapiens*. It therefore seems that Sartre, Nietzsche, and Ivan had good grounds for their sense of apprehension at the loss of God. On naturalism, our intuitions about, say, the goodness of caring for orphans and the badness of killing off the elderly are arbitrary illusions. Moreover, our feeling of revulsion upon this discovery is simply a part of the evolutionary package, not a reliable guide to truth—for, on naturalism, our brains are ill-equipped to make strong judgments about metaphysical truths.[73]

What if we consider the alternative? What if we regard our disgust at immorality and the intensity of our attraction to love and compassion as a clue rather than illusion? Such a possibility would enable us, as we described it in the last chapter, to live more comfortably within our own humanity, not needing to question our deepest instincts. It would simultaneously allow us to avoid the risk of falling into a kind of cultural elitism in which all humanity has been basically wrong about the questions that mattered most to them, while we few in the modern West have become undeceived. For almost every human culture throughout history has agreed with Mark Studdock that such a thing as "the Normal" really is out there. Only a narrow sliver of humanity ever doubted it.[74]

73. In its stronger forms, such skepticism about metaphysical knowledge verges on becoming self-defeating, since the rational faculties employed to determine that morality is driven by the evolutionary process are themselves the product of the evolutionary process. Why do they get a special exception? As Tim Keller asks, "If we can't trust our belief-forming faculties to tell us the truth about God, why should we trust them to tell us the truth about anything, including evolutionary science?" *The Reason for God: Belief in an Age of Skepticism* (New York: Dutton, 2008), 138.

74. Even among contemporary philosophers, in fact, moral realism remains the dominant position. A 2009 survey involving over three thousand participants, for example, found that 56 percent of philosophers accept or lean toward moral realism; 28 percent, antirealism; 16 percent, other. See "The PhilPapers Survey: Results," PhilPapers, accessed February 19, 2021, https://philpapers.org/surveys/results.pl.

The Theistic Story: Conscience as Divine Law (and What about the Euthyphro Dilemma?)

So here we ask, If there were a transcendent basis for morality beyond the natural realm, what might such a basis be? There might be a variety of ways that morality could be grounded in supernaturalistic reality, but at this point it's nearly impossible not to bring in God—for historically, morality has been closely linked with religion and, in Western civilization particularly, with God. The metaethical and metaphysical have developed together. Whether there is warrant for this association we cannot yet fully decide, but as a matter of history it is indisputable.[75]

How, specifically, could morality be related to God? There are various options, but one of the more prominent is that moral obligations exist as a kind of divine law or a set of divine commandments.[76] These commandments, in turn, reflect God's character, or perhaps his intellect.[77] This can be hashed out in various ways, but it is sufficient for our purposes to note that on such a view we are no longer obligated to regard with suspicion the various characteristics of morality we have observed, as we were on the naturalistic alternative. For instance, the lawlike significance of moral obligations, as described by Elizabeth Anscombe, would derive

75. For a historical overview of the attempt to affirm the existence of God on the basis of morality, see David Baggett and Jerry Walls, *The Moral Argument: A History* (Oxford: Oxford University Press, 2019). A significant figure in the moral argument was Immanuel Kant, who famously spoke of both "the starry heavens above and the moral law within me" as testimonies of the divine, yet ultimately sought to ground the knowledge of God in the moral realm rather than the metaphysical. Kant's influence in this regard has been massive. For instance, in Baggett and Walls, *The Moral Argument*, the moral argument effectively begins with Kant.

76. For a discussion of various alternatives, see Evans, *God and Moral Obligation*, 25–52. Evans argues that natural law ethics and virtue ethics are not necessarily rivals to a divine command theory of ethics. For a modified divine command theory of ethics that ably addresses many of the worries about this view, see Robert Merrihew Adams, *Finite and Infinite Goods: A Framework for Ethics* (Oxford: Oxford University Press, 1999).

77. This alternative is represented by Baggett and Walls, *Good God*, 87, who argue that morality is dependent on divine intellectual activity, calling this view "theistic actualism" and identifying various precursors to it in Augustine, Leibniz, Aquinas, Berkeley, and Edwards.

from the fact that they *are* laws. The immensity and fixedness of moral goodness, as conveyed by C. S. Lewis as "the Normal," would be a consequence of the fact that goodness *is* immense, fixed, and immovable as a mountain.

On such a view, our moral nature would not be tricking us, but just the opposite—it would function like a clue or sign about the great conflict driving the world. Decades ago J. B. Phillips noted that the Nazis disagreed with the moral values of the free world, and unless there is some objective standard of morality, then there is no means by which to adjudicate these competing moral visions. But almost everyone knows that the Nazis were wrong to do what they did. Phillips asked, "*Why* is there this almost universal moral sense? Why do we consider that 'good' is a better thing than 'evil'? Surely this recognition of good, so deeply rooted and so universal, is another far from negligible pointer to Reality."[78] On a theistic view, morality can function like this—clue rather than illusion.

Morality could even be a unique pathway of relation to God, more vigorous and lively than others. For however much we might find suggestions of God in a tragic poem or a lovely sunset, the realm of conscience works upon us at a more interior level, in a more personal and vivid way. John Henry Newman called conscience the "connecting principle between the Creator and the creature," distinguishing between a "notional assent" to the truth of God versus a "real assent," emphasizing the role of conscience in moving one from the former to the latter.[79] Thus, while other arguments for God work at the rational level, the realm of conscience would testify to him in a more existential way. Conscience would be a unique arena in the human-divine relationship, like a crucial hill contested by two armies, where the heaviest warfare concentrates.

78. J. B. Phillips, *Your God Is Too Small* (New York: Macmillan, 1979), 71 (italics original).

79. John Henry Newman, *An Essay in Aid of a Grammar of Assent* (Westminster, MD: Christian Classics, 1973), 117, quoted in Matthew Levering, *Proofs of God: Classical Arguments from Tertullian to Barth* (Grand Rapids: Baker Academic, 2016), 147.

However, it is crucial again to distinguish the ontological question of the basis for morality from the epistemological question of its potential revelatory role, just as it is imperative to distinguish it from questions of religious history. For almost immediately, when one says anything at all about morality related to divine law or commandments, concerns immediately arise about allegedly unjust laws in the Bible and questions of religious violence. Atheists like Christopher Hitchens draw attention to various atrocities committed by religion or in the name of God to argue that the particular set of ethics commanded in the Bible or another religious texts is itself immoral.[80]

So it is important to stress that the conception of morality as divine law does not, in itself, require any particular commitment to a particular set of perceived divine commandments given in history, nor does it involve any kind of confidence that those who believe in God will necessarily live out his commandments better than anyone else. The idea of God as the source of morality is not a claim that believers in God are more moral (which is a sociological question), or that religions have produced moral guidelines for society (a historical question), or that religious people know morality more accurately (which is an epistemological question).[81] The issue is *where morality itself comes from* (an ontological question). It is possible to affirm morality as ontologically grounded in God without accepting any of these other (sociological, historical, or epistemological) beliefs. Indeed, there may be good reasons to affirm the former but not the latter.[82] We will tackle questions of

---

80. E.g., Christopher Hitchens, *God Is Not Great: How Religion Poisons Everything* (New York: Twelve, 2007), 184–93. For a helpful response to concerns of this kind, see Paul Copan, *Is God a Moral Monster? Making Sense of the Old Testament God* (Grand Rapids: Baker Books, 2011).

81. This distinction is relevant to Sam Harris's claims that morality is based on reason and science, which confuses the epistemological and ontological bases for morality: doubtless we can *know* morality better with the aid of science and reason, but this does not mean that such enterprises can function as an *ontological basis* for morality.

82. Tim Keller, *Making Sense of God: An Invitation to the Skeptical* (New York: Viking, 2016), 177, points out that the claim that atheists are always immoral people

religious violence a bit in the next chapter; here we must recognize such questions are subsequent to the question of God.

But there is another objection that is seemingly always raised to the identification of God as the ground of morality, and which we must therefore deal with right away: the famous Euthyphro dilemma. Just as the "What caused God?" objection has become a kind of stock-in-trade response to the cosmological argument, so the Euthyphro dilemma, in its various formulations and applications, has this function against the moral argument. The objection goes all the way back to Socrates's dialogue with the character Euthyphro where, after establishing that piety is defined by the unanimous consent of all the gods, Socrates poses a new question: "Is the pious loved by the gods because it is pious, or is it pious because it is loved by the gods?"[83] Their discussion reveals problems that obtain on either alternative. If piety is pious because it is loved by the gods (the first horn of the dilemma), then a host of problems emerge. For instance, morality becomes arbitrary—impiety could be holy, had the gods loved it instead.[84] But, on the other hand, if piety is loved by the gods because it is pious (the second horn of the dilemma), then piety seems to come from something other than the gods. Piety would then not depend upon the gods, and consequently would need some other source.

Euthyphro's dilemma has a long tradition of discussion in relation to monotheistic traditions, up to the present day. Baggett and Walls, for instance, note the dilemma's "extraordinary staying power" and its abiding influence in twenty-first-century discussions

---

not only goes against common experience but that "Christians have additional reasons to doubt such a statement, because the New Testament teaches on the one hand that all persons, regardless of belief, are created by God with a moral conscience (Romans 2:14). On the other hand, the same text tells them that all people, including believers, are flawed sinners (Romans 3:9–12)." So Christians are equipped to approach this question recognizing good in unbelievers and bad in believers, because all people have both dignity and depravity at the same time.

83. In *Plato: Complete Works*, ed. John M. Cooper (Indianapolis: Hackett, 1997), 9.

84. Baggett and Walls, *Good God*, 34–35, list six objections to the radical voluntarism associated with the first horn of the dilemma.

of the relation of theism and morality.[85] Specifically, it is frequently
utilized to derive the implication that God cannot be the source
of morality. Bertrand Russell summed up the challenge posed by
the dilemma for monotheism, emphasizing in particular that the
first horn imperils God's goodness:

> If you are quite sure there is a difference between right and wrong,
> you are then in this situation: Is that difference due to God's fiat
> or is it not? If it is due to God's fiat, then for God Himself there
> is no difference between right and wrong, and it is no longer a
> significant statement to say that God is good. If you are going to
> say, as theologians do, that God is good, you must then say that
> right and wrong have some meaning which is independent of God's
> fiat, because God's fiats are good and not good independently of
> the mere fact that he made them. If you are going to say that, you
> will then have to say that it is not only through God that right and
> wrong came into being, but that they are in their essence logically
> anterior to God.[86]

But as has been frequently pointed out, the Euthyphro dilemma
has a fatal flaw. In requiring a choice between these two alternatives, it poses a false contrast—for these options are not mutually
exhaustive. According to classical Christian thought, for instance,
morality extends from God, not by divine fiat, but as a reflection
of his character (or, perhaps, his thoughts).[87] Goodness is therefore neither external to God nor dependent on his will; rather,
goodness is identical with God himself. As William Alston has
observed, Euthyphro's dilemma assumes a Platonic conception of
the objectivity of goodness, in which goodness is a kind of abstract

85. Baggett and Walls, *Good God*, 32, where they also note Antony Flew's intriguing comment that "a good test of a person's aptitude for philosophy is whether or
not she can grasp the Dilemma's force and point."

86. Bertrand Russell, *Why I Am Not a Christian: And Other Essays on Religion
and Related Subjects*, ed. Paul Edwards (New York: Simon & Schuster, 1957), 12.

87. For a defense of the identification of God with goodness, see also Adams,
Finite and Infinite Goods.

Idea, separate from God.[88] But historically, not only Christian theologians but also Jewish and Muslim theologians have conceived of God as simple, and therefore identical to his attributes, in part to avoid difficulties like this.[89]

What does all this entail? Unless we are willing to go down the dark path of Nietzsche, Sartre, and Ivan Karamazov, in which moral significance is illusion and moral choice is like art, then we will find theism a better explanatory environment for our moral experience than naturalism. That is to say, theism can provide a more plausible framework for the objectivity of moral values and obligations than naturalism can. And if this is right, it may be useful to go one step further and consider the practical effect of such a hypothesis. Suppose one thinks of moral values as Sartre did, only then to consider the possibility of Mark Studdock's "the Normal"—what emotional implications would such a change have?

The question feels vitally important, as though we were waiting to hear whether a loved one has survived an accident or to receive the results from a test determining whether we have an incurable disease. Morality is so deeply hardwired into our nature that an amoral world feels very close to a meaningless world. Almost no one can consistently live out a Nietzschean moral outlook (it does not appear that even Nietzsche could). We intuitively recognize that *it matters* whether we exploit or help the poor, whether we love our families or abuse them; to consider that such intuitions are illusory feels not like a minor loss but like something unspeakably horrible. The theistic story, by contrast, infuses nobility into

88. William P. Alston, "What Euthyphro Should Have Said," in *Philosophy of Religion: A Reader and Guide*, ed. William Lane Craig (New Brunswick, NJ: Rutgers University Press, 2002), 291. Alston proposes that instead of this Platonic conception of goodness, "we can think of God himself, the individual being, as the supreme standard of goodness" (291).

89. For a comparison of Jewish, Muslim, and Christian conceptions of divine simplicity, see my *Theological Retrieval for Evangelicals: Why We Need Our Past to Have a Future* (Wheaton: Crossway, 2019), 131–37.

human life and struggle; it has the potential implication that how you live will matter *forever.*

I propose that our thirst for a real, nonillusory morality is so foundational to our lives that we simply cannot live without it. And not only because we sense that good and evil are deeply meaningful categories, but because we instinctively long for good to ultimately triumph over evil. This longing is so basic to the human heart that it is almost impossible not to conceptualize our lives, and all of history, in terms of *moral hope.* One way we can draw attention to this intriguing fact is by noting the role of moral hope in the stories we tell.

The Longing for Moral Hope: Why Movies (Almost Always) Have Happy Endings

As we have noted, storytelling is one of the most fundamental ways human beings make sense of the world. In Western culture, movies are perhaps our primary form of storytelling. As Robert K. Johnston puts it, "We in the West are a movie culture. . . . Film has become our Western culture's major storytelling and myth-producing medium."[90] In three ways, movies (narrative movies, at least, as opposed to documentaries) display a kind of instinctive moral framework.[91]

First, the drama or conflict of a movie is virtually always organized along the lines of *good versus evil.* This is the essential plot

90. Robert K. Johnston, "Introduction: Reframing the Discussion," in *Reframing Theology and Film: New Focus for an Emerging Discipline*, ed. Robert K. Johnston (Grand Rapids: Baker Academic, 2007), 16. Johnston explores the power of film further, for both individuals and society, in *Reel Spirituality: Theology and Film in Dialogue*, 2nd ed. (Grand Rapids: Baker Academic, 2006), 25–39.

91. Of course, these characteristics are not only true of movies but reflect all mediums of storytelling to some extent. I've reflected previously on the theological implications of movies in "3 Ways Movies Are Searching for the Gospel," *The Gospel Coalition*, January 4, 2016, https://www.thegospelcoalition.org/article/3-ways-movies-are-searching-for-the-gospel/, from which I draw here. For further exploration of metaethical questions in movies, see Dan Shaw, *Morality and the Movies: Reading Ethics through Film* (New York: Continuum, 2012).

of almost every movie, rehearsed over and over and over again to the point that we don't even notice it:

- Good and evil clash.
- Good struggles and suffers for a while.
- Eventually, good defeats evil.

Often evil has an institutional advantage—we love Jason Bourne because he is on the run; we hate Warden Samuel Norton in *The Shawshank Redemption* because of his complacent power; and so forth. Often good is an underdog or somehow down on their luck. Think of Rocky Balboa, for instance, or Dr. Richard Kimble—or think of how many heroes in Disney films are orphans or experience the loss of one or both parents along the way.

Sometimes good and evil are cast in terms of a particular motif, like the "light side" versus the "dark side" in the Stars Wars franchise; sometimes they're cast in terms of different parties or groups (like the Autobots versus Decepticons in the Transformers franchise, or Charles Xavier's mutants versus Magneto's in X-Men); sometimes good is orchestrated around one individual (James Bond, Indiana Jones, etc.). Sometimes the struggle between good and evil is darker, like Batman versus the Joker; other times it's more implicit and/or lighthearted (say, Frank Dixon versus Viktor Navorski in *The Terminal*). Sometimes there are static "good guys" and "bad guys" or, in the case of superhero stories, heroes and villains; other times you can see a character struggling back and forth between good and evil (like Gollum in *The Lord of the Rings*). Sometimes the "evil" is located not in people but in nature (survival stories, *Jurassic Park*, *Jaws*, etc.), though even here you often find "bad guys" creeping in; other times good versus evil is depicted internally (*Frankenstein*, *The Godfather*, etc.); still other times it's depicted in terms of ideas or systems or even machines (*The Matrix*, *The Terminator*, etc.) or aliens (*Alien*, *Independence*

Day, etc.)—but again, there are usually good and evil human characters as well.

But the point is, movies are never just about different parties striving for survival and power. There is virtually always a moral dimension to the drama and therefore a heightened sense of significance. We don't just want one side to win: we sense one side *ought* to win. We know it's *right* that Simba dethrones Scar, and not simply his good fortune; and we feel resolution and satisfaction when Gene Hackman is sitting alone in that bar at the end of *Runaway Jury*.

But, secondly, movies aren't just about good fighting evil; they're about good *defeating* evil. Movies reflect not only an instinctive moral understanding but also an eschatological one. Once again, this is so common we don't even think about it. But a Happy Ending is an essential part of every good story.

In other words, whether good defeats evil is never a matter of indifference to the viewer. You never think, *Well, either Jim Braddock or Max Baer will win. Who cares?* No, when good triumphs at the end, it always restores some happiness and harmony that was disrupted during the struggle. You could summarize most plots in three phases:

- Happiness
- Loss of happiness
- Restoration to some greater and more permanent happiness

Sometimes there's the idea that everything is set back to normal, particularly in time-travel films like *Back to the Future* and *X-Men: Days of Future Past*. Usually the state of harmony at the end of the movie exceeds that at the beginning; something is permanently gained along the way. There are exceptions to this, but if you stop and think about it, you realize that they are very rare.

Third, in almost every film, good not only fights against and triumphs over evil but does so by means of suffering and sacrificial love. It would be an utterly lame superhero movie if the villain was weak and overthrown without any cost or pain involved for the hero. That never happens.

Take *Rudy*, for instance (one of my personal favorites). That scene where he's sitting at the park and discovers he gets in to Notre Dame—it never gets old to me. I could watch it over and over. But how lame would it be if Rudy was six feet five with a 140 IQ? It would never make a good movie. The sacrifice it took him to get there is what makes his story powerful to us: we sense there is some great meaning, not only to the triumph but also to the struggle along the way.

Or take the suffering John Nash endures in *A Beautiful Mind* (another personal favorite). The depth of his suffering throughout that film, the way his whole world is turned upside down, makes the speech at the end—and the way his wife sticks it out with him, too—all the more beautiful. What makes the story tick is that he triumphs, not over Soviet spy codes but over mental illness; it's a story not just about achievement but about love and redemption.

The motif of sacrifice almost always accompanies that of suffering. How many times have we seen one of the good guys give up their life, or think they're giving up their life, or give up something else important, in order to save the day? The choice of sacrificial love is the key trigger in so many plots, from *The Adjustment Bureau* to *Beauty and the Beast* to *Stranger than Fiction*, and on and on we could go. Someone gives up their life, sacrificing themselves for someone else, only to find their life return to them.

Occasionally, of course, movies deviate from this plot form. For instance, now and again a movie doesn't have a happy ending. But what is interesting is how emotionally unsatisfying that is. If the bad guys win in the end, you almost feel cheated.

Take the 2011 movie *The Grey*, for example, which can be interpreted as an exploration of death from a nihilistic standpoint. (Warning: spoilers ahead through the rest of this section and in the last few paragraphs of this chapter.) The film narrates the story of a group of oil workers stranded in the Alaskan wilderness after a plane crash, trying to survive attacking wolves. The film has surprising philosophical depth—the dialogue, the plot, the cinematography, even the harsh Alaskan setting all seem designed to highlight the ugliness and crushing inevitability of death. Before the crash, Liam Neeson's character, John Ottway, begins to attempt suicide, stopping at the last possible moment. There are flashbacks of him writing a suicide note, as well as flashbacks of happy memories with his wife, who is eventually revealed to be dead. (Interestingly, one of the reasons the director, Joe Carnahan, picked Liam Neeson for this role is that, in real life, Neeson lost his wife just two years prior to filming.)[92] After the crash, the characters all die, one by one, often reflecting on their impending deaths along the way.[93] In a particularly poignant scene toward the end of the film, after everyone else is dead, Ottway cries out to God, pleading for a sign, promising he will worship God to his dying day but needing help right now—only to hear nothing in return.

The film closes with Ottway discovering that he is in the wolf nest. As he prepares to fight the alpha wolf, we hear him recite a poem that has been referenced at critical moments earlier in the film, a poem that Ottway's father wrote and that Ottway read at his funeral:

> Once more into the fray
> Into the last good fight I will ever know
> Live and die on this day
> Live and die on this day[94]

92. Aaron Hatch, "The Grey: Battling Depression and Self-Worth," *The Artifice*, January 23, 2015, https://the-artifice.com/the-grey-battling-depression/.

93. There is discussion of the experience of death, how it "slides over you." One character accepts his death willingly, unable to keep fighting. While one character is in his dying moments soon after the plane crash, Ottway tells him to picture his daughter and says, "Let her take you there."

94. The poem is loosely inspired from a line in Henry V. It is interesting to note that the filmmakers changed the line in some promotional material for marketing purposes to "Live *or* die on this day." This implies more of a "man versus nature"

One way of interpreting the film, in line with this poem, is as a meditation on embracing the inevitability of death. The message would be something like, "Death is all there is—so go out with the bang." Ottway's final stand against the alpha wolf captures something of the noble despair of this sentiment. This theme recalls Dylan Thomas's poem "Do Not Go Gentle into That Good Night."

The tragic ending of *The Grey* seems to be an exception to the Happy Ending rule. This raises the question: *Why* is this ending tragic? When a movie lacks a Happy Ending, why does this affect us so profoundly?[95]

The film critic Roger Ebert watched many films throughout his career. But when he watched *The Grey*, toward the end of his life while battling cancer, he was so affected by the unrelenting darkness that, for the first time in his career, he could not stay for the second movie: "After this film, I was . . . stunned with despair. It so happened that there were two movies scheduled that day. . . . After 'The Grey' was over, I watched the second film for 30 minutes and then got up and walked out of the theater. It was the first time I've ever walked out of a film because of the previous film. The way I was feeling in my gut, it just wouldn't have been fair to the next film."[96] What was it that affected him so deeply? "The

adventure story rather than the philosophical meditation on death that is actually conveyed by *The Grey* and is better reflected in the actual words, "Live *and* die on this day."

95. A related question is, How, within the limits of a nihilistic worldview, are we to understand the brighter, more human moments in the film? For instance, in the final scene, just after his plea to God and before facing the alpha wolf, Ottaway collects the wallets of his dead companions and places all the pictures of their loved ones facing up on the ground, then adds his own to the pile. It is portrayed as an almost hallowed, sacred act. And his constant flashbacks throughout the film, both to happy moments with his wife as well as childhood memories with his father, convey a different emotional tone—one almost experiences these flashbacks as excursions into another world, a world of happiness and reunion. Within the boundaries of nihilism, what shall we make of the beauty in Ottway's relationship to his wife? *Does* his act of assembling the wallets of his companions mean anything? If death is all there is, *why* is it so tragic, so poignant, to face it in this way?

96. Roger Ebert, "I Sat Regarding the Screen with Mounting Dread," RogerEbert .com, January 25, 2012, https://www.rogerebert.com/reviews/the-grey-2012.

Grey advances with pitiless logic. There are more wolves than men. The men have weapons, the wolves have patience, the weather is punishing. I sat regarding the screen with mounting dread. *The movie had to have a happy ending, didn't it?*"[97]

Everyone understands how he feels. Nobody says, "Happy endings—but why would you care about that?" In fact, during test screenings of *The Grey* there was a massive backlash against the film's ending particularly *because* it lacks a Happy Ending. But Carnahan explained that he kept it the way it was to inspire philosophical reflection.[98]

Moreover, intriguingly, even *The Grey* seems to keep the door open to a Happy Ending. For despite the film's dark philosophical flavor, the brief "after credits" clip, combined with footage of the final fight that was not included in the film, seems to hint of something more.[99]

So again the question arises: Why is the longing for happy endings hardwired into our storytelling, such that Roger Ebert, and you and me, sense that something is missing without it?

Could Our Stories Reflect the Big Story?

In his essay "On Fairy Stories," J. R. R. Tolkien spoke of the "happy ending" or "eucatastrophe" of fairy stories—or more accurately,

97. Ebert, "I Sat Regarding the Screen with Mounting Dread" (italics added).

98. Stephen Saito, "Joe Carnahan Talks about the Alternate Ending He Shot for 'The Grey,'" *The Moveable Fest*, January 30, 2012, http://moveablefest.com/carnahan-grey-alternate-ending.

99. When I saw the movie at the theater, I left during the credits. The next time I watched it at home, I let it keep running, and I noticed there is a brief clip after the credits have run. It shows the alpha wolf that Liam Neeson began to fight as the movie ended lying on the ground, breathing slowly—perhaps dying? This clip is interpreted variously, but when combined with a behind-the-scenes image depicting John resting on the bloodied wolf after the fight, it seems to suggest that the film wants to leave room for hope that John killed the wolf. For discussion, see "THE GREY—Movie Endings Explained (2011) Joe Carnahan, Liam Neeson," YouTube video, 8:57, posted by JoBlo Videos, December 1, 2017, https://www.youtube.com/watch?v=_wES1Nm9jU0.

the "sudden joyous 'turn' (for there is no true end to any fairy-tale)."[100] For Tolkien, this aspect of stories is a little clue about reality itself: "The peculiar quality of the 'joy' in successful Fantasy can thus be explained as a sudden glimpse of the underlying reality or truth. . . . In the eucatastrophe we see in a brief vision that the answer may be greater—it may be a far-off gleam or echo of evangelium [gospel] in the real world."[101]

Thus, for Tolkien, Happy Endings can be seen as revelatory. They function as a clue about the kind of story we find ourselves in. On such a view, the feelings you get at the very end of your favorite movie or novel are a little foretaste of what is going to happen one day. Naturalism, by contrast, leaves us with a much bleaker future. Our movies are deceiving us. There is no Happy Ending, for our personal death will be the end of our consciousness, and the eventual extinction of human civilization will swallow up every memory or consequence of our lives.

It might be objected that the moral consequences of our lives need not be everlasting in order to be meaningful. Moral struggle can still be meaningful even though no Happy Ending is coming, because it can produce results in the here and now. But consider this thought experiment: Suppose for the sake of argument that five million years from now the human race is extinct (on naturalism, it seems doomed to happen sooner or later). What will be the significance, five millions years from now, of the distinction between the lives of Mother Teresa and Adolf Hitler? If every consequence from, and memory of, their lives has ceased to exist, can there be any abiding significance to the distinction between them? It is true that their lives had real, finite value, and finite value is still valuable. But here is the point: we seem to sense that there must be *more* than a mere finite value to good and evil—we long for something transcendent and lasting to emerge from moral

100. Tolkien, "On Fairy Stories," in J. R. R. Tolkien, *Tree and Leaf* (Boston: Houghton Mifflin, 1989), 62.

101. Tolkien, "On Fairy Stories," 64.

struggle. The thought that if you just wait long enough, the consequences of the lives of Hitler and Mother Teresa will eventually equal out is jarring, unsettling, disturbing. It runs contrary to the instinctive understanding of life that is reflected in nearly every movie ever made. We all long for moral victory that won't eventually evaporate.

On naturalism, it is therefore difficult to find a ground for ultimate moral hope. Nor is such a bleak outlook of the future particularly motivating for the pursuit of justice in the here and now. To be sure, atheists are often passionate advocates for justice, and believers sadly apathetic about justice. But which attitude is the more logical extension of the worldview? On naturalism, there will be no final justice in the universe. There is no final reward for good, nor any final redress for evil; our efforts at justice are relativized by the fact that whatever we accomplish, the consequences will eventually flatten out. On theism, by contrast, there remains the hope that moral accomplishment lives on after this world has ended. Good and evil are working their way toward an ultimate, lasting resolution. Our efforts, however tiny, might contribute to the final product. Such a perspective offers a dignity and significance to moral accomplishment, and therefore to the entirety of the human drama, that naturalism cannot provide.[102]

So you can think of these two options in terms of our earlier metaphor: our longing for moral justice is either like an opiate to a dying man, distracting him from the harshness of reality, or like a window to an imprisoned man, providing a little glimpse into what reality is ultimately like. Which alternative is more satisfying, to both heart and mind? Which gains more of your respect? Which can you actually live with?

---

102. Linville, "The Moral Argument," 443, summarizes the challenges for naturalism on this point: "The naturalist's obstacles in accounting for the dignity of persons are at least threefold, and they are interlocked: how to derive the personal from the impersonal, how to derive values from a previously valueless universe, and how to unite the personal and the valuable with the result of a coherent and plausible notion of personal dignity."

Conclusion

We are now in a position to ask: What do the considerations of this chapter add to our picture of the Supernature? What new information, particularly, do we glean from the moral realm? Previously we have been dealing with Something enormously intelligent, but now we find that it is also, in some way, good. It is not merely some great foreign entity, like a country we have heard of but never visited. It is Something we relate to at a more interior level, like a vivid dream we always remember, or a longing we have had since childhood. It is related to what we grapple with at the level of conscience. Whatever this Supernature is, we relate to it not as a kind of theory or postulate but at a gut level—at the same level at which we fall in love or face death.

We may still be dealing with something that we will not end up associating with any of the religions of the world. That is a question for the next chapter. But I think we have proceeded far enough to call the Supernature, in a loose and "nondenominational" sense of the word, *God*. For we are talking about something not only responsible for the universe in all its intricacy but also something both personal and moral. C. S. Lewis summed up how a consideration of morality contributes to our conception of metaphysics, calling it "inside information":

> We have two bits of evidence about the Somebody. One is the universe He has made. If we used that as our only clue, then I think we should have to conclude that He was a great artist (for the universe is a very beautiful place), but also that He is quite merciless and no friend to man (for the universe is a very dangerous and terrifying place). The other bit of evidence is the Moral Law which He has put in our minds. And this is a better bit of evidence than the other, because it is inside information. You find out more about God from the Moral Law than from the universe in general just as you find out more about a man

by listening to his conversation than by looking at a house he has built.[103]

So think about the passionate cry for justice you feel when you see evil. Think about the longing for the world to be set right again. Think of the feeling of hope at the conclusion of your favorite movie. On theism, one can call such feelings "inside information." They are telling you something you will not get anywhere else.

There is still much that we do not know—in fact, the introduction of moral considerations brings up new challenges, including perhaps the greatest challenge of all: the problem of evil. I don't address that challenge at length in this book,[104] but it may be useful to draw one observation as we close this chapter.

Whatever else we will say about theism, we must note that theism can and must acknowledge the real terribleness of evil. Any glib or casual response to the problem of evil is bound to be disastrous. The thoughtful theist might even be inclined to regard the nihilist as *almost* right or to think that the wrongness of nihilism cannot fully be shown but only experienced. For the pain of the world is truly titanic. Recall Ivan Karamazov's speeches, for example—or consider the gut-wrenching testimony of holocaust survivor Elie Wiesel: "Never shall I forget the little faces of the children, whose bodies I saw turned into wreaths of smoke beneath a silent blue sky. Never shall I forget those flames which consumed my faith forever. Never shall I forget that nocturnal silence which deprived me, for all eternity, of the desire to live."[105]

Theism has no neat and tidy answer to such devastation. But one thing theism can do, which naturalism cannot, is tell you why it hurts so badly. For on theism, evil really is a perversion,

103. C. S. Lewis, *Mere Christianity*, in *The Complete C. S. Lewis Signature Classics* (San Francisco: HarperSanFrancisco, 2002), 23.
104. Classical treatments of the problem of evil can be found in C. S. Lewis, *The Problem of Pain*, in *The Complete C. S. Lewis Signature Classics*, 365–433, and Alvin Plantinga, *God, Freedom, and Evil* (Grand Rapids: Eerdmans, 1974), 7–64.
105. Elie Wiesel, *Night* (1960; repr., New York: Bantam Books, 1986), 32, quoted in Baggett and Walls, *Good God*, 218.

a desacralizing, a "fall," a twisting of what things *should* be. Theism might not tell you *why* wrongness is there, just yet; but naturalism cannot even tell you *that* it is wrong. For naturalism has no supra-physical standard by which to pass judgment; again, on such a view all feelings of the grossness of evil are an illusion fobbed off on us by the evolutionary struggle that predated us. The world simply *is*, and no Happy Ending is coming.

When I first watched *The Grey*, it affected me like it affected Roger Ebert. I wrote these words in my review of the film (substitute the word "theist" for "Christian" here, since we are not yet to Christianity):

> It seems to me that the Christian and the nihilist can walk together a long way, side by side, in mutual defiance of evil, mutual resignation to fight it to the last choking breath. The Christian view acknowledges that evil is indeed staggering, unthinkable, blinding, oppressive. The Christian, I think, can weep with each dying character; he can walk into the wolf nest with the same grim determination that John Ottway shows; he can recite with full conviction, "do not go gentle into that good night." His grief is not less severe than that of the nihilist. But he also knows why he values the pictures of loved ones in those wallets. He also knows why Ottway wishes there were an afterlife, and cries out to God, even when he doesn't believe in God. In other words, the Christian is able to affirm *both* the chilling darkness and the aching beauty of the world. The Christian may struggle with evil, but the nihilist must struggle with good. Evil may be mysterious for the Christian, but good for the nihilist can only be incomprehensible.[106]

In other words, the problem of evil is indeed a real problem for theism. But at least you get to see it as that—a *problem*.

For a problem, at least, might have a solution. To that we now turn.

---

106. Gavin Ortlund, "Reflections on The Grey," *Soliloquium*, June 18, 2012, https://gavinortlund.com/2012/06/18/the-grey/.

4

The Hope of the World

*Why Easter Means Happiness
beyond Your Wildest Dreams*

Throughout this book we have been contrasting theism and naturalism as two rival ways of telling a story about the world. We have suggested that theism is the better story of the two—the more plausible, the more interesting, the more elegant, and the more dignifying to our humanity. At this point we turn from the general matter of whether God exists to a more concrete question: Supposing he does exist, how (if at all) might we locate him?

We are thus passing a crucial threshold from more abstract, philosophical reflection into the messier historical realities of religion. Accordingly, we begin by addressing criticism of religion in general, for there is an increasingly prevalent mentality in some circles that considers religion an inherently corrosive, evil phenomenon. We then consider a particular religious figure (Jesus of Nazareth) who stands out among other religious figures for claiming not merely to reveal God but to be God.[1] We suggest that the notion that Jesus was, in fact, divine is a plausible explanation of the historical data pertaining to (1) his divine claims and (2) his followers' belief in his resurrection. The *degree* of plausibility will doubtless depend on many factors—but unless one is closed in principle to the possibility of divine involvement in human history, a divine interpretation of Jesus is intriguingly compelling.

Finally, we reflect on the implications of this possibility, emphasizing its happiness and the resolution it brings to all of history. Thus, if the world is like a story, Jesus would be the hope on which the whole thing turns (what Tolkien calls the happy ending or eucatastrophe). On such a view, Christ's incarnation and resurrection are the true Story every other story is searching for—as Tolkien puts it, a "story of a larger kind which embraces all the essence of fairy-stories."[2]

Is Religion Inherently Evil and/or Ignorant?

We must begin by addressing worries about religion as such, for there is no reason to consider any particular religion if the whole phenomenon is poisonous and backward.[3] And this is an

---

1. Of course, any responsible investigation of religious questions would need to consider other religions and religious philosophies as well, but recall that we have limited our scope in this book to a comparison of these two options (Christian theism and naturalism). A brief account of Christianity's position in relation to other religions, and the uniqueness of the figure of Christ, can be found in C. S. Lewis, *Mere Christianity*, in *The Complete C. S. Lewis Signature Classics* (San Francisco: HarperSanFrancisco, 2002), 29–30; G. K. Chesterton, *The Everlasting Man* (1925; repr., San Francisco: Ignatius, 1993), 169–261; and Ravi Zacharias, *Jesus among Other Gods: The Absolute Claims of the Christian Message* (Nashville: Thomas Nelson, 2000).

2. J. R. R. Tolkien, "On Fairy Stories," in J. R. R. Tolkien, *Tree and Leaf* (Boston: Houghton Mifflin, 1989), 65, speaking specifically of Christ's incarnation and resurrection.

3. Some Christians respond to such worries by distinguishing the Christian gospel from religion. This can be a valid distinction in certain respects, and it is possible to adhere to Christianity (or any other religion) while worrying about the fruits of

increasingly common view. Steven Pinker's recent book *Enlightenment Now* provides a good example of this way of thinking about religion. He proposes the Enlightenment values of reason, science, humanism, and progress as the key to the future, and he is optimistic about their ability to guide humanity forward. Among the counter-Enlightenment forces that must be overcome is religion—in fact, Pinker thinks that religious faith is the "most obvious" hindrance to the progress of humanity.[4] For Pinker, religion has been a huge source of war and violence throughout history, and few sophisticated people maintain robust religious beliefs today.[5]

There are various oddities in Pinker's description of religion that we will pass over here—theological simplicities (for example, the Trinity is described as the belief that "God is three persons but also one person"),[6] biblical inaccuracies (for example, the claim that the Bible commanded the Israelites to commit mass rape),[7] and surprising dismissals of relevant arguments (for instance, regarding cosmological and ontological arguments, he simply writes, "The Cosmological and Ontological arguments for the existence of God are logically invalid"[8]—one is left without an argument or any indication of which variation of these proofs he

religion in general—but obviously Christianity is a religion in the basic sense that it affirms concepts like the supernatural, worship, and faith.

4. Steven Pinker, *Enlightenment Now: The Case for Reason, Science, Humanism, and Progress* (New York: Viking, 2018), 30.

5. Pinker, *Enlightenment Now*, 420–42, unpacks his overall stance to religion here. The claim that few sophisticated people maintain robust religious commitments today is made on p. 430 with respect to belief in heaven and hell, the literal truth of the Bible, and a God who performs miracles.

6. Pinker, *Enlightenment Now*, 359.

7. Pinker, *Enlightenment Now*, 429.

8. Pinker, *Enlightenment Now*, 421. Pinker offers some interesting recommendations on the climate change crisis, and his book presents solid data on the fields he is trained in, so its dismissive posture toward religion is particularly unfortunate. As with Sam Harris, one also worries whether science alone can fill the void created by rejecting philosophy and religion—for instance, grounding the various humanistic values Pinker advocates. See *Enlightenment Now*, 391–95, where he defends his very high view of science.

has in view). None of this engenders the impression of an analysis of religion that is particularly careful or responsive to detail.

But there is a more basic methodological issue in Pinker's outlook that is worth some attention here, since it is characteristic of the new atheist attitude more broadly: namely, the tendency to treat religion as a singular phenomenon rather than to deal with particular religions or particular religious ideas. For example, at one point Pinker appears to derive the conclusion that God does not exist from the claim that different religions "decree mutually incompatible beliefs about how many gods there are, which miracles they have wrought, and what they demand of their devotees."[9] But it is pure silliness to suppose that religions must be in agreement with each other for any one of them to be true. You might as well argue, "Different nations have different forms of government, and they are all incompatible with one another; therefore, away with government!" Later, responding to the terrible bloodshed caused by secular regimes, Pinker reasons, "If religion were a source of morality, the number of religious wars and atrocities ought to be zero."[10] This is a strange criterion! According to this way of thinking, the flaws in one religion will serve to discredit every other religion, as well as religion in general.

The problem with this approach, as David Bentley Hart puts it, is that "religion in the abstract does not actually exist, and almost no one (apart from politicians) would profess any allegiance to it."[11] Rather than take each expression of religion as representative of the whole, it would be better, and more authentic to the complexity of human history, to critically distinguish between different forms of religion. After all, religion is one of the oldest and most widespread aspects of human culture, virtually as diverse as human beings themselves. The subject matter called up under

9. Pinker, *Enlightenment Now*, 421.
10. Pinker, *Enlightenment Now*, 430.
11. David Bentley Hart, *Atheist Delusions: The Christian Revolution and Its Fashionable Enemies* (New Haven: Yale University Press, 2009), 7–8.

the label *religion* is simply enormous. Any reasonable historical outlook will admit that one religion will differ from another; one can find both good and evil throughout religions; and some religious ideas are conducive to violence and bigotry, others less so, and others not at all. Thus, in each case of religious violence, we must ask: Is it religion *as such* or the particular religious ideas in question that have caused the violence? Simply documenting religious evils and then condemning religion wholesale is an instance of the fallacy of composition (inferring a truth about the whole from analysis of the parts). This logic is akin to saying, "Wendy's, Subway, and Arby's are terrible; therefore, fast food is bad," or, "Baseball and golf are boring; therefore, I dislike sports."

The tendency to treat religion in too general terms is a common feature in the new-atheist literature, and it often leads to a distortion of the relevant historical and sociological data. Christopher Hitchens, for example, believes that "religion poisons everything"; and throughout the book bearing this subtitle he makes many related claims: "Religion is not unlike racism,"[12] "Religion . . . is not just amoral but immoral,"[13] and on and on. It is certainly a logical possibility that all religions without exception could be both false and bad, and such a claim could theoretically be born out with empirical support. The problem is that the empirical support doesn't fit; so it has to be stretched. Thus, we read that Martin Luther King Jr. was not a Christian in any *real* sense,[14] that all the churches without exception blessed the slave trade (William Wilberforce is not discussed; William Lloyd Garrison is downplayed),[15] that the chance that Christianity inspired resistance to the Nazis is "statistically almost negligible" (Dietrich Bonhoeffer and Martin Niemöller must have acted from other

12. Christopher Hitchens, *God Is Not Great: How Religion Poisons Everything* (New York: Twelve, 2007), 35.
13. Hitchens, *God Is Not Great*, 52.
14. Hitchens, *God Is Not Great*, 176.
15. Hitchens, *God Is Not Great*, 176–77.

motives), and many other such claims. If Hitchens had restrained his claim to say "Religions often poison" or "Many religions poison," we might have agreed with him to a degree, and he would not have needed to exaggerate.

It would also have been more interesting if Hitchens had engaged the *ideas* in question in these various figures; for example, whatever Martin Luther King Jr.'s personal faults were (Hitchens makes much of them), the whole rationale for his philosophy of civil disobedience, as articulated in his "Letter from a Birmingham Jail," was explicitly theistic and religious to its roots. In this letter, King anticipates anxiety regarding his willingness to break laws and responds thusly:

> One may well ask: "How can you advocate breaking some laws and obeying others?" The answer lies in the fact that there are two types of laws: just and unjust. I would be the first to advocate obeying just laws. One has not only a legal but a moral responsibility to obey just laws. Conversely, one has a moral responsibility to disobey unjust laws. I would agree with St. Augustine that an unjust law is no law at all.
>
> Now, what is the difference between the two? How does one determine whether a law is just or unjust? A just law is a man-made code that squares with the moral law or the law of God. An unjust law is a code that is out of harmony with the moral law. To put it in the terms of St. Thomas Aquinas: An unjust law is a human law that is not rooted in eternal law and natural law.[16]

King proceeds to unpack this philosophy with reference to Christian philosophers and biblical examples, like the refusal of Shadrach, Meshach, and Abednego to obey the laws of Nebuchadnezzar, or early Christians who faced the lions for disobeying the Roman emperor.[17] Throughout, King's conception of civil

16. Martin Luther King Jr., "Letter from a Birmingham Jail," in *Arguing about Law*, ed. John Oberdiek and Aileen Kavanagh (New York: Routledge, 2009), 257.
17. King, "Letter from a Birmingham Jail," 258.

disobedience rests on this conviction of the superiority of the eternal divine law to human laws. So when Hitchens insists that "King's legacy has very little to do with his professed theology,"[18] he would have better served his reader by at least offering a guess as to how King's philosophy of civil disobedience could have survived without the eternal, divine moral law as its foundation.

Not only is it hard to establish a general association between religion and evil, but in the opposite direction, the "religion poisons everything" mentality must also account for secular atrocities, particularly in the twentieth century. Hitchens references this as the common question he and his atheist friends get from religious audiences.[19] Why was humanity's most secular century simultaneously its bloodiest? If religion is the problem, why are the atheistic regimes (Stalin, Mao, etc.) seemingly the cruelest of all?[20]

In a new afterword to his *The End of Faith*, Sam Harris likewise notes that this question was one of the most common responses to the book's initial printing. In response, he observes, "While some of the most despicable political movements in human history have been explicitly irreligious, they were not especially rational."[21] It is difficult to discern how this observation is relevant to the point at hand, since Harris has been arguing that violence and irrationality are the result of religious belief; the question is, on such a view, why there are so many counterexamples. Perhaps Harris is operating with so elastic a definition of religion that he associates it with any kind of blind dogmatism, whatever the actual content of its beliefs. This would fit with his claim earlier in the book that tyrants like Stalin and Mao were leaders of a

18. Hitchens, *God Is Not Great*, 180.
19. Hitchens, *God Is Not Great*, 230.
20. Another interesting question, which we cannot pursue here, concerns the universality of violence in the nonhuman realm. As is often pointed out, chimpanzees, for example, are very violent but not very religious.
21. Sam Harris, *The End of Faith: Religion, Terror, and the Future of Reason* (New York: Norton, 2004), 231.

"political religion."[22] Other secular voices have said similarly—
Bill Maher, for example, when challenged by the example of the
Soviet Union as contrary to his thesis that religious ideas are
the primary historical cause of violent behavior, categorizes the
Soviet Union as a "secular religion."[23]

However we define terms like "political religion" or "secular
religion," using such labels for the Soviet Union seems more conve-
nient than illuminating. The complete elimination of religion was
a fundamental tenet of the Marxist-Leninist philosophy that was
embraced as the official state ideology of the Soviet Union (and
various other countries in the Eastern Bloc) for several decades in
the early to mid-twentieth century.[24] Not only was the official Soviet
policy explicitly materialistic and atheistic at the core, but it engaged in a persecution of religious belief and practice of staggering
proportions, executing for several decades a ruthless campaign of
propaganda, ridicule, harassment, incarceration, and mass execu-
tion. This took place from when the Bolsheviks took over in 1917
till Stalin's death in 1953 (with a later revival in the 1960s) and was
at times particularly severe, especially throughout the antireligious
campaign from 1928 to 1941.[25] In 1937 alone, for example, over
eighty-five thousand Russian Orthodox priests were shot.[26] The
vast majority of churches, mosques, and synagogues were shut
down by the start of World War II. From 1917 to 1941, the number

22. Harris, *The End of Faith*, 79: "Consider the millions of people who were killed
by Stalin and Mao: although these tyrants paid lip service to rationality, communism
was little more than a political religion."

23. This is a point Maher makes in his dialogue with Ross Douthat on *Real Time
with Bill Maher* (season 10, episode 13, aired on April 20, 2012, on HBO); Maher's
general posture toward religion can also be seen in his film *Religulous*.

24. In his classic text on the Marxist-Leninist outlook, Otto Wille Kuusinen de-
voted the first chapter to philosophical materialism. *Fundamentals of Marxism-
Leninism* (New York: U.S. Joint Publications Research Service, 1960), 9–50.

25. For a phase-by-phase overview, see Philip Walters, "A Survey of Soviet Policy,"
in *Religious Policy in the Soviet Union*, ed. Sabrina Petra Ramet (Cambridge: Cambridge University Press, 2005), 3–30.

26. Alexander N. Yakovlev, *A Century of Violence in Soviet Russia* (New Haven:
Yale University Press, 2002), 165.

of Russian Orthodox churches, for instance, had decreased by 95 percent; the number of active bishops from 130 to between 4 and 7; and the number of priests from 51,105 to less than 500.[27]

In light of these facts, the Soviet Union could only be regarded as a "religion" in some unconventional, vague sense of the word—and even this possibility was rigorously rejected by Soviets. Lenin, for instance, emphatically denied that communism could be construed as a "political religion" or as analogous to religion in any way, denouncing those who conceived of it as a kind of "religion of humanity" as betraying the communist vision.[28] Ultimately, the claim that the communism of the Soviet Union was a kind of religion can be made only on the basis of the most tenuous and superficial meaning of the word "religion," such that to the extent the statement is true, it becomes irrelevant to the criticism of "religion" in the more traditional sense. The whole effort seems as ad hoc as the insistence that Martin Luther King Jr. was not *really* a Christian.

We would do well to remember this recent history. I worry profoundly that the buoyant tone of much twenty-first-century secularism subsists by forgetting, or failing to take seriously, the brutal facts of the twentieth century. Consider this: the bloodiest chapter in the human story was simultaneously an experiment in secularism on an unprecedented scale.[29] Humanity at its most

27. These figures come from the Soviet antireligious specialist A. Veshchikov, quoted in John B. Dunlop, "Gorbachev and Russian Orthodoxy," *Problems of Communism* 39 (July–August 1989): 107.

28. See the discussion in Victoria Smolkin, *A Sacred Space Is Never Empty: A History of Soviet Atheism* (Princeton: Princeton University Press, 2018), 13, where she quotes Lenin as regarding these communism-religion comparisons as a "despicable 'flirtation' with God." As Smolkin explains, "As Lenin saw it, the distinction between Communism and religion was not trivial. Whereas religion was an irrational illusion, Communism was a science grounded in reason; whereas religion appealed to the supernatural to explain the wonders of the universe, Communism relied on materialism to explain the workings of nature" (13–14).

29. R. J. Rummel, an authority on genocide and government mass murder, puts it like this: "Of all religions, secular and otherwise, that of Marxism has been by far the bloodiest—bloodier than the Catholic Inquisition, the various Catholic crusades, and the Thirty Years War between Catholics and Protestants. In practice, Marxism

ruthless was without gods or temples. This does not automatically prove that the loss of religious belief leads to violence, though some have argued that.[30] But it does make it impossible to agree with those who regard religion as the cause of the violence, such that once religion is taken away, mercy and tolerance and rationality will reign unhindered. Hart marvels at this atheistic optimism: "Given that the modern age of secular governance has been the most savagely and sublimely violent period in human history, by a factor (or body count) of incalculable magnitude, it is hard to identify the grounds of their confidence."[31]

Is religion, on balance, a greater force for evil or for good? It's not easy to say. In the United States, studies routinely show that religion has a variety of positive psychological, social, and even medical effects, and tends to promote certain virtuous behaviors, such as giving to charity.[32] On the other hand, it is sometimes diffi-

---

has meant bloody terrorism, deadly purges, lethal prison camps and murderous forced labor, fatal deportations, man-made famines, extrajudicial executions and fraudulent show trials, outright mass murder and genocide. In total, Marxist regimes murdered nearly 110 million people from 1917 to 1987. For perspective on this incredible toll, note that all domestic and foreign wars during the 20th century killed around 35 million. That is, . . . Marxism is more deadly than all the wars of the 20th century, including World Wars I and II, and the Korean and Vietnam Wars." R. J. Rummel, "The Killing Machine That Is Marxism," *The Schwarz Report*, December 15, 2004, https://www .schwarzreport.org/resources/essays/the-killing-machine-that-is-marxism. Elsewhere Rummel describes these estimates as a "prudent or conservative mid-range estimate." R. J. Rummel, *Death by Government* (New Brunswick, NJ: Transaction, 1994), xx.

30. Alexandr Solzhenitsyn, upon receiving the Templeton Prize in 1983, said: "If I were asked today to formulate as concisely as possible the main cause of the ruinous Revolution that swallowed up some sixty million of our people, I could not put it more accurately than to repeat: 'men have forgotten God; that's why all this has happened.'" Solzhenitsyn, "Men Have Forgotten God: The Templeton Address," in *In the World: Reading and Writing as a Christian*, ed. John H. Timmerman and Donald R. Hettinga (Grand Rapids: Baker Academic, 2004), 145.

31. Hart, *Atheist Delusions*, 14. And later: "Christian society certainly never fully purged itself of cruelty or violence; but it also never incubated evils comparable in ambition, range, systematic precision, or mercilessness to death camps, gulags, forced famines, or the extravagant brutality of modern warfare" (107).

32. For example, Jonathan Haidt notes, "Studies of charitable giving in the United States show that people in the least religious fifth of the population give just 1.5 percent of their money to charity. People in the most religious fifth (based on church

cult to tell whether the benefits of religion come from religion per se or from the social involvement it tends to encourage. General statements about "religion" are very difficult; and I am not attempting here a blanket defense of religion in general. Even if this were possible, it would not be desirable with respect to the goals of this book. The point here is simply that religion is sufficiently complex to warrant a more guarded, case-by-case evaluation.

This more nuanced view of religion allows us to steer clear of the cultural elitism that is often endemic to the wholesale rejection of religion in some secular circles. Because secularism is rare throughout premodern and Eastern contexts, the "religion poisons everything" attitude is eerily conducive to a snobbish mentality in which humanity has been basically always poisoned by ignorance and backwardness, while we few here in the modern West have managed to extricate ourselves. Often this cultural prejudice is thinly veiled, if at all. Christopher Hitchens, for instance, virtually equates "premodern" with "ignorant," as such a view has facility in helping him lampoon religion. Thus: "Religion comes from the period of human prehistory where nobody . . . had the smallest idea what was going on."[33] Such a view also steers close to scientism, since apparently there is nothing important worth knowing apart from that which is known through science. "Religion has run out of justifications. Thanks to the telescope and the microscope, it no longer offers an explanation of anything important."[34] Being open to religion enables you to take a milder, more liberal attitude toward ancient and non-Western humanity.

---

attendance, not belief) give a whopping 7 percent of their income to charity." Haidt, *The Righteous Mind: Why Good People Are Divided by Politics and Religion* (New York: Vintage, 2012), 308. Similarly, Robert Putnam and David Campbell, after conducting a number of studies on how religious and nonreligious Americans differ, concluded, "By many different measures religiously observant Americans are better neighbors and better citizens than secular Americans—they are more generous with their time and money, especially in helping the needy, and they are more active in community life." Quoted in Haidt, *The Righteous Mind*, 310.

33. Hitchens, *God Is Not Great*, 64.
34. Hitchens, *God Is Not Great*, 282.

It enables you to see yourself in solidarity with, rather than in isolation from, the majority of human beings in the face of the fundamental mysteriousness of life and the universe.[35]

One final point: we must also reject the claim that religion is purely the product of one's sociocultural context, that people adhere to religions simply, or nearly simply, based upon where they live. Dawkins, for example, writes early on in *The God Delusion*, "If you are religious at all it is overwhelmingly probable that your religion is that of your parents. If you were born in Arkansas and you think Christianity is true and Islam false, knowing full well that you would think the opposite if you had been born in Afghanistan, you are the victim of childhood indoctrination."[36] Years earlier, Bertrand Russell claimed that "with very few exceptions, the religion which a man accepts is that of the community in which he lives, which makes it obvious that the influence of environment is what has led him to accept the religion in question."[37]

It is uncertain how such a correlation could be drawn with any confidence between one's environment and one's beliefs—the question draws us into the age-old nature-versus-nurture dilemma. But the real fatal flaw in this way of thinking is that it backfires on the secularist: for if religious beliefs are explainable in terms of one's context, are not secular beliefs, too? After all, secularism is extremely rare outside the modern West. If Richard Dawkins thinks that you would not be a Christian if you were born in Afghanistan, we may likewise wonder if he would be an atheist had *he* been born there. It is impossible to know, and to think that in either case the belief in question is thereby discredited is to commit the genetic fallacy, in which the validity of a belief is determined by how it arose. With this in view, we are left with the

35. Consider, as a fascinating example of this kind of cultural broadening, Jonathan Haidt's description of living in India for three months, and the impact it had on him, in *The Righteous Mind*, 118–24.
36. Richard Dawkins, *The God Delusion* (New York: Houghton Mifflin, 2006), 3.
37. Bertrand Russell, *Why I Am Not a Christian: And Other Essays on Religion and Related Subjects*, ed. Paul Edwards (New York: Simon & Schuster, 1957), v.

more modest claim (one that is fairer to both believer and skeptic alike) that our beliefs are doubtless *influenced* by our environment but must be finally evaluated by their evidential merits.

Speaking of evidential merits for religious belief, it's time we got there.

Moving beyond the "Lord, Liar, Lunatic" Trilemma

Most religions make claims about some kind of divine or ultimate spiritual reality and how this reality should be related to. Yet of all religious figures throughout human history, Jesus of Nazareth made spiritual claims of a unique and unparalleled nature. For while most religious figures claimed to manifest or offer the way to spiritual reality or God, Jesus claimed to *be* God.[38] This is the Christian claim—that the unique, transcendent Creator God has not revealed himself to his creation in some indirect, ambiguous manner but rather has himself become a part of it—like an author writing himself into his story as one of the characters.

If you are Hamlet looking for Shakespeare, such a possibility changes the situation dramatically. The whole task is potentially redirected. So it is worth investigating the claim to see if it has any merit.

As a historical phenomenon, Jesus of Nazareth must be interpreted some way or another. He is often regarded as the most influential human being who ever lived, and the largest and most diverse group of adherents was founded in his name. We must make *something* of this. A few generations ago C. S. Lewis famously suggested that there are basically three broad categories by which we might interpret Jesus:

38. To be sure, there are many stories of gods taking human form in antiquity, but they differ fundamentally from the Christian idea of the *incarnation* in that they did not arise in the strict monotheistic context of Judaism—more on this, and on the idea that Jesus claimed to be God, in just a bit.

I am trying here to prevent anyone saying the really foolish thing that people often say about Him: I'm ready to accept Jesus as a great moral teacher, but I don't accept His claim to be God. That is the one thing we must not say. A man who was merely a man and said the sort of things Jesus said would not be a great moral teacher. He would either be a lunatic—on the level with the man who says he is a poached egg—or else he would be the Devil of Hell. You must make your choice. Either this man was, and is, the Son of God, or else a madman or something worse. You can shut Him up for a fool, you can spit at Him and kill Him as a demon or you can fall at His feet and call Him Lord and God, but let us not come with any patronizing nonsense about His being a great human teacher. He has not left that open to us. He did not intend to.[39]

It's worth referencing Lewis's argument here because of its huge influence and because it helpfully introduces some initial options for how we might understand Jesus. However, it has often been pointed out that the argument suffers from a crucial weakness: it assumes that Jesus did, in fact, claim to be God. How do we know he made this claim? Thus, we must consider at least four possibilities: lord, liar, lunatic, or legend.[40]

Those who go the "legend" route typically don't conceive of Christ as *only* a legend or a myth, having no existence at all as a historical figure. You hear such a claim now and again, but it's very rare among professional historians. Bart Ehrman, for example, a popular historian of the New Testament and early Christianity, and an evangelical-Christian-turned-agnostic whose

---

39. Lewis, *Mere Christianity*, 36.

40. Dawkins, *The God Delusion*, 92, offers yet another alternative: "A fourth possibility, almost too obvious to need mentioning, is that Jesus was honestly mistaken. Plenty of people are." It's not easy to see, however, how one can pronounce oneself the judge of the world, superior to angels, preexistent with God, and so on because one is "honestly mistaken." Errors on such points do seem to call into question the overall trustworthiness of the speaker, particularly when his broader moral teaching is rooted in his authoritative claims about himself; this may well have been part of what motivated Lewis to include "lunatic" as an option.

views we will engage more in just a moment, claims, "The view that Jesus existed is held by virtually every expert on the planet," and he describes many efforts to prove the contrary as displaying the same level of historical sophistication as *Monty Python and the Holy Grail* or *The Da Vinci Code*.[41] The more common claim among thoughtful skeptics is that Jesus indeed existed, and had great religious influence of some kind or another, but did not claim to be God. One common view, for example, represented by modern scholars like Ehrman as well as earlier generations of German scholars, is that Jesus understood himself as a kind of apocalyptic preacher heralding the kingdom of God and possibly as the Jewish Messiah—but not as divine.[42]

Considering such possibilities draws us into an enormously complicated subject to which we cannot do full justice here but that we must engage as best we can more briefly: namely, the historical reliability of the New Testament Gospels. To what extent do the four canonical Gospels of Matthew, Mark, Luke, and John give us an accurate portrayal of the "historical Jesus"? So here we will offer some brief reflections on the nature of the Gospels as historical documents and then engage Bart Ehrman's proposal that belief in Jesus as divine was a later "legend" that developed after his death.

How Reliable Are the Gospels?

A compelling case can be made that the New Testament Gospels give us a great deal of reliable information about the historical

41. Bart D. Ehrman, *Did Jesus Exist? The Historical Argument for Jesus of Nazareth* (New York: HarperOne, 2013), 4.

42. Bart D. Ehrman, *How Jesus Became God: The Exaltation of a Jewish Preacher from Galilee* (New York: HarperOne, 2014), 112–28. The most famous earlier proponent of "apocalyptic Jesus" is Albert Schweitzer in his famous *The Quest of the Historical Jesus*, ed. John Bowden (Minneapolis: Fortress Press, 2001; the first edition was published in German in 1906). In this chapter we focus on Ehrman as a good representative of this view in its modern articulation. Of course, there are all kinds of other depictions of the "historical Jesus," and their variety is often taken to reduce the plausibility of the effort.

figure Jesus of Nazareth.[43] How much this is the case is highly contested, of course—the emphasis of a whole tradition of scholarship
is to downplay this claim. The Jesus Seminar in the 1990s famously
claimed that only 18 percent of the sayings of Jesus as recorded in
Matthew, Mark, Luke, John, and the Gospel of Thomas go back
to the historical Jesus. Even if this were so, this 18 percent would
not be negligible as historical information; it would surpass what
we know about many other ancient figures. But, as is often pointed
out, the Jesus Seminar is not representative of mainstream scholarship on the historical Jesus.[44] Paul Eddy and Greg Boyd have com-
piled a range of data from ethnography, folkloristics, and orality
studies, demonstrating the basic reliability of the traditions that
fed into the Synoptic Gospels. They point out that the assumptions that lead scholars to question their reliability are generally
rooted in Eurocentric, ethnocentric, and/or academic biases that
impose modern literary models on first-century oral culture.[45] In

43. Note that this is a more modest claim than a defense of the full trustworthiness of the Gospels. Lewis's trilemma is sometimes unfairly tied to belief in the written Gospels as completely true—thus, Christopher Hitchens describes it as follows:
"Either the Gospels are in some sense literal truth, or the whole thing is essentially a
fraud and perhaps an immoral one at that." *God Is Not Great*, 120. But there is an
annoying carefreeness here in the pivot from Jesus's historical claims to the integrity
of the *written* Gospels, alongside the introduction of the category "literal." Questions of the genre and trustworthiness of the Gospel records are a quite distinct issue
from Jesus's historical claims about his identity. Immediately afterward, Hitchens
uses John 8:3–11 to attempt to debunk biblical inspiration (he probably should have
referenced 7:53–8:11), but this is a passage almost everyone admits is not in the earliest manuscripts (see Hitchens, *God Is Not Great*, 120–22).

44. See the discussion in Craig Blomberg, *The Historical Reliability of the Gospels*, 2nd ed. (Downers Grove, IL: IVP Academic, 2007), 16–17, who calls the Jesus
Seminar "eccentric, unrepresentative scholarship" (16), noting that "one of the better
kept secrets of the last quarter of a century is the growth of what has been dubbed
the third quest of the historical Jesus, in which a large number of scholars, and by
no means just conservative Christian ones, have been growing in their confidence in
how much we can know about the Jesus of history and in how reliable the New Testament Gospels are" (17). See also Ben Witherington III, *The Jesus Quest: The Third
Search for the Jew of Nazareth*, 2nd ed. (Downers Grove, IL: IVP Academic, 1997).

45. Paul Rhodes Eddy and Gregory A Boyd, *The Jesus Legend: A Case for the
Historical Reliability of the Synoptic Jesus Tradition* (Grand Rapids: Baker Academic, 2007).

his groundbreaking work on the subject, N. T. Wright summarized a newer wave of scholarship on the historical Jesus (what he terms the "third quest") that moves beyond the positivistic naivete of the Jesus Seminar and displays more rigorous attention to various aspects of Jesus's historical context, such as his Jewishness.[46] For scholars like Wright, the question of the "historical Jesus" is urgently important, but the results need not be so skeptical: "We can know quite a lot about Jesus; not enough to write a modern-style biography, including the colour of the subject's hair, and what he liked for breakfast, but quite a lot."[47]

While this subject is too vast to cover thoroughly here, consider just a few basic facts about the Gospels. By most estimates, Mark is the earliest Gospel, written perhaps in the 60s, while John was the last Gospel, written perhaps in the 90s. There is some wiggle room in these dates, but not much.[48] By comparison to other ancient works of history, this places them in relatively close proximity to the events they describe.[49] Richard Bauckham summarizes: "The Gospels were written within living memory of the events they recount. Mark's Gospel was written well within the lifetime of many of the eyewitnesses, while the other three canonical Gospels were written in the period when living eyewitnesses were

46. N. T. Wright, *Jesus and the Victory of God*, Christian Origins and the Question of God 2 (Minneapolis: Fortress, 1996), 28–124.

47. Wright, *Jesus and the Victory of God*, 123; cf. also his summary on 657–62.

48. A minority of scholars would place Mark in the early 70s; conservative and liberal scholars sometimes date John a little earlier or later, respectively; but such possibilities do not impinge greatly on the present point.

49. For example, as Blomberg notes, "The detailed life of Alexander the Great, however, which most historians believe can be reconstructed with a fair amount of accuracy, depends on Arrian and Plutarch's late first and early second-century biographies of a man who died in 323 B.C." Craig L. Blomberg, "The Historical Reliability of the Gospels," in *Evidence for God: 50 Arguments for Faith from the Bible, History, Philosophy, and Science*, ed. William A. Dembski and Michael R. Licona (Grand Rapids: Baker Books, 2010), 230. Michael R. Licona, *The Resurrection of Jesus: A New Historiographical Approach* (Downers Grove, IL: IVP Academic, 2010), 589, makes the same point in comparison with the biographies of the Roman emperor Augustus.

becoming scarce, exactly at the point in time when their testimony would perish with them were it not put in writing."[50] Furthermore, it is likely that some of the material that went into the Gospels was written before the completion of the first Gospel—for example, Q (the document purportedly containing material found in both Matthew and Luke) probably dates to the 50s.[51]

In the period between Jesus's life and the writing of the Gospels, the stories of Jesus's life were transmitted primarily through oral traditions. On the one hand, one might think that over a period of three or four or five decades, memories of Jesus's words and deeds would be significantly altered as they were passed along. On the other hand, first-century Palestinian Judaism was an oral culture, placing strong emphasis on memory in education and following particular practices of preservation and transmission that sought to preserve accuracy. Older generations of modern scholarship, championing form criticism, emphasized that Jesus traditions would have changed based upon the needs and goals of the community in which they were passed along. But more recent scholars like Bauckham have shown how unlikely this would be, within the time frame imagined, in light of the way oral tradition works. Bauckham points to a fascinating range of material in the Gospels that indicates that Jesus traditions were connected to named and known eyewitnesses and carefully passed down through formal methods of transmission.[52] Other scholars have pointed to evidence that the various communities of followers of Jesus that are proposed by the form critics were conversant with each other, which undercuts the plausibility that the stories were drastically warped from one group to another.[53]

50. Richard Bauckham, *Jesus and the Eyewitnesses: The Gospels as Eyewitness Testimony* (Grand Rapids: Eerdmans, 2006), 7.

51. See the discussion in Blomberg, *The Historical Reliability of the Gospels*, 54.

52. E.g., Bauckham, *Jesus and the Eyewitnesses*, 9, 93, 264, 472. See also Blomberg, *The Historical Reliability of the Gospels*, 58–62.

53. Martin Hengel, "Christology and New Testament Chronology: A Problem in the History of Earliest Christianity," in *Between Jesus and Paul* (London: SCM, 1983).

The fact that the Gospels were written and circulated within the lifetime of many who would have remembered the events described is especially significant in light of the Gospels' concrete, historical character, in keeping with their now widely recognized literary status as *ancient biographies*.[54] Matthew, Mark, Luke, and John are anchored in the first-century world of Roman politics, Palestinian geography, and Jewish religion. One can read many of the later Gnostic Gospels as more philosophical and timeless in nature; but the canonical Gospels are teeming with little details tethered to historical events (like the census of Caesar Augustus), places (like the Sea of Galilee), and people (like Pontius Pilate).[55] Therefore, much of what the Gospels claimed to receive on the basis of eyewitness testimony (e.g., Luke 1:2) would have been, in principle, verifiable at the time of its writing. If the Gospels had concocted or dramatically warped historical events, this could have been pointed out by people still alive—just as a history book about the Great Depression published in the 1970s could be judged by people who had lived through the events described.

We can also have good confidence that the Gospels were copied fairly accurately after their initial composition. In trying to identify what the original autographs said, we are working with more than 5,600 manuscripts of the New Testament *in Greek alone*—most

54. The key book that shifted the scholarly view on this was Richard A. Burridge, *What Are the Gospels? A Comparison with Graeco-Roman Biography* (Cambridge: Cambridge University Press, 1992); more recently, see Craig Keener, *Christobiography: Memory, History, and the Reliability of the Gospels* (Grand Rapids: Eerdmans, 2019).

55. I remember being inspired to investigate the Gospel of Philip after reading Dan Brown's 2003 novel *The Da Vinci Code* when I was a college student. The novel had created quite a stir for suggesting that Jesus was married to Mary Magdalene; even though the claim is not well founded historically, I wanted to consider the passage in the Gospel of Philip that this theory is supposedly based on. I remember being struck by how different the Gospel of Philip felt from the New Testament Gospels, particularly in its lack of historical texture. Like many of the other Gnostic Gospels, it is essentially a compilation of sayings and teachings, without narrative or historical context. Matthew, Mark, Luke, and John, by contrast, reflect a high level of historical detail and situatedness.

other ancient Latin or Greek texts have closer to a dozen.[56] As Daniel Wallace puts it, "In terms of extant manuscripts, the NT textual critic is confronted with an embarrassment of riches. . . . The NT is by far the best-attested work of Greek or Latin literature in the ancient world."[57] In these and many other ways, the Gospels are, particularly in comparison to other ancient documents, historically impressive documents.[58]

None of this requires that the portrait of Jesus we find in the Gospels is infallible, of course. It does suggest, however, that a wholesale skepticism about them is unwarranted (and, if not paralleled by a comparable skepticism of other ancient history, arbitrary). By any reasonable standard, the canonical Gospels certainly tell us *some* information about the historical Jesus, and it is worth the hard labor of attempting to discern just how much they do so. Specifically: Are the claims to be God that Jesus makes in the Gospels historically authentic? Do we have historical reasons to believe that Jesus understood himself as divine?

Could Jesus's Claims to Be God Be a Legend?

Bart Ehrman proposes that Jesus did not claim to be God in his lifetime but that this is a subsequent belief that arose among his

56. Daniel B. Wallace, *Revisiting the Corruption of the New Testament: Manuscript, Patristic, and Apocryphal Evidence* (Grand Rapids: Kregel Academic, 2011), 27.

57. Wallace, *Revisiting the Corruption of the New Testament*, 29–30.

58. It is sometimes claimed that the disciples were uneducated and thus would not have been able to write such literarily and theologically sophisticated documents as the Gospels (e.g., Ehrman, *How Jesus Became God*, 90). But even Ehrman figures that the literacy rate among Jews at the time was around 5 percent. Statistically, it would therefore be unlikely that *all* of the disciples were illiterate; there are little indications that John, e.g., was familiar with the Jewish leaders and likely benefited from Jewish education himself (e.g., cf. John 18:15). It is not at all improbable that two of the twelve should have been able to write the kind of Gospel we find in the New Testament; and this would explain why Mark and Luke were written by others—in Mark's case, reportedly in dialogue with Peter; in Luke's case, on the basis of careful investigation of the transmitted eyewitness testimonies available to him (Luke 1:1–4). Such a situation is not certain on strictly historical grounds, of course; but it is eminently plausible.

followers after his death. Ehrman thinks that when the earliest followers of Christ became convinced that Jesus was risen from the dead, they initially posited that he had been exalted to heaven, becoming an angel or angel-like being (Ehrman calls this an "exaltation Christology"). Later Christians came to believe that Christ was not simply a man-become-angel, but preexisted his earthly life as some kind of angelic or divine being (an "incarnation Christology").[59] Christological development then continued all the way up through the councils of the early church to a full trinitarian conception of Christ. Ehrman thinks the incarnation Christology may have begun extremely early, perhaps in the 50s, and perhaps even earlier.[60] However, it did not begin in Jesus's own lifetime. Thus, with regard to the Gospels, Ehrman argues that Jesus makes explicit claims of divinity only in John's Gospel because it was written later; by contrast, we don't see any comparable claims in the portions of the Synoptic Gospels that he regards as tracing back to the historical Jesus.[61] Thus, for Ehrman, the Jesus of John is very different from the Jesus of Mark.

On face value this historical reconstruction has a kind of plausibility, for it is undeniably true that Jesus's claims of divinity are the clearest and strongest in John, the latest Gospel to be written. On closer examination, however, several problems emerge. First, an important pillar of Ehrman's case is his claim that there are a wide variety of senses in which human beings could become "god" in ancient Greco-Roman, as well as in ancient Jewish thought.[62] He argues that in modern thought, God and humanity are fundamentally discontinuous, while in the ancient world, divinity and humanity existed along a vertical continuum that had points of

---

59. Ehrman, *How Jesus Became God*, 279.
60. Ehrman, *How Jesus Became God*, 262–69.
61. See the discussion in Ehrman, *How Jesus Became God*, 94–98, where he lists three principles of textual criticism by which we can start to make evaluations of what material in the New Testament traces back to earlier sources and what material traces back to later sources.
62. Ehrman, *How Jesus Became God*, 11–84.

overlap (he particularly emphasizes the role of angels in Jewish thought).[63] This enables him to argue, "If human could be angels (and angels could be humans), and if angels could be gods, and if in fact the chief angel could be the Lord himself—then to make Jesus divine, one simply needs to think of him as an angel in human form."[64]

There are good reasons, however, to think that in first-century Palestinian Jewish thought, the qualitative uniqueness of God was firmly held and strongly emphasized.[65] Larry Hurtado has written several books exploring early Christian devotion to Jesus, arguing that it was completely unparalleled in Jewish thought: "The accommodation of Christ as a recipient of cultic worship in the devotional practice of early Christian groups was a most unusual and significant step that cannot be easily accounted for on the basis of any tendencies in the Roman-era Jewish religion."[66] When it comes to the Jewish texts Ehrman considers, the examples he provides do not violate the uniqueness of belief in Jesus's incarnation. Many concern angels, and he mainly documents cases of angels *appearing* as human, not necessarily *becoming* human,[67] or human beings *sharing* in angelic glory in the afterlife, not necessarily *becoming* angels.[68] It is a stretch to see these as parallels to

63. Ehrman, *How Jesus Became God*, 39; cf. 4.

64. Ehrman, *How Jesus Became God*, 61, 270–71.

65. On this point, see Richard Bauckham, *Jesus and the God of Israel* (Grand Rapids: Eerdmans, 2008), 5; and Michael F. Bird, "Of Gods, Angels, and Men," in *How God Became Jesus: The Real Origins of Belief in Jesus' Divine Nature—A Response to Bart Ehrman* (Grand Rapids: Zondervan, 2014), 28–30.

66. Larry W Hurtado, *Lord Jesus Christ: Devotion to Jesus in Earliest Christianity* (Grand Rapids: Eerdmans, 2005), 31; cf. Hurtado, *One God, One Lord: Early Christian Devotion and Ancient Jewish Monotheism*, 3rd ed. (London: Bloomsbury, 2015).

67. Ehrman, *How Jesus Became God*, 55–59. He focuses especially on "the angel of the Lord," as well as Psalm 82:6 and *Apocalypse of Abraham* 10–11. While these examples show that angels could appear in human form, they do not depict a permanent, ontological transformation from angel to human.

68. Ehrman, *How Jesus Became God*, 59–61, where he references the description of the glorification of the righteous in 2 Baruch 51:3–10, as well as Enoch and Moses. But in all of these examples, people are described as becoming *like* angels in

belief in Jesus's incarnation in any relevant way. Moreover, while in Jewish thought divine language can be applied to angels, and angels can receive a kind of authority and veneration, none of these are exactly parallel to early Christian worship of Jesus. As Michael Bird points out, in Jewish thought "a sharp line was drawn between the veneration of intermediary figures and the worship of the one God, . . . based on the fact that such beings were not part of God's divine identity."[69] Thus, while there are examples of angels sharing in God's authority or honor, the early church worshiped Jesus *as* God. The origin of this practice is not easy to explain in terms of parallel beliefs.

Regarding the development of this belief in Jesus as God, it is remarkable how quickly the fundamental pillars came into place. Even Ehrman acknowledges that Philippians 2:6–11 is a pre-Pauline tradition that Paul quotes and thus dates earlier than the book of Philippians.[70] Because of factors like this, Ehrman is open to Jesus being regarded as an angel or an angel-like being earlier than the 50s, perhaps even in the first few years of the Christian movement.[71] While there is certainly development in the early church's under-standing of Jesus, it is striking how the main thing—the worship of a man as God—seems to have happened either immediately or almost immediately. Martin Hengel, describing christological development during the span of time between Jesus's death and Paul's writing, puts it like this: "More happened in this period of less than two decades than in the whole next seven centuries, up to the time when the doctrine of the early church was completed."[72]

Now for the main issue: Do we have good historical reasons to doubt that Jesus claimed to be God, as Ehrman suggests? Let us,

---

possessing heavenly glory; this is not necessarily a change from human to angel—an "angelification," as Ehrman calls it.

69. Bird, "Of Gods, Angels, and Men," 35.

70. Ehrman, *How Jesus Became God*, 262–69.

71. Cf. Ehrman, *How Jesus Became God*, 279.

72. Martin Hengel, *The Son of God: The Origin of Christology and the History of Jewish-Hellenistic Religion* (London: SCM, 1975), 4.

for the sake of argument, accept the critical principles by which
Ehrman determines which material in the Gospels is authentic
to the historical Jesus, particularly his criterion of *independent
attestation*, which I take to be the least controversial.[73] In passing
I would simply point out that the critical principles undergirding Ehrman's reconstruction are highly disputed; for example,
Richard Bauckham has argued powerfully that even the Gospel of
John should be understood as eyewitness testimony.[74] But even if
we restrict ourselves to material attested in the purportedly more
reliable sources, we still hear Jesus making claims that assume
an astonishing weight of divine authority, beyond what we could
reasonably expect from a merely human messiah and preacher.

As an entry point, consider Jesus's declaration of forgiveness of
sins to the paralytic man in Mark 2:5. The Jewish scribes who are
present understand Jesus to be forgiving sins by his own authority, thinking, "He is blaspheming! Who can forgive sins but God
alone?" (Mark 2:7). On Ehrman's reading of this story, the scribes'
worry is misplaced—for Ehrman claims that "when Jesus forgives
sins, he never says, 'I forgive you,' as God might say, but 'your sins
are forgiven,' which means that *God* has forgiven the sin."[75] But
this misses the whole point of this story. For in response to the
scribes, Jesus claims that his authority to heal demonstrates his
own authority to forgive: "But that you may know that the Son
of Man has authority on earth to forgive sins . . ." (Mark 2:10).
The idea that Jesus is simply informing the paralytic that *God*
has forgiven him overlooks the climactic purpose of the story.[76]

73. Ehrman, *How Jesus Became God*, 95, describes this principle as follows: "If a
story is found in several of these independent traditions, then it is far more likely that
this story goes back to the ultimate source of the tradition, the life of Jesus itself."
    74. Bauckham, *Jesus and the Eyewitness*, 358–471.
    75. Ehrman, *How Jesus Became God*, 127 (italics original).
    76. One of the curious features of Ehrman's account is that he seems to suggest that
Jesus does not refer to himself with the phrase "Son of Man"; see *How Jesus Became
God*, 106–7. This is an eccentric suggestion that might work for some of the sayings
of Christ about the son of man, but certainly not all of them (for instance, in Mark
2:10 Jesus refers to his own actions—i.e., forgiving sin—as those of the son of man).

This little episode is a good example of how the Gospels (including John) reveal Jesus's divine identity—through *the exercise of divine authority*. No one thinks that Jesus walked around announcing, "God is a Trinity, and I am the Second Member!" In fact, Jesus often *concealed* his identity, charging both his disciples and others not to reveal who he is (e.g., Mark 1:43–44; 8:30). Instead, Jesus's divine self-understanding was revealed through what he did and said in the context of his ministry inaugurating the kingdom of God. Take the presentation of Jesus in Mark's Gospel, for example—his authoritative teaching (1:22), his power over demons (1:27), his ministry (11:28), his power to heal (1:41), his transfiguration (9:2–8), his requirement of absolute devotion to himself (8:34–38), and so forth. Think of the disciples' terror after Jesus calms the storm: "Who then is this, that even the wind and the sea obey him?" (4:41; cf. Luke 8:25, and also the story in Matt. 14:22–33, where they worship Jesus as the Son of God after he walks on the water). Consider his claims to be the "lord even of the Sabbath" (Mark 2:28); his detailed predictions of future events (10:34; 14:30); and his equation of devotion to himself with devotion to the gospel (8:35; 10:29). One might quibble with this text or that, but the cumulative portrait conveys a particular kind of authority, an authority that goes well beyond the realm of any human prophet or teacher.

This is why Jesus's ministry increasingly merits the charge of blasphemy from the Jewish leadership. This climaxes at the end of Mark's Gospel in the high priest's question just before his crucifixion, "Are you the Christ, the Son of the Blessed?" Jesus responds, "I am, and you will see the Son of Man seated at the right hand of Power, and coming with the clouds of heaven" (Mark 14:61–62; cf. the slightly different accounts in Matt. 26:64; Luke 22:67–69). In response, the chief priest tears his clothes and accuses Jesus of blasphemy, just as the Jewish leaders do when Jesus makes comparable claims in John's Gospel. The charge of blasphemy arises because Jesus is claiming not merely to be the Messiah but, in addition to this, to stand in the unique position of divine authority associated with future judgment.[77]

This is in broad alignment with the claims to deity in John's Gospel. John's Gospel *as a whole* (i.e., not merely its quotations of Jesus) emphasizes the deity of Christ more than Matthew, Mark, or Luke, just as it is different from the other Gospels in so many other respects as well—style, theological emphases, events reported, overall narrative shape, and so on. So it's less surprising to find unique claims of divinity by Jesus in the Fourth Gospel. Yet Jesus doesn't stroll around in John's Gospel saying, "Listen up everyone, I am God!" Rather, there are a few occasions in which he makes a claim to this effect (e.g., 8:58; 10:30), occasioned by specific circumstances—particularly his extended dialogues with the Jewish leaders. Thus, the contrast that Ehrman draws between John and earlier material is too strong—it is eminently possible to read all four Gospels as offering a consistent portrait of Christ, though in different ways and with different points of emphasis. Whether we are in Mark or John, we are dealing with a figure who acts and speaks with a divine authority that would be blasphemous if not authentic.

In light of considerations like these, the category of *legend* is not an obvious or easy alternative to *liar*, *lunatic*, or *lord*. For even if we accept the questionable historical reconstruction it requires, we are still confronted with an astonishing and unprecedented historical figure—a man who forgave sins by his own authority, a man who healed and cast out demons in his own name, a man who claimed that in his own person the kingdom of God had arrived. Among his followers, explicitly divine language is applied to him from the earliest documents of the New Testament, and from the traditions they quote (e.g., Phil. 2:6), coming from within two decades of his

---

77. There are a number of issues in this passage that need to be explored; but suffice to say that Jesus is likely drawing from both Daniel 7:13 and Psalm 110:1 here. See the discussion in Michael F. Bird, "Did Jesus Think He Was God?," in *How God Became Jesus*, 65–66.

death. In short, deity is attributed to Jesus in the earliest material
of the New Testament. As G. B. Caird put it, reflecting on the high
Christology of the letters of Paul in the 50s, "The highest Christology of the NT is also the earliest."[78] This is not the stuff of legend,
like the stories we tell about King Arthur or Robin Hood.

If *legend* is off the table, then we are back to Lewis's trilemma.
Which of these other three alternatives is most likely? *Lunatic* and
liar obviously remain difficult for anyone who is struck by the
moral beauty and authority of Jesus's life. One might choose to
fall back on them, or on some other alternative, if one is strongly
disinclined on other grounds to accept any supernatural explanation of Jesus. But there is something disconcerting about positing
either deceit or madness at the font of humanity's biggest religion.
The more time I spend reading the Gospels, the more difficult I
find it to take these options seriously. I have had many experiences
with those suffering from mental illness. That is not what we
are up against in Matthew, Mark, Luke, and John. And the liar
alternative seems equally awkward. Speaking for myself, at least,
I'm convinced, deeply so, that Jesus is *good*.

Openness to the *lord* alternative will obviously depend on many
factors, such as whether one is open to the divine in general. But
the notion that Jesus was a genuine revelation of God is one plausible way to make sense of the historical data we have. For there
are a limited number of explanations for this person's astonishing existence and claims to be God, and none of them can be
embraced casually and easily. All of them are bracing. The notion that Jesus was actually telling us the truth is one of the more
consistent of them and has a broad explanatory power. Unless
we are constrained by an antisupernatural bias, why should we
consider this explanation impossible? Why couldn't Jesus really
be the Creator God's point of entry into our world?

78. G. B. Caird, *New Testament Theology*, ed. L. D. Hurst (Oxford: Clarendon,
1994), 343, quoted in Bird, "The Story of Jesus as the Story of God," in *How God Became Jesus*, 207n7; this corresponds to similar claims by Richard Bauckham and others.

The Resurrection of Jesus

There is another point of historical data that furthers the plausibility of a divine account of the historical Jesus: the sudden emergence of the conviction among his followers that he had risen from the dead. Just as there must be *some* historical explanation for the birth of worship of Jesus, there must be some reason for the birth of the belief in his resurrection and the church it inspired. Since the Enlightenment, historians and scholars of religion have offered various proposals: perhaps the women went to the wrong tomb; perhaps Jesus never fully died (the "swoon theory"); perhaps the disciples were mistaken in some manner (e.g., they had grief-induced hallucinations); perhaps the disciples stole the body and lied about the resurrection. These and many other explanations have been seriously considered.

The reason that scholars have historically put forward such explanations, rather than simply writing off the whole idea as a legend that requires no alternative explanation, is that there are certain historical facts concerning the early Christian movement that almost all historians agree upon. Michael Licona summarizes three facts that are so strongly supported by historical data that they are affirmed as factual by "a nearly unanimous and heterogeneous consensus of scholars":

1. Jesus died by crucifixion.
2. Very shortly after Jesus's death, the disciples had experiences that led them to believe and proclaim that Jesus had been resurrected and had appeared to them.
3. Within a few years after Jesus's death, Paul converted after experiencing what he interpreted as a postresurrection appearance of Jesus to him.[79]

---

79. Licona, *The Resurrection of Jesus*, 617.

He includes four other "second-order facts" that enjoy a strong but not as widespread attestation among historians: the conversion of Jesus's brother James, the empty tomb, Jesus's predictions of his death and resurrection, and the proclamation of the earliest apostles that Jesus was raised bodily.[80] When New Testament scholars and historians argue for the historical plausibility of the resurrection, they are claiming that the hypothesis that Jesus was actually bodily raised explains these data better than the alternative theories.[81]

So there are basically two ways that those who deny the resurrection can go. First, they can simply dismiss all these historical points of reference as uncertain or legendary. Second, they can accept them, or some of them, but argue that the naturalistic explanations of them are more plausible. It is important to stress that this second route is, by far, the pathway most represented among serious-minded historians. John Dominic Crossan, a critical scholar involved with the Jesus Seminar who interprets Jesus's resurrection in terms of metaphor, claimed that the fact that Jesus was crucified under Pontius Pilate "is as sure as anything historical can ever be."[82] Gerd Lüdemann, an influential New Testament scholar who is an atheist, wrote, "It may be taken as historically certain that Peter and the disciples had experiences after Jesus' death in

80. Licona, *The Resurrection of Jesus*, 468–69.

81. N. T. Wright, *The Resurrection of the Son of God*, Christian Origins and the Question of God 3 (Minneapolis: Fortress, 2003), 696, builds his argument for the resurrection of Christ from the empty tomb and the postmortem appearances of Christ, arguing that the combination of these two facts form a set of both necessary and sufficient conditions for the rise of early Christian belief in the resurrection. William Lane Craig builds an argument for the historicity of Jesus's resurrection on three facts: the empty tomb, the appearances of Jesus to his disciples, and the origins of the Christian faith. See William Lane Craig, *Assessing the New Testament Evidence for the Historicity of the Resurrection of Jesus*, Studies in the Bible and Early Christianity (New York: Edwin Mellen, 1989); and Craig, *The Son Rises: The Historical Evidence for the Resurrection of Jesus* (Chicago: Moody, 1981), 45–134.

82. John Dominic Crossan, *Who Killed Jesus? Exposing the Roots of Anti-Semitism in the Gospel Story of the Death of Jesus* (San Francisco: HarperSanFrancisco, 1995), 5.

which Jesus appeared to them as the risen Christ."[83] Gary Habermas has worked through an enormous body of writing on Jesus's resurrection and has observed how rarely skeptical historians deny that the disciples had a powerfully transformative experience of the risen Jesus. It may have been a hallucination, or a vision, or some kind of grief-induced religious experience, or something else—but *something* happened that led the disciples to this belief.[84]

Those who are new to the debate may wonder why so many nonbelieving historians would concede so much ground. Why should we consider the disciples' transformation and witness, for instance, to be historically secure, or at least historically very probable? Why not simply question everything?

The crucial thing to see here is how strong the historical data is concerning facts like these.

Earlier we commented that even the more skeptical New Testament scholars and historians rarely question that Jesus existed. There is just too much evidence for him. For example, we noted that even the radically skeptical Jesus Seminar regarded 18 percent of the sayings of Christ as recorded in Matthew, Mark, Luke, John, and the Gospel of Thomas to be authentic to the historical Jesus. This is a sillily low percentage, but it also reflects a far larger body of information than we have concerning many other ancient figures. If you want to say that Jesus was a "legend," there are other ways of going about it—denying his existence altogether reflects an *unreasonable* historical skepticism.

Something comparable is true with respect to the historical data concerning Jesus's resurrection. It is unreasonable to reject any and every fact that the New Testament mentions in relation to Easter and the early Christian movement. For example, many of the basic

83. Gerd Lüdemann, *What Really Happened to Jesus: A Historical Approach to the Resurrection*, with Alf Özen, trans. John Bowdon (Louisville: Westminster John Knox, 1995), 80.
84. Gary R. Habermas and Michael R. Licona, *The Case for the Resurrection of Jesus* (Grand Rapids: Kregel, 2004), 60.

facts that need to be explained have *early, independent attestation* in the New Testament. To give one example, Jesus's burial is attested to by Mark, by the tradition Paul quotes from in 1 Corinthians 15:3–5, by the sources used by Matthew and Luke, by John, and by the sermons in Acts. For ancient history, this is an impressive amount of attestation quite soon after the event in question.[85]

The strength of the data concerning the basic facts that led to a sudden transformation among the disciples of Jesus can be seen by the speculative and arbitrary feel of the arguments typically set against them. Take, as an example, Bart Ehrman's questioning of the historicity of Jesus's burial by Joseph of Arimathea. Ehrman stresses that the Sanhedrin *as a whole* had condemned Jesus to crucifixion, since Mark 14:64 records, "They all condemned him as deserving death" (the word "they" here refers back to the chief priests and the entire Sanhedrin, mentioned in v. 55). Ehrman finds it odd that Joseph of Arimathea, one of the members of the Sanhedrin, would then be involved in the burial: "Why, after Jesus is dead, is he suddenly risking himself (as implied by the fact that he had to gather up his courage) and seeking to do an act of mercy by arranging for a decent burial for Jesus's corpse?"[86] On this basis, Ehrman questions the historicity of Joseph's burial of Jesus.

But this is a rather unimaginative argument. In the first place, the fact that "the whole council" is referenced need not require that every single member was present. The New Testament frequently speaks of groups in general terms, with language that does not require that there are no exceptions.[87] (It is unlikely that

85. There are many fine resources that catalog such data, so I won't reproduce it all here. A good starting point for those interested would be Habermas and Licona, *The Case for the Resurrection of Jesus.*

86. Ehrman, *How Jesus Became God*, 152.

87. It is this same literalism with respect to groups and individuals that enables Ehrman to claim that Acts 13:28–29 represents a different tradition than that of burial by Joseph, since it mentions the Jewish leadership *as a whole* burying Jesus rather than Joseph or Nicodemus specifically (see *How Jesus Became God*, 154). But the referent here is not "the Sanhedrin as a whole," as Ehrman claims, but rather "those who live in Jerusalem and their rulers" (Acts 13:27). This is a good

all seventy-one members would have been present at Jesus's trial; it was a hastily drawn meeting in the middle of the night; only twenty-three members were needed for a quorum.)[88] But second, more to the point, even if Joseph had been present, obviously the Sanhedrin as a whole entity could act in ways at variance with the opinion or wishes of particular individual members. Is there any group of any kind, anywhere, that doesn't? Has Ehrman never been a part of a committee or board? It is not difficult to the slightest degree to imagine that Luke 23:51 records the truth when it states that Joseph was a member of the Sanhedrin but "had not consented to their decision and action." This would be precisely why Joseph's action would be courageous, just as other members of the Sanhedrin who were sympathetic to Jesus would visit him only *at night* (as Nicodemus does in John 3:2).

It is therefore difficult to sympathize with Ehrman's conclusion: "My hunch is that the trial narrative and the burial narrative come from different sets of traditions inherited by Mark. Or did Mark simply invent one of the two traditions himself and overlook the apparent discrepancy?"[89] There is only a "discrepancy" here if one supposes that groups and their individual members never conflict.

Elsewhere Ehrman claims that Joseph's burial of Jesus was a later tradition because it is not included in the creed Paul quotes in 1 Corinthians 15:3–5.[90] But this is simply an argument from silence that amounts to the requirement that the tradition Paul is quoting must have been exhaustive with respect to detail. Why

example of how the New Testament can refer to groups more loosely, without assuming the involvement of every individual (unless Ehrman thinks that Paul intends to say that every citizen of Jerusalem without exception participated in the burial of Jesus).

88. For further discussion, see D. A. Carson, "Matthew," in *The Expositor's Bible Commentary*, vol. 8, ed. Frank E. Gaebelein (Grand Rapids: Zondervan, 1984), 553; and Michael Green, *The Message of Matthew*, The Bible Speaks Today (Downers Grove, IL: InterVarsity, 1988), 306.

89. Ehrman, *How Jesus Became God*, 152–53.

90. Ehrman, *How Jesus Became God*, 139–43.

should we accept this requirement for a moment? Ehrman's main argument in favor of it seems to be rooted in his perception of parallelism in the passage. He divides the creed into two major sections of four statements, in which "he was buried" in verse 4 corresponds to "he appeared to Cephas" in verse 5. Thus, he argues, "If the author of that creed *had* known such a thing, he surely would have included it, since without naming the party who buried Jesus . . . he created imbalance with the second portion of the creed where he does name the person to whom Jesus appeared (Cephas)."[91] Again, this is speculative; but even if we accepted the reasoning, the parallelism only works if one omits from the creed the final clause "then to the twelve" (1 Cor. 15:5). Ehrman himself points out that there is no reference to "the twelve" anywhere in Paul's writings; accordingly, he seems to regard this clause as part of the creed, stipulating that "the original form of the creed was simply verses 3–5."[92] So it is unclear why Ehrman omits this clause from his analysis of the structure of the creed. If it is a part of the original creed, then the inclusion of Joseph would *not* have balanced the parallelism.

The deeper methodological concern here is that Ehrman treats 1 Corinthians 15:3–8 as a kind of comprehensive historical summary rather than a compact creedal formula. For this reason, he also uses this passage to derive the conclusion that the women visiting the tomb on Sunday morning is a later tradition.[93] His reason for claiming that Paul was intending to give an exhaustive list of people to whom Jesus appeared in 1 Corinthians 15:5–8 is that Paul refers to himself as "last of all" in verse 8. But the fact that Paul references his *temporal* relation to previous appearances does not require that Paul intends an exhaustive list. On the

91. Ehrman, *How Jesus Became God*, 153 (italics original).

92. Ehrman, *How Jesus Became God*, 139. For further discussion as to the extent of the creed, see Gordon D. Fee, *The First Epistle to the Corinthians* (Grand Rapids: Eerdmans, 1987), 722–29.

93. Ehrman, *How Jesus Became God*, 142–43.

contrary, Paul's focus in naming individuals here has to do with *apostles*, since he is seeking to defend his own apostolicity (1 Cor. 15:9–11; being an eyewitness to the risen Christ was a criteria for apostleship [Acts 1:21–26]). It is unwarranted to infer that because Paul doesn't mention the women here it must be a later tradition.

Ehrman's treatment of the creed in 1 Corinthians 15:3–8 serves as a good example of the kind of undue skepticism reflected in critical reconstruction of the development of the stories that eventually were included in the New Testament. The effort is speculative and tendentious; it must rely heavily on arguments from silence. The fact is simply this: the historical data we have concerning the basic facts associated with the launch of the Christian movement is remarkably good. Compared to the sources for other ancient history, we have a wealth of data to work with. For instance, the fact that in 1 Corinthians 15:3–8 we have a summary of various witnesses to the resurrection that dates from within *two decades* of Jesus's death, possibly even sooner, is remarkable—John Rodgers calls it "the sort of data that historians of antiquity drool over."[94]

So it appears that Jesus's original followers, and very soon many others, came to a sudden and life-changing belief that he had been raised from the dead. It is reasonable to accept this much on historical grounds. The question then is, How and why did this belief come about? The nature and details of the various historical data concerning the early Christian belief in the resurrection create difficulties for many of the common naturalistic explanations. Consider the following facts:

- The disciples began preaching the resurrection almost immediately after it allegedly occurred, in the very city in which it allegedly occurred. The message was therefore highly falsifiable. If the women had simply gone to the wrong tomb,

94. Quoted in Richard N. Ostling, "Who Was Jesus," *Time*, June 24, 2001, http://content.time.com/time/magazine/article/0,9171,149895,00.html.

or if the disciples were simply mistaken about Jesus being risen, the opponents of the early Christians could have likely gone to the tomb and produced the body.

- Numerous eyewitnesses of the resurrection were identified by name. More than sixteen are mentioned in the New Testament, including many women, whose inclusion is significant because they had little social status in the culture of the time, and so strengthens the plausibility of their testimony being true. This is a large, diverse, and identifiable array of witnesses, several of which appear to be independent of each other (e.g., Paul, and Jesus's brother James). It is difficult to hypothesize how all these eyewitnesses together could have been either mistaken or lying. If they were mistaken, how did this particular mistake arise among so many different parties? If they were lying, it is a stunningly impressive group act that no one "broke."

- There are grounds to believe that the disciples were willing to die for their belief in the resurrection, and, in most cases, did.[95] Many people are willing to die for their convictions, to be sure—*if* they believe they are true. But the disciples were claiming to have *seen* Jesus. There is a difference between being willing to die for an ideology one has inherited and being willing to die for an empirical fact one has personally witnessed.[96]

- None of the disciples are portrayed sympathetically throughout the Gospels. On the contrary, they consistently lack faith, fail to understand Jesus's purposes, abandon him in his final

95. For a discussion of the historical evidence of the apostles' martyrdom, see Timothy McGrew and Lydia McGrew, "The Argument from Miracles: A Cumulative Case for the Resurrection of Jesus of Nazareth," in *The Blackwell Companion to Natural Theology*, ed. William Lane Craig and J. P. Moreland (Malden, MA: Wiley-Blackwell, 2020), 614–16.

96. For more on the difference between the early disciples' willingness to die and other religious zealots' willingness to die for their beliefs, see McGrew and McGrew, "The Argument from Miracles," 624.

hour, and so forth.[97] They initially do not even believe the
resurrection (Luke 24:11). There is a kind of credibility
associated with a movement whose leaders are presented
in such a way. One feels it less likely one is being duped, or
grappling with a piece of propaganda.

- There is much in the Gospels that would have been embarrassing to include if it were not true. We have already
  mentioned the Gospels' countercultural respect for women,
  who were among Jesus's most loyal followers, share in his
  ministry (e.g., Luke 8:1–3), and are the first witnesses of the
  empty tomb. This is a beautiful aspect of the gospel story,
  but it would not have seemed so in the historical context of
  the early church. To this we could add many other features of
  the Gospels that would have been unpleasant for the original
  followers of Jesus—the notion of a crucified Messiah, the
  claim of an individual resurrection in the middle of history,
  the unsavory crowds following Jesus, and so on.[98] Even the
  little discrepancies reflected in the Gospel accounts are of
  the kind that one generally finds in eyewitness testimony.[99]

When I began to research the historical reliability of the Gospels, I was skeptical that a strong case could be built. I expected
that one could make a plausible case for God, but to accept the
resurrection would be more a matter of faith. However, the nature
and detail of the various data concerning Christ's resurrection in
the New Testament have converged to give them, in my mind, a

97. As Blaise Pascal put it in his *Pensées*, if Jesus did not rise from the dead, the
apostles were either deceived or deceivers in proclaiming this fact. See *Pensées* 322,
in Peter Kreeft, *Christianity for Modern Pagans: Pascal's* Pensées *Edited, Outlined,
and Explained* (San Francisco: Ignatius, 1993), 266.
98. See the discussion of these and other "embarrassing aspects" of the Gospel
stories in Eddy and Boyd, *The Jesus Legend*, 452.
99. McGrew and McGrew, "The Argument from Miracles," 598: "In law, it has
long been recognized that minor discrepancies among witnesses do not invalidate
their testimony—indeed, that they provide an argument against collusion."

ring of plausibility. They have a kind of endearing quality to them that is difficult to brush off. Detectives and those familiar with evaluating eyewitness testimony have often been impressed with the Gospels in this way, observing the kinds of qualities and details in their reports that tend toward credibility.[100] There is also the intriguing way the whole gospel narrative hangs together with all the symmetry of a good story and in seeming fulfillment of various Old Testament prophecies (e.g., Isa. 53). Hans Urs von Balthasar marveled at the beauty and unity of the story of Christ's passion and resurrection, wondering "How could all this have been fabricated by the clever mystifications of a few isolated individuals?"[101]

Above all else, there stands the sheer stature of Jesus. He is truly a titanic personality. Across the centuries, all kinds of people have been captivated by the diverse qualities represented by his personality—for instance, his radical inclusiveness and grace for outcasts and his simultaneous sternness against hypocrisy and oppression.[102] Or think of the combination of *authority* and *gentleness* one detects in his various interactions in the Gospels. He leaves a powerful impression on the imagination. *Something* very powerful and intriguing stands behind the early Christian movement. Some kind of dynamic force lurks behind the pages of the New Testament. If it was not a resurrection of the historical Jesus, what was it?

There is another fact that makes its own intriguing contribution to the quality of the New Testament witness: how radically unexpected, for first-century Jews, an individual bodily resurrection in

100. J. Warner Wallace, *Cold-Case Christianity: A Homicide Detective Investigates the Claims of the Gospels* (Colorado Springs: David C. Cook, 2013), draws from his career as a homicide detective to suggest the trustworthiness of the New Testament Gospels as eyewitness accounts.

101. Hans Urs von Balthasar, *The Glory of the Lord: A Theological Aesthetics*, vol. 1, *Seeing the Form*, trans. Erasmo Leiva-Merikakis, ed. Joseph Fessio, SJ, and John Riches (San Francisco: Ignatius, 1982), 475.

102. Tim Keller, *Making Sense of God: An Invitation to the Skeptical* (New York: Viking, 2016), 237, states that the diverse qualities of Jesus's personality combine to make him "the most beautiful life of humanity."

the middle of history would have been. N. T. Wright has emphasized this point, drawing attention to discontinuity with the uniqueness of the early Christian belief in Jesus's resurrection and the Jewish milieu in which it arose, which affirmed only a general resurrection at the end of history. According to Wright, "No second-Temple Jewish texts speak of the Messiah being raised from the dead. Nobody would have thought of saying, 'I believe that so-and-so really was the Messiah; therefore he must have been raised from the dead.'"[103]

This makes it more difficult to be sympathetic to proposals that the disciples came to believe in the resurrection because of psychological factors such as wish fulfillment. There is already a challenge to this hypothesis on the grounds that several of those claiming to have encountered the risen Christ were *not* hoping to do so (think of Saul, for example, on the road to Damascus).[104] But there is also the difficulty that even those who *had* believed in Jesus would not likely have turned to a hope in his bodily resurrection in their hour of need. This would have been more of a scandal than a comfort. As Wright puts it: "Something had *happened*, something which was not at all what they expected or hoped for, something around which they had to reconstruct their lives and in relation to which they had to redirect their energies. They were not refusing to come to terms with the fact that they had been wrong all along. On the contrary, they were indeed coming to terms with, and reordering their lives around, dramatic and irrefutable evidence that they had been wrong."[105]

The bottom line is this: something very powerful occurred to launch the Christian movement; and the naturalistic accounts of

103. Wright, *The Resurrection of the Son of God*, 25.
104. George Eldon Ladd pointed this out in his older study: "It is often contended that Jesus is never said to have appeared to unbelievers, only to believers. This simply is not true on two scores. The disciples were not believers after Jesus' death and burial; and James and Paul never had been disciples—they were both unbelievers when Jesus appeared to them." *I Believe in the Resurrection of Jesus* (Grand Rapids: Eerdmans, 1975), 138.
105. Wright, *The Resurrection of the Son of God*, 700 (italics original).

this fact generally struggle to account for it, in one way or another. Gary Habermas notes that none of these naturalistic accounts are particularly favored, even among modern critical scholars.[106]

For this reason, some have argued that the resurrection of Jesus is, on historical grounds, apart from the intrusion of an antisupernatural bias, very probable.[107] For instance, Michael Licona concludes his meticulous historical examination of the resurrection of Jesus with the claim that "the only legitimate reasons for rejecting the resurrection hypothesis are philosophical and theological in nature: if supernaturalism is false or a non-Christian religion is exclusively true."[108] N. T. Wright draws a similar conclusion: "If we were faced with some other historical problem which had brought us to a secure and interrelated pair of conclusions, and if we were looking for a fact or event to explain them both; and if we discovered something which explained them as thoroughly and satisfyingly as the bodily resurrection of Jesus explains the empty tomb and the 'meetings'; then we would accept it without a moment's hesitation."[109]

Here I'm claiming slightly less (though not because I disagree): I'm simply saying that it's plausible, on historical grounds, to believe in the resurrection of Christ. Granted, a miracle is never easy to believe. But if you're open to a miracle ever happening, this seems about as good a candidate as you are likely to find. It concerns the most stunning figure of human history and spawned the world's largest religion. If miracles are not inherently impossible, why couldn't this be a real one?

If it is, it has massive implications. So it's worth briefly considering: Supposing Christ was indeed the Lord God among us and did indeed rise from the dead, what difference would it make?

106. Gary Habermas, *The Historical Jesus* (Joplin, MO: College Press, 1996), 170.
107. Wright, *The Resurrection of the Son of God*, 687, discusses the nature of historical probability, in contrast to certainty or plausibility.
108. Licona, *The Resurrection of Jesus*, 608.
109. Wright, *The Resurrection of the Son of God*, 710.

The Unmaking of Sadness: What Easter Ultimately Means

The resurrection of Jesus is a unique concept among the religions of the world. N. T. Wright calls the resurrection "life after life after death," because it entails not merely mental consciousness after death but the restoration and transformation of the physical body.[110] Such an emphasis on physicality is already rare among religious conceptions of the afterlife—but it is the particular *kind* of physicality involved in Jesus's resurrection that makes it so novel.

Christians believe that when Jesus rose from the dead, he did not merely return to life but to a new *kind* of life. Many people had been raised from the dead in the Bible, including by Jesus himself—but they all died again. Jesus's resurrection is unparalleled in that he came into a new, permanent kind of body. The New Testament describes the quality of this resurrection as "the power of an indestructible life" (Heb. 7:16). Hence we find clues in the Gospels that Jesus's resurrected body was not completely normal: he seems able to appear and disappear quite suddenly, for example, including entering a locked room (John 20:26). At the same time, it is the same physical body that had been crucified: Jesus can eat (Luke 24:41–43), and the disciples can touch his scars with their hands (John 20:27).

We can put it like this: on Easter morning a new kind of reality emerged, without precedent in history or eternity. The resurrection of Jesus was as significant a turning point in the course of created reality as the initial moment of creation itself. Many theologians, noting Paul's reference to Christ's resurrection as the "firstfruits" of that of believers (1 Cor. 15:20), have spoken of Jesus's resurrection body as a kind of prototype of heaven, a proleptic anticipation of what God will one day do to the whole universe.[111] Thus, Easter has been called "the emergence within

110. Wright, *The Resurrection of the Son of God*, 31.
111. The term "firstfruits" is a farming metaphor, referring to the first batch of the crop that serves as a representative sample of all the rest.

history of the life of the world to come,"[112] "the embryonic principle of cosmic transformation,"[113] "the womb of the new aeon,"[114] and "the beginning of the new and final world-order."[115]

Thus, if you want to know what kind of Happy Ending reality is ultimately headed toward on the Christian view of things, the best clue you have is what happened to Jesus's flesh on Easter morning. The resurrection was not a random or arbitrary stunt: it was the first installment of the new, physical-yet-immutable glory that will one day characterize the world.

Consider for a moment that Jesus's resurrected body retains scars from crucifixion. For all eternity he will have scars in his wrists and ankles. Thus, Easter morning did not simply reverse Jesus's terrible suffering and death, bringing him back to his original state. Rather, some greater good has been brought about through Jesus's suffering. In fact, Christians believe that through this very thing—the worst evil ever committed—our salvation has been achieved. Jesus's resurrection does not erase his suffering from having happened; it redeems it and accomplishes through it the greatest good.

In this way, the Easter story reflects the character of the redemption envisioned by Christian hope for the whole world. God will not merely end pain and evil; he will mend them. The sorrows of this life will not be simply concluded or even washed away from memory; rather, for those who reap the benefits of Jesus's resurrection, those sorrows will be transformed into something glorious and beautiful. For instance, in the New Testament heaven is depicted as a realm in which God wipes away the tears of his

112. Ladd, *I Believe in the Resurrection of Jesus*, 12.

113. Sinclair Ferguson, *The Holy Spirit*, Contours of Christian Theology (Downers Grove, IL: InterVarsity, 1997), 254.

114. Geerhardus Vos, *The Pauline Eschatology* (Philipsburg, NJ: Presbyterian and Reformed, 1994), 156.

115. Richard B. Gaffin Jr., *Resurrection and Redemption: A Study in Paul's Soteriology* (Philipsburg, NJ: Presbyterian and Reformed, 1987), 89–90. For more discussion of these various statements, see my "Resurrected as Messiah: The Risen Christ as Prophet, Priest, and King," *Journal of the Evangelical Theological Society* 54, no. 4 (2011): 750–51.

people (Rev. 21:4). The imagery suggests not merely the cessation of earthly suffering but *consolation for* earthly suffering. Not only will we stop weeping; God will wipe away the tears previously shed. Thus, not only will earthly sadness not enter heaven; heaven will enter our earthly sadness and forever transform it.

The import of all this is that if Christ's resurrection really happened, it is unspeakably happy news. It entails not just any old afterlife but the best imaginable afterlife. Tim Keller puts it like this: "The Biblical view of things is resurrection—not a future that is just a *consolation* for the life we never had but a *restoration* of the life you always wanted. This means that every horrible thing that ever happened will not only be undone and repaired but will in some way make the eventual glory and joy even greater."[116]

Just imagine: What if there was a world in which your deepest pain was not simply ended or forgotten but transformed into glory, like the scars on Jesus's resurrected body?

To be clear, I am not arguing that every person will experience this resurrection joy: in the Bible it is a promise specifically to those who suffer with Christ in this life (e.g., Rom. 8:17). Indeed, the essence of this joy lies in encountering Jesus himself: in finally meeting the one who made you and has known you exhaustively every moment of your life, like Hamlet at last facing Shakespeare.

Toward the end of J. R. R. Tolkien's *The Lord of the Rings*, the character Sam wakes up after having suffered terribly on his long quest to destroy the One Ring. He is greeted by his old friend Gandalf, whom he had thought was dead. Gandalf asks him how he feels. Sam responds:

> For a moment, between bewilderment and great joy, he could not answer. At last he gasped: "Gandalf! I thought you were dead! But then I thought I was dead myself. Is everything sad going to come untrue? What's happened to the world?"

116. Timothy Keller, *The Reason for God: Belief in an Age of Skepticism* (New York: Dutton, 2008), 32 (italics original).

"A great shadow has departed," said Gandalf, and then he laughed, and the sound was like music, or like water in a parched land; and as he listened the thought came to Sam that he had not heard laughter, the pure sound of merriment, for days upon days without count. It fell upon his ears like the echo of all the joys he had ever known. But he himself burst into tears. Then as sweet rain will pass down a wind of spring and the sun will shine out the clearer, his tears ceased, and his laughter welled up, and laughing he sprang from his bed.

"How do I feel?" he cried. "Well I don't know how to say it. I feel, I feel"—he waved his arms in the air—"I feel like spring after winter, and sun on the leaves; and like trumpets and harps and all the songs I have ever heard!"[117]

Sam's emotions in this passage capture the quality of the hope inspired by the Christian idea of resurrection. There is such darkness, such pain—but somehow, in the end, against the odds, all is set right again. Everything sad comes untrue. I often imagine that how Sam experiences Gandalf's laughter—"the echo of all the joys he had ever known"—is what the first few seconds of heaven might be like.

So as a thought experiment, think back on the happiest moment of your life. Perhaps an idyllic childhood memory, when the world was safe and calm. Perhaps being truly known by another person and for the first time loved rather than rejected. Perhaps the attainment of a dream, or reconciliation with a friend, or a simple moment of contentment out in nature—happiness often sneaks in during quiet moments like that.

Now imagine, just for the sake of supposal, that you knew in your deepest heart of hearts that you would have that feeling of happiness back permanently—that, in fact, it was only ever an anticipation or foreshadowing of that final, settled Happiness that

117. J. R. R. Tolkien, *The Lord of the Rings*, 50th anniv. ed. (New York: Houghton Mifflin, 2004), 951–52.

you will experience forever, with ever-increasing awareness and enjoyment. In other words, imagine that your happiest moments are not gone from you once they are over—instead, they will return to you in some deeper yet all-familiar form.

If you knew this was ahead of you, how would it change you? Can you even imagine the indestructibleness of the hope it would inspire?

Another way to capture the implications of resurrection is, drawing from the last chapter, to think of the way the ending of your favorite movie makes you feel. For me, I think of the ending of *X-Men: Days of Future Past*, when Hugh Jackman wakes up in Professor X's mansion and discovers to his astonishment that all is somehow right again. Defeat and death were just a dream. After so much suffering, all is well. There is a kind of bright aura to the scene. On the Christian view of things, that is a little picture of where the world is ultimately headed.

Now think of the alternative. On naturalism, there is no hope for life beyond this realm—for naturalism is the philosophy that this realm is simply all there is. Thus, reality is headed toward simple extinction, not a Happy Ending. Consider how such a philosophy will equip you to function in the face of the pain of this world. Imagine, for instance, sitting with a child with a terminal illness in a hospital room. They have just a few moments to live. Such a worldview is completely bereft of hope to offer this child. Operating from within the parameters of naturalism, what would you even *say* in such a circumstance?

The difference between these alternatives is stark indeed. The stakes couldn't be higher.

Conclusion

This chapter has felt different from the previous three in the writing, as I suspect it has in the reading. We've moved broadly from philosophy to history, from metaphysics to religion.

At the same time, our approach in this chapter has remained abductive. For it's very difficult to leverage historical arguments in the direction of an ironclad conclusion. No matter how powerful the data, it usually funnels toward a probability, not a certainty.

Accordingly, our goal throughout this chapter has not been to demand a conclusion but to push in the direction of two basic points: (1) it's plausible on historical grounds to believe in a divine, rather than strictly human, account of Jesus of Nazareth; (2) it's also wonderful to do so—happy beyond imagination.

Whether someone personally comes to affirm such beliefs about Christ will depend on many factors. But if the arguments of this chapter have been successful, such a view will be recognized at least as a *reasonable* interpretation of the historical data—and also as a matter of tsunami-like emotional consequence.

The only reasonably sane response, then, will be to keep working at it until you've made up your mind one way or the other.

Conclusion

Moving Forward with Probabilities

n this book we've canvased four arguments suggesting that theism, and Christian theism in particular, makes a certain kind
of sense of the world. As we have said, these four arguments
can be seen in a narrative form—origins, meaning, conflict, and
hope are four anchors of any good story. You might regard them
as the four building blocks of any story: every story comes from
someone, means something, is shaped by conflict, and then ultimately resolves. What emerges, then, if we draw these arguments
together into a more coherent picture? What kind of story does
the Christian one turn out to be?

According to the way of thinking we have pursued throughout
this book, the Christian story is not only a more plausible story
than its naturalistic counterpart but more interesting, more elegant, more dignifying to humanity, and more hopeful.

In the Christian story, our physical universe is just one tiny contribution to reality, like an island in an immense ocean; therefore
the beauty we observe around us does not enclose us but merely
whispers of this vast beyond. In the Christian story, music and
poetry tug at our hearts for a reason: they are the ancient language
by which the world was written. In the Christian story, ideas and

math and logic have a kind of stable energy to them; learning them is like discovering an encoded message from someone highly intelligent. In the Christian story, love is at the core of reality; it is what spawned the world, and it will have the final word. In the Christian story, you have every right to be furious with injustice; goodness is real, and your life can be nobly spent in its service. In the Christian story, evil will one day be defeated; happiness will reign forever; every movie you ever watch is whispering to you about this.

Above all, the Christian story makes sense of the fact that the world does not make sense. For we live in the midst of chapter 3, in the raging conflict between good and evil. The Christian story thus explains our intuitive sense that the world is both valuable and broken—that it is good, and yet something has gone deeply wrong with it. The Christian story thereby gives us ground to both love and hate the world—or, as G. K. Chesterton put it, to be both astonished at it and at home in it.[1]

In this way, Christianity ultimately entails neither despair nor relaxed indifference but *hope*. The result of accepting Christian theism would be something like Hamlet deciding that, because Shakespeare is out there, the slings and arrows of fortune are not outrageous, however much they might feel like it; to be is better than not to be.

In short, the Christian story has a deep and abiding beauty to it, the kind of beauty to make Puddleglums of us all, if we look at it long enough—if we really let it touch us.

How Do We Decide from Probability?

But there is one way in which this conclusion may feel incomplete. The chapters of this book have pursued abductive arguments—and abductive arguments, even in cumulative force, do not result in

1. G. K. Chesterton, *Orthodoxy* (Peabody, MA: Hendrickson, 2006), 4.

the decisive commitment associated with faith. Suppose, based on a consideration of all the various factors, one winds up 90 percent certain of some kind of supernaturalism, 85 percent certain of theism, but only 65 percent certain of Christianity. What, then, does one do? How does one move from intellectual probability to existential certainty?

For many years I was plagued by such questions. I remember in college discovering existentialist philosophy and deeply resonating with its emphasis on being hurled into existence yet ill-equipped for it. Life seemed bizarrely unfair. You don't choose to be born; existence is simply thrust upon you. Then you must decide how to live. You cannot avoid the question. Not to think about it is itself a decision. But to make this decision is the one thing that is most difficult to do: for what is needed is some kind of certainty, and every effort to understand life inevitably produces something less than certainty.

One night in December 2005 I wrote the following in my journal:

> The only thing worse than the pain of life is its utter randomness. We are hurled into consciousness and struggle without any explanations or answers to accompany them. Life is like a test that we are forced to take, the answers to which are impossible for us to know. The ideas with which we fill in the blanks of the questions of life are at best guesses and usually merely unexamined prejudices. Life is like a battle that we are forced to fight but the objective of which is unclear to us. We are hurled into the contest, but unsure of what is required of us. We sense that we must strive, but are unsure to what end we strive, or by what means. The great dilemma of life is not its failure or pain but its uncertainty and chaos.[2]

There was one thing, however, I never considered: What if the very uncertainty concerning ultimate questions, and the existential angst it produces, exists for a reason?

2. This is a journal entry of mine from December 8, 2005, slightly edited.

Søren Kierkegaard reflected a great deal on the psychology of faith and its relation to the anxiety and dread associated with uncertainty. In his *Concluding Unscientific Postscript* (and in his earlier *Philosophical Fragments*), he considered how eternal happiness could ever be related to historical knowledge. Kierkegaard noted that faith involves an infinite personal interest in the truth of Christianity, which is essentially disproportionate to the kind of knowledge yielded by historical investigation. As he put it, "Even with the most stupendous learning and perseverance, and with the heads of all critics placed on a single neck, one never gets further than an approximation, and that there is an essential disproportion between that and a personal, infinite interest in one's own eternal happiness."[3] But then Kierkegaard asks, Supposing one *could* arrive upon a complete factual certainty of Christianity—would this result in the reality of faith? On the contrary, he thinks, "In this objectivity one loses the infinite, personal, impassioned interestedness that is the condition of faith, the *ubique et nusquam* [everywhere and nowhere] in which faith can come into being."[4] For Kierkegaard, faith is bound up with inwardness and pathos—it no more emanates from certainty than falling in love does.

Blaise Pascal also reflected on the role of uncertainty in relation to faith. He wrote much about the hiddenness of God and the disturbing anxiety it produces.[5] He vividly described the preposterousness of the human condition: we are neither nothing nor everything, and thus we are incapable of either certain knowledge or complete ignorance. We are floating about in a stormy sea, as it were, incapable of landing on a fixed point of reference for the

3. Søren Kierkegaard, *Concluding Unscientific Postscript to the Philosophical Crumbs*, ed. and trans. Alistair Hannay, Cambridge Texts in the History of Philosophy (Cambridge: Cambridge University Press, 2009), 22.

4. Kierkegaard, *Concluding Unscientific Postscript*, 26.

5. Hans Urs von Balthasar, *The Glory of the Lord: A Theological Aesthetics*, vol. 1, *Seeing the Form*, trans. Erasmo Leiva-Merikakis, ed. Joseph Fessio, SJ, and John Riches (San Francisco: Ignatius, 1982), 1470: "Pascal is the Christian thinker who has best seen and thought out the dimension of hiddenness in Christian evidence and who has best understood its necessity."

one question that matters most: namely, what to do about God and death.[6] But Pascal argued that this very circumstance serves a purpose. The truth *must* be difficult. It *must* produce angst. For, Pascal argued, this is one aspect of the context in which love develops, and love is an essential ingredient to faith.

Pascal did not think of faith as an irrational passion (though his famous wager is often caricatured in this direction).[7] Read in light of his own concerns, Pascal is not absolutely divorcing faith and reason, nor does he assert that there are no rational grounds for belief. On the contrary, he argued explicitly that there is enough light for those who want to believe and enough obscurity for those who don't.[8] For Pascal, God has arranged things this way because certainty is not our main need, just as ignorance is not our main problem. "God wishes to move the will rather than the mind. Perfect clarity would help the mind and harm the will."[9] Pascal thus emphasized that the evidence for God is both accessible and resistible. C. Stephen Evans calls these the "Wide Accessibility Principle" and "Easy Resistibility Principle."[10] To put it simply: if

6. E.g., *Pensées* 199, in Peter Kreeft, *Christianity for Modern Pagans: Pascal's* Pensées *Edited, Outlined, and Explained* (San Francisco: Ignatius, 1993), 124–25.

7. *Pensées* 418, in Kreeft, *Christianity for Modern Pagans*, 294: "If you win you win everything, if you lose you lose nothing." When Pascal's wager is read in context of the rest of the *Pensées*, it is easier to keep in mind his audience: it addresses those undecided, i.e., those who are halfway between belief and unbelief. This is very much the kind of audience I have in mind in this book as well. Some object that Pascal's wager is at odds with Paul's assertion in 1 Corinthians 15:17. But I believe that a nuanced expression of the wager, used in conjunction with other arguments and with sensitivity to human psychology, is compatible with the suffering of this life. For Pascal is addressing the question from the ultimate standpoint of eternity, while Paul is genuinely considering the counterfactual—if Christ did not rise—for its implications in this life. For more on Pascal's Wager and 1 Cor. 15:17, see the helpful argumentation in Michael Rota, *Taking Pascal's Wager: Faith, Evidence, and the Abundant Life* (Downers Grove, IL: IVP Academic, 2016), 76–79.

8. E.g., *Pensées* 149, in Kreeft, *Christianity for Modern Pagans*, 69.

9. *Pensées* 234, in Kreeft, *Christianity for Modern Pagans*, 247.

10. C. Stephen Evans, *Why Christian Faith Still Makes Sense: A Response to Contemporary Challenges*, Acadia Studies in Bible and Theology (Grand Rapids: Baker Academic, 2015), 24–25. "It thus seems plausible to assume that, though the evidence for God would be widely available and easily accessible [Wide Accessibility

you are looking for God, you will likely succeed; if you are avoiding him, you will also likely succeed.

What all this amounts to is this: those who feel trapped by uncertainty, as I did in college, must ask themselves if they are quite certain about their need for certainty. For, ultimately, the demand for certainty springs from the assumption that we know what we need and that we know what we want. But do we? Hasn't most happiness and truth already come to us through experiences that involve surprise, surrender, and risk? Perhaps certainty is overrated.

Taking the Wager

In the meantime, what do we do? As Pascal emphasizes, we must choose. We must *wager*. We must make the *best* decision that we can in light of the information that we *do* have. And why, after all, should we expect certainty before we have done this?

For Pascal, it is here that the beauty of the gospel becomes most acutely relevant. One of his briefer entries simply reads thus: "An heir finds the deeds to his house. Will he say, perhaps, that they are false, and not bother to examine them?"[11]

This is our situation in relation to the gospel. It is a message that concerns our infinite happiness and the everlasting good of the world. It claims that our world has an author, a meaning, a struggle, and a hope. If anything ever deserved to be longed for, it is this. If anything was ever important, it is this. It is as though you have confessed your secret feelings to your true love and are even now awaiting a reply.

Are you almost convinced? Would you give anything, as would I, for it to be true? Then *believe*. Give yourself to that belief as you give your heart to the one you love. In that posture, you will find certainty, and you will find yourself.

Principle], it would also be the kind of evidence that a person who wished to do so could dismiss or reject [Easy Resistibility Principle]" (p. 25).

11. *Pensées* 632, in Kreeft, *Christianity for Modern Pagans*, 203.

Author Index

Subject Index

abductive argument, 11–13, 18, 37n49,
    207, 210–11
"absolute nothingness," 37, 41
absurdism, 108–9
"accidental collocations of atoms,"
    107, 111
aesthetics, theology of, 5
agent causation, 43n70
agnosticism, 122n19, 130
Alice in Wonderland (Carroll), 46
allegory of the cave (Plato), 15n30
alternative universes, as speculative
    hypothesis, 66
angels, 184
  music of, 95–96
"Anscombe intuition," 122, 138
anthropic principle, 39, 63–66
antirealism, 73–74, 143n74
apathy about truth, 6
apocalyptic Jesus, 177n42
apologetics
  approaches to, xii
  Pascal on, 3
argument from causality, 27
argument from contingency, 27
argument from motion, 27

art
  disembedded from metaphysical as-
    sumptions, 87, 89
  as imitation of reality, 87
astrology, 51
atheism
  and cruel regimes, 169–71
  different strands of, 130
  as tradition of thought, 122
  See also new atheism; old atheism
author and story metaphor, 45, 57–58.
    See also Shakespeare/Hamlet
    metaphor

Bach, Johann Sebastian, 88, 91,
    98n129, 111
Beautiful Mind, A (film), 153
beauty, 111
  of Christianity, 4
  criteria for, 82
  cutting through disenchantment and
    apathy, 7
  and the distracted, 8
  of the gospel, 214
  of music, 99
  and truth, 5–6, 15, 83

as malleable, 132
and metaphysics, 159–60
Nietzsche's skepticism of, 127–29
objectively grounded in science, 124
ontological dependence on God, 121n16
reducible to biology, 142–43
transcendent basis, 144–46
moral justice, 113
moral realism, 113n1, 143n74
moral relativism, 139
movies, 10n23, 150–56
Mozart, Wolfgang Amadeus, 88
multiverse theory, xiii, 33, 39, 64–68
music, 60, 87–101, 111
as accidental product of nature, 96
as "auditory cheesecake," 92–93
and evolution, 91–93
as gift, 99
impoverished in naturalistic world-view, 105
as ineffable, 97
metaphysical significance, 94–96
points to God himself, 89
power of communication, 97, 98
and transcendence, 89–93, 99–100

naïve teleological arguments, 61
Narnia, 4
narrative, and worldview formation, 10n23
narrative apologetics, 9, 14
Nash, John, 82, 153
natural causes, sufficiency of, 20
naturalism, xii–xiii, 4, 14
account for music, 101
despair of, 108–9
limitations of, 50
and love, 104–6
and mathematical realism, 78–79

and morality, 122–24, 138–43, 149, 158
no final justice in the universe, 158
no hope in, 206
not a requirement for evolution, 140
as "philosophy of the unhappy man," 47
physical reality as a cement wall, 50–51
natural law ethics, 144n76
natural laws, 20
natural selection, 70, 103, 138, 139
nature and Supernature, 45–54
nature-versus-nurture dilemma, 174
Nazi Germany, 132, 145
necessary being, 27, 28, 43
negative atheism, 122n19
neo-Darwinism, 70
new atheism, xii, 53, 124, 130, 166–67
Nicodemus, 194
Nicomachus, 80
Niemöller, Martin, 167
nihilism, 7, 16, 109, 127n34, 131
"no boundary proposal," 34
nonstandard cosmology, 32, 41–42
"Normal," 116–17, 141, 143, 145, 149
nothing, 21–22, 36–41, 50–51
notional assent, 145

old atheism, 126, 130, 138
ontological argument, 15, 165
ontological duality, 28–29
oral traditions, 180
orderliness of the universe, points to God's existence, 60

pantheism, xiii
parallel universes, 68. See also multi-verse theory
Pascalian wager, 13, 213, 214
philia, 106
philosophy, xii
physical reality, 49–51, 71–72, 75, 84